THE
EVERYTHING

WEEKNIGHT
PALEO COOKBOOK

Dear Reader,

As a mother of two girls, I know how important educating yourself and your children about food can be. I also know how day-to-day stressors can derail even the best-laid plans. However, with a little preparation and the use of *The Everything® Weeknight Paleo Cookbook*, you can get your body and family on a healthy track in no time.

Forget about fast food and boxed, processed food. It's time to start embracing fresh, local, honest meals. This cookbook contains 300 healthy, easy recipes. By picking up this book, not only do you have the comfort of knowing these simple recipes are forever at your fingertips, you'll also find information and food lists to help get you started on your food journey. With all of the misinformation regarding "diets" and "quick fixes" available, isn't it time to just start eating real food and concentrating on living again?

The Paleo diet is an anti-inflammatory diet that concentrates on pure foods. Give this way of eating a full month before you say no. I truly believe that you will lose some weight, sleep better, notice clearer skin and brighter hair, and have increased energy. Who can argue with that? I double-dog dare you to do this for yourself!

Happy eating,

Michelle Fagone
Cavegirl Cuisine

Welcome to the EVERYTHING® Series!

These handy, accessible books give you all you need to tackle a difficult project, gain a new hobby, comprehend a fascinating topic, prepare for an exam, or even brush up on something you learned back in school but have since forgotten.

You can choose to read an Everything® book from cover to cover or just pick out the information you want from our four useful boxes: e-questions, e-facts, e-alerts, and e-ssentials.

We give you everything you need to know on the subject, but throw in a lot of fun stuff along the way, too.

We now have more than 400 Everything® books in print, spanning such wide-ranging categories as weddings, pregnancy, cooking, music instruction, foreign language, crafts, pets, New Age, and so much more. When you're done reading them all, you can finally say you know Everything®!

QUESTION

Answers to
common questions

FACT

Important snippets
of information

ALERT

Urgent
warnings

ESSENTIAL

Quick
handy tips

PUBLISHER Karen Cooper

MANAGING EDITOR, EVERYTHING® SERIES Lisa Laing

COPY CHIEF Casey Ebert

ASSISTANT PRODUCTION EDITOR Alex Guarco

ACQUISITIONS EDITOR Lisa Laing

ASSOCIATE DEVELOPMENT EDITOR Eileen Mullan

EVERYTHING® SERIES COVER DESIGNER Erin Alexander

THE
EVERYTHING®
WEEKNIGHT
PALEO
COOKBOOK

Edited by Michelle Fagone

Founder of CavegirlCuisine.com

Avon, Massachusetts

I would like to dedicate this book to Samantha and Calla. You are a constant source of inspiration, and you bring daily joy and love to my heart.

An Everything® Series Book.
Everything® and everything.com® are registered trademarks of F+W Media, Inc.

Published by Adams Media, a division of F+W Media, Inc.
57 Littlefield Street, Avon, MA 02322 U.S.A.
www.adamsmedia.com

Contains material adapted and abridged from *The Everything® Glycemic Index Cookbook, 2nd Edition* by LeeAnn Smith Weintraub, MPH, RD, copyright © 2010, 2006 by F+W Media, Inc., ISBN 10: 1-4405-0584-5, ISBN 13: 978-1-4405-0584-3; *The Everything® Paleolithic Diet Book* by Jodie Cohen and Gilaad Cohen, copyright © 2011 by F+W Media, Inc., ISBN 10: 1-4405-1206-X, ISBN 13: 978-1-4405-1206-3; and *The Everything® Paleolithic Diet Slow Cooker Cookbook* by Emily Dionne, copyright © 2013 by F+W Media, Inc., ISBN 10: 1-4405-5536-2, ISBN 13: 978-1-4405-5536-7.

ISBN 10: 1-4405-7229-1
ISBN 13: 978-1-4405-7229-6
eISBN 10: 1-4405-7230-5
eISBN 13: 978-1-4405-7230-2

Printed in the United States of America.

10 9 8 7 6 5 4 3 2 1

Library of Congress Cataloging-in-Publication Data
The everything weeknight paleo cookbook / edited by Michelle Fagone, founder of CavegirlCuisine.com.
pages cm
Includes index.
ISBN-13: 978-1-4405-7229-6 (pb)
ISBN-10: 1-4405-7229-1 (pb)
ISBN-13: 978-1-4405-7230-2 (eISBN)
ISBN-10: 1-4405-7230-5 (eISBN)
1. High-protein diet--Recipes. 2. Reducing diets--Recipes. 3. Low budget cooking. 4. Prehistoric peoples
--Nutrition. I. Fagone, Michelle, editor of compilation.
RM237.86.E94 2014
641.5'638--dc23
2013033175

This book is available at quantity discounts for bulk purchases.
For information, please call 1-800-289-0963.

Contents

Introduction 9

1 An Introduction to the Paleo Lifestyle 11
The Paleolithic Diet 12
Health Benefits of the Paleo Lifestyle 13
The Standard American Diet 15
Paleo-Approved Foods 18
Increase in Refined Sugars 21
Mood Swings and Blood Sugar Levels 22
Foods the Entire Family Will Love 23
Paleo Lifestyle Beyond the Home 25
Getting Started 25
Cooking and Flavoring Meals 27
You Can Do This! 31

2 Appetizers and Snacks 33

3 Sauces and Spreads 57

4 Salads and Dressings 79

5 Stocks, Soups, and Stews 107

6   Beef, Pork, and Lamb 145

7   Poultry. 171

8   Fish and Seafood 195

9   Sides 221

10 Children's Favorites 243

11 Grilling Time 257

Appendix A: Paleo "Yes" Foods 269
Appendix B: Paleo "No" Foods. 273
Appendix C: Paleo Substitutions 275
Appendix D: Six Weeks of Weeknight Paleo Meals 276
Standard U.S./Metric Measurement Conversions 277

Index. 279

Acknowledgments

Sam, your love and support is neverending. Thanks for being the best taste-tester a cavegirl could ask for!

Much love to my parents, Steve and Janet. You two are truly the best (and craziest) parents. Thank you for always being adventurous and dedicated to fitness . . . as well as to fun!

Last, I would like to thank my friends and partners-in-crime in the Paleo community—you have been such a source of learning and support. Your encouragement, honesty, and laughs keep me going. Thank you!

Introduction

THE PALEO LIFESTYLE IS not like most modern-day diet plans. In fact, it is probably the oldest diet in the world. The Paleo way of eating takes you back to the wisdom your ancestors possessed in the Paleolithic era, when man hunted and gathered his food. Back then, there were no fast-food restaurants or packaged microwavable meals. In fact, exercise and nutrition went hand-in-hand (man had to sprint after an animal to obtain his meal). Berries, nuts, and plants were foraged in their natural state. Fish were caught, not farmed. The simplicity and honesty of Paleolithic-era food produced bodies that were free of inflammation and distress.

Ridding your body of toxins found in inflammatory foods will contribute to increased energy levels. Your natural circadian rhythm, or body clock, will start working better, allowing you to pop out of bed after a great night's sleep. Your prescription medication and over-the-counter drugs may become a thing of the past. Aches and pains from arthritis or swelling joints will subside because you are consuming foods that do not irritate your body.

If this sounds too easy to be true, it's not. You can do it—though it might not be as simple as you think. It depends on your starting point. If you are accustomed to quick-fix drive-thrus and processed packaged foods, then this lifestyle will take some planning, some overhauling of old ways, and a willingness to commit to your health.

The first step is becoming educated on how to fuel your body with chemical-free nutrition. For example, oftentimes you can get much better food at your local farmer than from most grocery stores, which get their meat from chemically-enhanced animals raised on cattle farms and livestock farms. At these farms, thousands of animals are stuffed into feedlots and live in their own manure. Not only is the large quantity of manure destroying our soil, it is also a breeding ground for bacteria. And guess how the farmers kill these bacteria? They put more chemicals in and on the animals. Think about this the next time you dive into a store-bought steak with no labels.

An informed consumer makes better decisions. Become an army of one and make changes with your wallet. You may pay a little more for your food up front, but the money you will save on medicine and future health issues will way outshine the initial costs.

You may have noticed that the CrossFit community largely claims this diet as its own, but the athletic community in general has latched on to this way of eating. Clean and organic foods prepared simply and tastefully are helping athletes increase performance and strength because the diet aligns their nutrition with the genetic needs of their bodies. You don't have to run a marathon to be considered an athlete. Start moving your body. Start playing outdoor games with your family. Just start. You will be surprised at how soon you will call yourself an athlete.

In the following pages, you'll find 300 easy-to-follow, simple-to-prepare recipes, along with the tools to start your healthy journey. Isn't it time for you to take charge of your and your family's health? You are definitely worth it.

CHAPTER 1

An Introduction to the Paleo Lifestyle

The Paleolithic diet or "Paleo lifestyle" has become increasingly popular in recent years. Also known as the "Caveman Diet," the name refers to a period of time when people only ate grass-fed game, wild-caught fish, nuts, vegetables, berries, and occasionally, other fruits. These people lived before the time of modern agriculture and the domestication of animals. They hunted for their meat and gathered their berries and nuts. There were no grains planted in fields, no milk past weaning, and, subsequently, the population wasn't plagued by many of the diseases that are seen today.

The Paleolithic Diet

Even though they had to find, hunt, and kill most of their food, your Paleolithic ancestors were still eating better-quality foods than most of the world is today. Not only are the hundreds of quick-fix weight loss products wreaking havoc on the human body, but the Standard American Diet (SAD) with grains at the helm is believed to contribute to a number of diseases caused by inflammation.

FACT

Modern-day humans are only one-tenth of 1 percent genetically different from their Paleolithic ancestors. During the last 10,000 years, their diets have changed dramatically, though humans have changed very little.

Paleopathology, the study of disease in prehistoric times, shows that when humans became reliant on corn and rice, signs of iron-deficient anemia began to appear. According to the World Health Organization (WHO), over 30 percent of the world's population is anemic. This is largely due to phytates found in corn and rice, which inhibit the absorption of iron, says Robb Wolf, author of *The Paleo Solution*. Furthermore, after the rise of agriculture and food processing, there was an increase in tooth decay and infant mortality. Just like the rings of a tree can be used to determine its age, our ancestors' bones tell a story, too.

Today's Paleolithic Diet

So right now you're thinking that you need to move to the forest and take up hunting, fishing, and gardening to be on today's Paleolithic diet? That could not be further from the truth. The Paleo lifestyle simply requires a shift in your thinking. First, you will need to learn what foods are considered Paleo "yes" or Paleo "no." From there, all you need to start on your journey toward Paleo success is a simple shopping list, an open mind, and a whole bunch of recipes. Switching over to eating Paleo does not have to be an arduous task. In fact, many of the recipes adored by families the world over can easily be converted to Paleo with a few carefully chosen ingredients and some fun substitution.

Health Benefits of the Paleo Lifestyle

One of the most significant benefits of adhering to a Paleo lifestyle is the potential for decreasing your risk of developing a number of chronic diseases, such as cancer, diabetes, cardiovascular disease, and osteoporosis. Decreasing the risk of developing diseases can, of course, also be achieved by consuming a well-balanced, nutrient-dense, modern-day diet low in unhealthy fats, processed foods, refined carbohydrates, and preservatives. However, the popularity of Paleo nutrition continues to expand, and people of all ages, demographics, and fitness levels are climbing aboard and sailing back to ancient ways, perhaps in an effort to reverse the negative impact that years of unhealthy eating habits and sedentary lifestyles have caused.

Heart Healthy

The high-fiber, low-saturated fat, high-antioxidant, and high-micronutrient content of the Paleo diet has many heart-healthy benefits. Such a diet composition can result in improved cholesterol profiles, decreased cardiac-risk scores, and improved blood-pressure status. It can promote a healthier heart and an overall healthier future.

Cancer-Fighting Possibility

The Paleo diet provides a number of disease-fighting, cancer-preventing components. Its high dietary-fiber content, coupled with an abundance of vitamins, minerals, and antioxidants, as well as the strict avoidance of processed trans fats and refined, processed sugars, creates a strong line of defense against numerous types of cancer.

Optimization of Overall Health and Wellness

Adherence to a Paleolithic lifestyle can also help in the prevention and management of chronic diseases like obesity, diabetes, and osteoporosis. It also encourages a naturopathic-based and organic approach to health, as well as a greater ownership of one's well-being. Being self-aware and establishing a more health-conscious perception of yourself are important steps in becoming and staying well.

Prehistoric Metabolism

It was more than just what the cavemen ate that allowed them to maintain healthier weight profiles and a better overall body composition than their modern-day counterparts. Resting metabolism (your metabolic rate) naturally declines with age. This is due to the decrease in one's muscle mass over time, which in turn is due to the decline in physical activity over time. Paleolithic times did *not* promote or even allow for any sort of sedentary lifestyle. To survive meant one had to move, hunt, gather, keep moving, and so on, thus preserving one's muscle mass for a longer period during adulthood.

Health Without Medicine

Health and metabolism may have been more easily maintained in prehistoric times, despite the fact that advances in modern medicine were not available. If the two worlds collided—prehistoric lifestyle meets modern medicine—it could very well be the best of both worlds. Hence the current popularity of Paleo nutrition.

The Standard American Diet

Some believe that the Standard American Diet needs to be completely restructured. They say that grains, dairy, beans, and alcohol should be avoided. What? That sounds crazy! Not necessarily, though. If you look at the science behind how these food groups relate to the body, you'll find that they all contribute to inflammatory issues that can lead to arthritis, heart disease, cancer, diabetes, and other health problems. Over the years America has increasingly become a sick and obese nation, possibly due to a diet comprised of an addicting combination of refined sugars, salts, and carbohydrates.

Processed and "fat-free" food has replaced the multitude of beautiful produce we have available to us. Change begins with retraining your brain and breaking some habits. You probably don't need to buy that candy bar when you stop to fill up at the gas station. Do you really need that bagel along with that large morning coffee? Is ordering Chinese take-out every Tuesday really necessary? Planning ahead will help bypass old rituals.

The Truth about Fat-Free

Fats have gotten a bad rap in diets today. Most people trying to lose weight think it is important to avoid them at all costs, but that isn't necessarily true. In the 1980s, Americans were introduced to, among other things, fat-free cookies. Unfortunately, the fat was replaced with sugar, and a lot of it. What a great marketing plan to convince people that this was a healthy way to eat. What is even scarier is that it worked. Processed cottage cheese and refined white rice became staples of American "diet" food. As people tried to lose weight, they looked for quick fixes and tried every new diet that came along, with little success. There were pills and body wraps and unfounded theories. But none of these seemed to work. It's time to get rid of everything that you ever "learned" about fat-free foods being healthy and start eating real food.

Good Fats, Bad Fats

Despite what you've heard, fat is not the devil. It is a macronutrient that your body needs every day to absorb vitamins and nutrients. The important differentiation is in the type of fat you consume. Saturated fats, those that are solid at room temperature, are the types that clog arteries and promote heart disease. Unsaturated fats, those that are liquid at room temperature, are completely different in their structure and impact on the human body. These types of fats protect you from illness and disease.

For example, vegetable oil is high in inflammatory omega-6 fatty acids. Other commonly used, highly processed oils with similar omega-6 drawbacks are canola, safflower, peanut, and soybean oils, as well as margarine and shortening. So where can one find good fats? Avocados, olive oil, salmon, tuna, raw nuts, and pumpkin seeds are just a few good sources of healthy fats. Saturated animal fats from humanely-raised, free-range animals are an excellent source of fats needed for proper functioning of the body. According to Mark Sisson, "Fat will fuel your everyday activities, your walking, your shopping, your working and reading. Fat can even provide the bulk of the energy required by your brain. Your brain still needs glucose, mind you, but becoming metabolically healthy will allow you to access both glucose and fat for energy." Eat fat in moderation, but eat it.

Good Carbohydrates

People new to the Paleo lifestyle often wonder about carbohydrates. Will they have to give up this food group? The answer is no—followers of the Paleo lifestyle give up grains, refined sugars, and white potatoes. These foods can lead to inflammation and are low in health benefits. But you don't need to give up carbohydrates completely. Vegetables are beautiful, nutrient-dense foods that deliver a big punch of carbs along with a variety of vitamins and minerals.

FACT

Grains, beans, and potatoes are poor sources of vitamins A, B, and C, and folic acid. They have a negative impact on your blood-sugar levels, causing a spike in insulin released from your pancreas. Additionally, they have low mineral and antioxidant profiles.

Try to eat a vegetable with every meal. Take the extra few minutes to throw some mushrooms and peppers in your scrambled eggs. Slice a few tomatoes on any plate of food. Steam some fresh zucchini. Substitute parsnips for potatoes in traditional chowders. If you're an athlete or very active person, enjoy an occasional sweet potato.

Beans and Legumes

Beans and legumes, including peanuts, are also restricted. Beans and legumes contain phytic acid and lectins. In the digestive system, phytic acid grabs onto any nutrients in your stomach and makes that nutrition indigestible. Your body also has a hard time breaking down lectins, which can tear at the intestinal lining. Both lectins and phytic acid are irritating to gut health and can cause inflammation, heartburn, cramps, and abdominal pain commonly referred to as leaky gut syndrome.

Dairy Doesn't Always Do a Body Good

Dairy is another area of concern for gut health, especially if you are lactose intolerant. Some people include limited dairy foods in their Paleo lifestyle. These folks are generally labeled as "Primal" rather than "Paleo." The primal enthusiasts occasionally enjoy full-fat organic cream and cheeses that have been sourced from grass-fed cows. Stay away from processed cheese and fat-free milk. Repeat this saying often: "Fat-free is *not* good."

You might be wondering how will you get calcium without dairy? Your mom always told you to drink your milk for strong bones. But feedlot cows are injected with growth hormones. When you don't know the precise source of your milk or meats, you are most likely ingesting these hormones. Calcium can be obtained in many other ways. Greens are very high in calcium. Try kale, broccoli, collard greens, and Swiss chard. Sweet potatoes on occasion are also a good source.

GMOs

A lot of food today contains genetically modified organisms (GMOs). GMOs are currently a subject of controversial debate about their associated health effects and environmental risks. Although these foods are a relatively new idea, some people believe that these GMOs will start cross-pollinating, creating a multitude of new crops that could upset our ecosystem. Another concern is that not enough research has been done to conclude how safe these altered crops are on the human body. Relying on fresh, local ingredients without GMOs is the backbone of Paleo. The fact that farmers' markets are sprouting up everywhere makes it easy to support local businesses and eat sustainably. If you don't have time for the farmers' market, you can even have a box of fresh goodies put together for you on a weekly basis through a Community Supported Agriculture program (CSA). Most CSAs will establish pick-up points in your community, while some will even deliver food to your door. Go to *www.localharvest.org/csa* to find a CSA near you.

Paleo-Approved Foods

Back in the Pleistocene Epoch, humans ate anything that they could find or hunt. That included game meat, organ meat, fish, chicken, eggs, fruit, vegetables, root vegetables, nuts, and seeds. There are a huge number of everyday foods that fall within this list. Some of the foods are common: beef, turkey, salmon, swordfish, almonds, avocados, strawberries, apples, spinach, and broccoli. Some of the foods are more obscure: venison, quail, moose, bear, kumquats, ugly fruit, and dandelion leaf. It's ideal to eat what is in season and locally produced as much as possible, but eating an apple grown six states away is better than eating a cupcake baked next door!

FACT

Paleo uses coconut sugar crystals, raw honey, and pure maple syrup as sweeteners.

Although the list of Paleo acceptable foods is long, there are some choices that are more beneficial than others. Foods rich in omega-3 fatty acids promote optimal health and well-being. Some great omega-3 choices include:

PROTEIN SOURCES OF OMEGA-3
- Wild-caught salmon
- Cold-water fish such as mackerel, herring, and sturgeon
- Free-range poultry
- Grass-fed beef

FAT SOURCES OF OMEGA-3

- Walnuts (particularly black walnuts)
- Brazil nuts
- Flaxseed

CARBOHYDRATE SOURCES OF OMEGA-3

- Broccoli
- Collard greens
- Raspberries
- Strawberries

ADDITIONAL PROTEIN SOURCES

- Grass-fed beef and veal
- Organic pork, chicken, and duck
- Offal
- Bison, venison, and elk
- Wild-caught fish, crab, shrimp, and oysters

QUESTION

Does grass-fed really make a difference?
According to *New York Times* investigative journalist and bestselling author Jo Robinson, compared with feedlot meat, meat from grass-fed beef, bison, lambs, and goats has less total fat, saturated fat, cholesterol, and calories. It also has more vitamin E, beta carotene, vitamin C, and a number of health-promoting fats, including omega-3 fatty acids and "conjugated linoleic acid" or CLA.

When eating Paleo, you will want to find fruits and vegetables with lower glycemic levels. These foods will not have a big impact on your blood sugar and insulin levels. By keeping these levels lower and in balance you will promote wellness and reduce any unnecessary inflammation. Foods with lower glycemic levels include:

LOW GLYCEMIC LEVEL FRUITS
- Apple
- Grapefruit
- Kiwi
- Orange
- Pear
- Plum
- Strawberries
- Raspberries

LOW GLYCEMIC LEVEL VEGETABLES
- Asparagus
- Beet greens
- Broccoli
- Cabbage
- Cauliflower
- Celery
- Swiss chard
- Collard greens

Organic vegetables and fruits are preferred when eating Paleo. Avoid corn, peas, and white potatoes. Eat sweet potatoes in moderation if you are active. Limit those fruits with a higher glycemic index, like bananas, mangoes, and pineapple.

A Family Affair

Deciding to switch your and your family's lifestyle to eat as your ancestors once did can be a very rewarding choice. Not only is the Paleo lifestyle beneficial for children and adults alike, it only requires a little effort and a bit of planning in order to make it work for you and your family. Start with baby steps. For example, instead of including foods with high glycemic carbohydrates like white potatoes and pasta in your meals, try replacing them with a vegetable or a sweet potato. To keep your children from getting bored with their vegetables, try adding new spices to your meals, varying the flavors with each new recipe. Don't underestimate your children's palate, but be sure to listen to their feedback every time you try something new. You may be surprised by what they like and dislike.

Benefits of Paleo Lifestyle in Children

You might be a bit concerned about putting your children on a "diet," but remember, the Paleo lifestyle is not a diet. It is not calorically limiting. It does not leave people feeling hungry and deprived. A true Paleo follower eats bountiful macronutrients in the form of protein, carbohydrates, and fat. Post-agricultural dieters also eat all three macronutrients, but the percentages favor refined sugar and high glycemic load carbohydrates that cause massive fluctuation in insulin levels and are poor contributors to healthy macronutrients. The secret to good nutrition for your family is not from grains, dairy, and legumes. It is in the vast array of Paleo choices chockfull of vitamins and minerals that your children and family need.

Increase in Refined Sugars

In the past forty years, the amount of refined sugar in the Westernized diet has increased astronomically. Is it a coincidence that the rate of illness has increased as well? The following table shows a trend in sugar consumption that is alarming.

▼ **REFINED SUGAR CONSUMPTION IN KG**

Year	Sucrose	High-Fructose Corn Syrup	Glucose
1970	48.2	.2	8.6
1980	37.9	8.8	8.9
1990	29.2	22.5	9.9
2000	29.8	28.9	9.9

American Journal of Clinical Nutrition, Vol. 81, No. 2, 341–354, February 2005, *Origins and Evolution of the Western Diet: Health Implications for the Twenty-First Century*, Loren Cordain, S. Boyd Eaton, Anthony Sebastian, Neil Mann, Staffan Lindeberg, Bruce A. Watkins, James H. O'Keefe, and Janette Brand-Miller.

Refined sugar consumption has increased overall from 57 Kg in 1970 to more than 68.6 Kg in 2000. More interestingly, the amount of high-fructose corn syrup consumption has tripled. High-fructose corn syrup, often referred to as maize syrup, is derived from corn. It was first developed in 1957 for three main reasons:

- It is about as sweet as table sugar.
- It is cheaper in the United States as a result of corn subsidies by the government and sugar tariffs placed on sucrose.
- Because it is liquid at room temperature, it is easy to blend and transport.

FACT

According to the Environmental Working Group and the *New York Times*, the United States government spent $41.9 billion on corn subsidies from 1995 to 2004. This could be a major contributing factor as to how high-fructose corn syrup took over the sugar market in the United States.

High-fructose corn syrup can be found in many items around the supermarket. It is added to soft drinks, fruit juice, condiments, processed snacks, bars, ice cream, frozen yogurt, cereal, canned fruit, bread and bread products, and canned soup. It sneaks into places you would not expect like mustard, salad dressing, peanut butter, frozen meals, and deli meats. If you look at the typical child's diet, high-fructose corn syrup is rampant. This sugar is not the kind of carbohydrate your child needs to fuel them. This type of sugar will spike their blood sugar and then immediately cause a crash as insulin tirelessly works to get the blood sugar levels normalized. This will lead to mood swings, hunger pangs, and attention issues as they fight to stay awake.

Mood Swings and Blood Sugar Levels

If you have a young child at home you know about mood swings. Children of all ages have varying moods that can, at times, be challenging to the adults around them. Mood swings have been directly linked to insulin and blood sugar levels. If your child's blood sugar is going up and down, so will their mood. Diabetes, the most common blood sugar imbalance disease in the world today, lists mood swings as a frequent symptom of the disorder. This, too, is because of their increase and decrease of blood sugar levels.

QUESTION

What are good snack choices for my kids that will not spike their insulin?
An easy way to successfully maintain good insulin and blood sugar levels throughout the day for children is to choose a snack that contains all three macronutrients: protein, fat, and carbohydrate. An apple with almond butter or organic, no-salt-added turkey jerky trail mix with added nuts and goji berries are both great balanced choices.

Foods the Entire Family Will Love

You are ready to try the Paleo lifestyle, but you are unsure what to serve your family. The first step is to shop. If shopping with the family is an option, it will help to identify the foods your family will enjoy. Bringing the family to the local organic produce store is a great place to start. These stores are full of colorful and unusual fruits and vegetables and herbs and spices. You will usually find a grass-fed or organic meat department with a large meat selection. Additionally, you will have the advantage of having a bulk section that will likely contain a vast array of nuts, oils, and superfoods such as spirulina, wheat grass, goji berries, mulberries, and cacao. The best part of a mostly organic store is you can rest assured that you can find no-salt-added variety items, and high-fructose corn syrup items are excluded. If it is your first time, bring a shopping list. This will curtail the anxiety of not knowing what to purchase. Some great food items for those with young children include:

- Apples
- Oranges
- Strawberries
- Raspberries
- Grapes
- Bananas
- Broccoli

- Asparagus
- Tomatoes
- Romaine lettuce
- Cucumber
- Carrots
- Red peppers
- Lemons
- Sweet potatoes
- Spaghetti squash
- Free-range chicken
- Grass-fed ground beef
- Cage-free eggs
- Salmon
- Flax oil
- Nut butter (excluding peanut butter)
- Avocado
- Walnuts
- Dark chocolate (72% or higher)
- Goji berries
- Organic, no-sugar-added applesauce
- Cans of no-salt-added diced tomatoes or tomato paste
- Dried spices, such as thyme, black pepper, chili powder, oregano, basil
- Fresh spices, such as dill, rosemary, cilantro, parsley, basil

The list above hits all the basics: fruits, vegetables, lean proteins, and good fats but also adds in the items you need to keep it fresh and exciting. Dried spices and fresh herbs will add flavor to the proteins and sauces. Lemon can be used to brighten up any dish. Rotating fruits and vegetables around from day to day will help reduce boredom and is best for getting the full benefit of vitamin and mineral profiles. Sweet potato and squashes will help to satiate children who are used to eating high carbohydrate choices. By no means is this list complete and it will not satisfy the tastes of every family. It is merely a starting point.

ESSENTIAL

Nut butters are a great and flavorful way of enrolling your children into the Paleolithic lifestyle. There are a few different varieties to satisfy lots of tastes and they provide a good source of essential fatty acids that growing children need for brain development.

Paleo Lifestyle Beyond the Home

When considering a lifestyle change it is difficult to imagine all the ways in which it will affect you. You do not live in a bubble. You interact with people outside of your home, at school, and at your workplace. It is important to find a way to make the Paleo lifestyle work in all those situations or you will feel unsuccessful once you leave your home. Planning and preparation are crucial. Making and preparing foods in advance and transporting them to your work or school will become commonplace. Invest in a good set of glass or BPA-free plastic containers with lids and lunchboxes for yourself and your children. As long as you are prepared in advance with food and the ability to transport it, you will be successful outside of your home.

Family Gatherings

Family gatherings with non-Paleo eaters do not need to be stressful or difficult. Paleo foods are tasty and pleasing to the eye and palette. Break out a new recipe or two that contain strong herbs and spices. Or, convert a favorite family recipe into a favorite Paleo recipe by excluding grains, legumes, or dairy. Substitute squashes for starch, diced tomatoes for sauces, and flavors like lemon and herbs in place of salt. If you are a little crafty you can turn any recipe into a Paleo recipe.

Getting Started

You may wonder where to start when it comes to eating Paleo. Some of the ingredients in this cookbook may seem a little foreign to you. Although an all-out pantry cleanse may be ideal, it may not be financially realistic. However, it is important to get rid of the heavy hitters and only bring good foods back into your home. Start by throwing out anything in the refrigerator or pantry with five or more ingredients listed and anything that contains more than 1 gram of sugar per serving. Then swap out your vegetable oils for olive, avocado, and nut oils. Trash those potato chips and crackers and add nuts, unsweetened dried fruits, and gluten- and soy-free jerky. Change out your white flour for coconut flour. Go through your refrigerator and start reading the labels. Even ketchup contains sugar. Get rid of those items. Add some new spices and dried herbs to your spice rack.

FACT

Not only is coconut flour gluten-free and a source of protein, it contains almost double the fiber content of whole-wheat flour.

Take things one recipe at a time. Eat simply. Try to buy food around the perimeter of your grocery store and stay away from processed, boxed items typically found in the aisles. Don't stress yourself out trying to be perfect. You will ultimately set yourself up for failure if perfection is your goal.

Preparation and Planning

Meal planning is crucial to eating Paleo. Jotting down recipes and planning what you're going to eat throughout the week eliminates last-minute headaches and/or overbuying. Not only does this cookbook have many options and yummy recipes, there is a world of great Paleo recipes at your fingertips on your computer. There is a wealth of information on the Internet and Facebook groups where people can exchange recipes and learn from each other. Check out *www.cavegirlcuisine.com* for additional Paleo recipes.

Have a prep day once a week. Saturdays and Sundays are good prep days after a trip to the grocery store or farmers' market. Dice your onions, mushrooms, and peppers. Cook a whole chicken and then make broth afterwards for a homemade soup. Wash all of your fruit. Hard-boil some eggs for snacks. Preparing the food makes it easier to use. Having your veggies prepped beforehand is crucial for saving time as well as assuring that you will actually use what you purchased.

Cooking Day and Storage

After prepping, have a cooking day. Invest in a good set of glass containers, as most plastics contain bisphenol A (BPA), which has been associated with health risks since 2008. Cook in bulk and divide into serving sizes. Freezing soups in portion sizes allows you to cook a double recipe of soup and then store for quick-fix dinners. If you don't prepare, there is a good chance that you will be dialing for take-out.

ALERT

BPAs have been a hot topic in recent years. There have been a variety of studies that point to a link between BPAs and issues related to brain development in fetuses and infants, asthma, and an increased likelihood of obesity. While further studies are being conducted, use glass containers or BPA-free plastics and metals.

For snacks, throw some unsalted nuts and soy- and gluten-free jerky in small containers. Try a variety of nuts, as each one has different nutritional properties. Having snacks on hand will help derail that little devil on your shoulder begging you to eat some chips! Really utilize one day a week to get on top of your meal planning and you'll be surprised how easy it is to stay on track.

Cooking and Flavoring Meals

A very important component of any meal plan is the consistency. In order to be consistent you must find a way to escape boredom. If you ask anyone who has ever been on a traditional diet, even those who have been successful on one, they will often complain that they are eating the same foods meal after meal, day after day. That's where cooking and flavoring foods becomes an important component. Experimenting with recipes and trying new foods will keep your plan exciting and fresh instead of mundane and boring.

Preparation of Protein

There are main ways to cook and prepare food: air heated and moist heated. Each of these ways of preparation cook food in various amounts of time and certain foods cook better under different conditions. Roasting and broiling foods are examples of air heat cooking and are good methods for steak, chicken, most seafood, lamb, and veal. These meats can stand higher temperatures and cook in shorter amounts of time. Braising and pot roasting of foods are usually done on meats that are not as lean and require longer cooking at lower temperatures. They are often cooked with sauces or in broths to help retain moisture. Examples of meats that would benefit from this style of preparation are pot roasts, pork loin and shanks, whole turkeys, beef chuck, and beef flank.

Alternatives for the Experienced Chef

Once you have your chef's hat on for a while, you might want to try some other more sophisticated ways to cook. High-heat options are good for quick cooking. They are best for thinner cuts or for meats that do not need to be fully cooked, such as high-end, sushi-grade seafood. Searing food is an indirect high-heat method that is done on the top of the stove, preferably over a gas flame. It will cook the outside of meat to add a little flavor and sear in the juice on the inside. This is ideal for tuna steak and high-quality cuts of beef. Broiling in the oven is a method of direct heat with a flame. It brings the flavor of outdoor grilling to the indoor kitchen. Pork and veal chops work well with this type of cooking and quick grilling of seafood can be accomplished this way. Sautéing meats is a medium to medium-high heat method that is great for cooking foods that have smaller surface areas. It is quick, convenient, and does not take much experience to prepare delicious Paleo-friendly meals for the entire family.

Vegetable Preparation

Vegetables are best when eaten raw as they retain their full vitamin and mineral profile. When they must be cooked there are several methods that will produce different tastes and textures. Steaming vegetables is the next best way to eat them next to raw. It is also an easy way to prepare vegetables in bulk to be used over several meals. Just as with meat, sautéing vegetables in oil is a great way to prepare your food. Be aware, however, that you must account for the fat used in cooking the food into your daily fat allowance. Additionally, you must keep in mind that not all oils behave the same way when exposed to heat. When choosing an oil to cook with, you want to consider its viscosity, the way it keeps the food from sticking to itself, and its smoke value (the amount of smoke it produces when it's burned). If an oil produces a great deal of smoke when heated, it will burn off of the food and not provide much for actual cooking.

ALERT

Flax oil is best used in its natural state. When flax is exposed to high heat it can increase the risk of releasing free radicals, which has been linked to diseases such as cancer.

Obtaining Fat in Your Diet

There are several ways to include good fats into your diet. You can add it directly onto your food so it is eaten in its natural state. It can be mixed with other items to make a great salad dressing or marinade. As stated previously, it can be used while sautéing foods. Fats used to cook with produce different results and flavors and are nice additives to a recipe. Olive oil is a viscose and great-tasting oil for cooking. Coconut oil is nice to add a crispy effect to food. Walnut and grapeseed oils are best for low temperature heating and for use in dessert or marinade recipes. Sesame oil is a great additive at the very end of cooking for a bit of flavor.

Bring on the Flavor

Spices are dried seasonings that come from the bark, buds, fruit, roots, or seeds of plants while herbs are from the leaves. Herbs are fresh and have a short shelf life, a week or less. Spices will generally last up to six months in a cool, dark storage area. Spices and fresh herbs should become a mainstay for the Paleolithic eater. There are a plethora of different fresh and dried spices from around the world that can be used to liven up any dish or recipe. As a Paleo eater, you need to avoid cooking and eating the same things time and time again. This is the absolute worst trap for a Paleolithic cook to fall into. Preparing every meal the same way will not only become boring, but all of your food will start to taste the same, thus causing you to dislike the plan. Spices and a variety of cooking styles will ensure that you engage many of your taste buds in your meals and keep your interest high. Following are examples of good spices and herbs to try and their accompanying food items best used for:

▼ **SPICES**

Spice/Herb	Best Use
Basil	Tomato, pesto, salads
Cilantro	Salsa, salad dressing, tuna
Cinnamon	Carrot, sweet potato, winter squash
Clove	Pork, turkey, winter squash
Curry	Meats, poultry, soups, eggs
Lemon	Steamed vegetables, fish, poultry
Mustard seed	Meat, fish, poultry, salad dressing
Onion	All dishes
Oregano	Salads, sauces
Rosemary	Lamb, chicken, fish
Sage	Pork, veal, tomato sauces
Tarragon	Meat, poultry, fish
Thyme	Slow-cooked meals, slow-cooker meats

FACT

Spices from around the world are used to maintain freshness of food. You'll notice that warmer climates tend to have "spicier" food. This is because food spoilage is more of an issue in warmer climates. Additionally, some spices have antibacterial properties to promote better health.

Although this previous list is helpful to start, the best way to learn to use spices and herbs is to experiment. Open and smell every spice you can get your hands on and throw the spices that pique your interest into your dishes. A good rule is to use fresh, leafy herbs toward the end of your cooking, but also in the beginning of recipes that are uncooked to absorb flavor such as cilantro in guacamole. Spices are usually used at the beginning of recipes so that their flavors will be well established in the dishes such as sage and thyme added to a roasted chicken.

You Can Do This!

Still not convinced? Give it four weeks. In this time, you should start to notice some weight loss, clearer skin, and a better night's sleep. You may feel a slight headache for the first couple of days as your body craves the sugar that it is accustomed to. Although you may not be eating sugar by the spoonful each day and think that this theory does not apply to you, start reading food labels. Sugar is in almost all processed food products. It's not always called "sugar." Sometimes it's called glucose, corn syrup, fruit juice concentrates, lactose, maltose, syrup, or sucrose. Be aware. Being an informed consumer will lead you to make better buying decisions.

A Lifestyle, Not a Diet

This way of eating is called a lifestyle for good reason. It's not a diet that you follow for a few months and then go back to your old way of eating. It's a change in the way you live. You need to embrace moderation and find that sweet spot between exercise and food that helps your body run at its peak. Really start to listen to your body. Does dairy mess with your gut health? Are you allergic to nuts? Do you feel better when you add a side of veggies to each meal? Do you sleep better when you stop eating after a certain hour?

There is no set way to follow Paleo. Use it as a guideline to determine what works best for you. If once a week you want to add a little cheese to your burger patty, do it. Just choose a high-quality cheese sourced from grass-fed cows. Skip the processed slices. If you are going to splurge, splurge with quality ingredients. You didn't fall off the proverbial wagon; you are just living your life. If you have a glass or two of wine at dinner one night, don't use this as an excuse to inhale a pizza the next day. Enjoy your wine. Enjoy your evening. Enjoy your life. Plan a hike the next day or go to a Zumba class. Get out and move. Smile. Stay active and aware.

Let's Go!

You are ready to begin, and this cookbook can help you tackle those busy weeknights. Make your plan on the weekends and follow these simple, easy-to-pull-together recipes for the busy nights during the week. A healthy dinner on the table does not have to take longer than thirty minutes. There are also a lot of hands-off slow-cooker meals included. With a little preparation in the morning, your family can enjoy a flavorful homecooked meal waiting for them at the end of the day. Enjoy!

CHAPTER 2

Appetizers and Snacks

Roasted Kale
34

Deviled Eggs
34

Baked Stuffed Clams
35

Scallop Ceviche
36

Scallops Wrapped in Bacon
36

Stuffed Mushroom Caps
37

Exotic Fruit Guacamole
38

Baked Chicken Wings
38

Buffalo Chicken Wings
39

Lollipop Lamb Chops
40

Stuffed Mushrooms (Crabmeat or Shrimp)
41

Stuffed Mushrooms (Spicy Beef)
42

Stuffed Mushrooms (Bacon and Herbs)
42

Clams Casino
43

Deviled Eggs with Capers
44

Paleo Chips
45

Roasted Parsnip Chips
46

Sardines in Red Pepper Cups
46

Shrimp Cocktail
47

Roasted Spicy Pumpkin Seeds
48

Hot and Spicy Nuts
48

Stuffed Grape Leaves
49

Slow-Cooked Almonds with a Kick
50

Eggplant Relish
50

Spiced Hazelnuts
51

Appetizer Meatballs
51

Slow-Cooked Paleo Party Mix
52

Spinach Dip
53

Hot Cinnamon-Chili Walnuts
54

Roasted Pistachios
55

Asparagus and Avocado Lettuce Wraps
56

Roasted Kale

This simple recipe makes a crisp, chewy kale that is irresistible. You can also slice up some collard greens or Swiss chard as a substitute for kale, or mix them all together for a tasty medley.

INGREDIENTS | SERVES 2

6 cups kale
1 tablespoon avocado oil
1 teaspoon garlic powder

1. Preheat oven to 375°F.

2. Wash, dry, and trim kale by pulling the leaves off the tough stems or running a sharp knife down the length of the stems.

3. Place leaves in a medium-size bowl; toss with oil and garlic powder.

4. Roast for 5 minutes on a roasting pan; turn kale over and roast another 7–10 minutes, until kale turns brown and becomes paper-thin and brittle.

5. Remove from oven and serve immediately.

PER SERVING | Calories: 160 | Fat: 8 g | Protein: 6 g | Sodium: 249 mg | Fiber: 4 g | Carbohydrates: 20 g

Deviled Eggs

Eggs are a staple in the Paleo diet. This is a quick recipe that can be whipped up in no time. Kids and adults will love these, and they can be easily served at parties or family gatherings.

INGREDIENTS | SERVES 10

10 large eggs, hard-boiled
2 green onions, finely chopped
2 cloves garlic, finely chopped
1 stalk celery, finely chopped
1 teaspoon dry mustard
1 teaspoon black pepper
Sweet paprika, to taste

1. Peel eggs, cut in half lengthwise, and separate yolks from whites.

2. Combine egg yolks, onions, garlic, celery, dry mustard, and black pepper. Mix well to form paste.

3. Stuff egg whites with yolk mixture.

4. Sprinkle paprika over eggs and serve.

PER SERVING | Calories: 76 | Fat: 5 g | Protein: 7 g | Sodium: 63 mg | Fiber: 0 g | Carbohydrates: 1.5 g

Baked Stuffed Clams

Try to use fresh clams rather than canned in this dish. Once you do, you'll never go back to canned! Cherrystone clams are hard-shell quahogs and are generally 2½" in diameter.

INGREDIENTS | SERVES 4

4 fresh cherrystone clams, well-scrubbed and opened, meat removed

1 tablespoon lemon juice

¼ cup almond flour

1 egg

1 tablespoon Homemade Mayonnaise (see Chapter 3)

½ teaspoon dried dill

2 tablespoons organic butter or ghee, melted

Salt and pepper, to taste

1. Preheat the oven to 350°F. Place the clam shells on a baking sheet.

2. Add the clam meat and the rest of the ingredients to a food processor or blender and pulse until mixed but not puréed.

3. Spoon the stuffing into the clam shells and bake for about 20 minutes. Serve immediately.

PER SERVING | Calories: 185 | Fat: 14 g | Protein: 12 g | Sodium: 77 mg | Fiber: 1 g | Carbohydrates: 4 g

Follow Your Nose and Your Ears!

When buying any kind of seafood, ask to smell it first. A fresh, salty aroma is fine; anything else is suspect—don't buy it! When selecting clams, make sure that they are tightly closed and make a sharp click when you tap them together.

Scallop Ceviche

This recipe calls for overnight preparation, so plan accordingly.

INGREDIENTS | SERVES 8

2 pounds small bay scallops

1 cup lime juice

1 large onion, chopped

20 black olives, chopped

½ cup water

3 medium tomatoes, peeled and diced

½ cup extra-virgin olive oil

1 teaspoon oregano

⅛ teaspoon white or black pepper

1. Marinate scallops in lime juice for 3–4 hours.

2. Drain and rinse scallops in cold water.

3. Place scallops in a medium-size bowl and add remaining ingredients. Mix and store overnight in refrigerator.

4. Serve chilled.

PER SERVING | Calories: 163 | Fat: 3.5 g | Protein: 27 g | Sodium: 494 mg | Fiber: 1.5 g | Carbohydrates: 4.5 g

Eating Raw Food

Many people advocate eating only raw food. However, you should be aware that the cooking process kills bacteria and small organisms that can cause illness. Eating uncooked food is a risk, no matter how tasty the dish.

Scallops Wrapped in Bacon

This common party appetizer has been revamped for Paleo with nitrate-free bacon.

INGREDIENTS | SERVES 10

2 tablespoons almond oil

20 large scallops

2 tablespoons minced garlic

20 slices uncured, nitrate-free bacon

1. Heat oil in a large frying pan over medium-high heat. Sauté scallops in oil with garlic 3–4 minutes, or until scallops are lightly browned. Set aside to cool.

2. Cook bacon about 1 minute on each side and use to wrap scallops. Make sure bacon is not overcooked or it will not wrap around scallops.

3. Secure each appetizer with a toothpick and serve warm.

PER SERVING | Calories: 159 | Fat: 15 g | Protein: 13 g | Sodium: 291 mg | Fiber: 0 g | Carbohydrates: 0 g

Stuffed Mushroom Caps

These appetizers are a bit more exciting than traditional recipes using bread crumbs. They are stuffed with protein and fats to ensure more macronutrients in each bite.

INGREDIENTS | SERVES 10

20 white mushrooms
2 tablespoons walnut oil
½ pound ground turkey
¼ cup minced onion
4 cloves garlic, minced
½ cup finely chopped walnuts
½ teaspoon sea salt
½ teaspoon black pepper

1. Preheat oven to 350°F.

2. Remove stems from mushrooms and hollow out mushroom caps. Dice mushroom stems and place in medium-size bowl.

3. Heat walnut oil in a medium-size frying pan and cook ground turkey, onion, and garlic for 5–8 minutes, or until turkey is no longer pink.

4. Add mushroom stems, walnuts, salt, and pepper to the ground turkey and cook until mushroom stems are soft, about 8 minutes.

5. Stuff turkey mixture into mushroom caps and place on baking sheet.

6. Bake for 20 minutes or until golden brown on top.

PER SERVING | Calories: 99 | Fat: 8 g | Protein: 5 g | Sodium: 139 mg | Fiber: 1 g | Carbohydrates: 2 g

Exotic Fruit Guacamole

Papaya and mango add an exotic twist to a traditional dish.
The mix of sour and sweet will make your taste buds pop.

INGREDIENTS | SERVES 4

1 medium papaya, peeled and cubed

1 medium mango, peeled and cubed

1 medium ripe avocado, pitted, peeled, and diced

1 tablespoon lime juice

2 cups seeded, diced tomato

¼ cup diced onion

2 tablespoons minced fresh cilantro

1 teaspoon seeded, finely chopped jalapeño pepper

1 garlic clove, minced

In a medium-size bowl, combine all ingredients. Mix well and serve.

PER SERVING | Calories: 120 | Fat: 6 g | Protein: 2.5 g | Sodium: 13 mg | Fiber: 5 g | Carbohydrates: 18 g

Baked Chicken Wings

Cayenne pepper is known for its metabolism-boosting properties. Blended with paprika and garlic, cayenne is sure to kick up the heat in these chicken wings.

INGREDIENTS | SERVES 4

12 chicken wings

3 tablespoons coconut aminos

½ tablespoon garlic powder

1 teaspoon paprika

1 teaspoon cayenne pepper

2 teaspoons raw honey

½ teaspoon salt

¼ teaspoon pepper

1 tablespoon avocado oil

1. Wash the chicken wings and pat dry with paper towels.

2. Combine remaining ingredients, except oil, in a bowl. Add wings and coat with mixture. Cover and refrigerate for 1–2 hours or overnight.

3. Preheat oven to 425°F. Line a baking dish with aluminum foil. Drizzle foil with oil. Place wings in one layer in baking dish.

4. Bake for 40 minutes or until golden brown. Turn the wings over after 20 minutes for even cooking.

PER SERVING | Calories: 395 | Fat: 29 g | Protein: 27 g | Sodium: 405 mg | Fiber: 0 g | Carbohydrates: 5 g

Buffalo Chicken Wings

These spicy wings make the perfect tailgate treat.

INGREDIENTS | SERVES 12

4 tablespoons almond oil

4 tablespoons hot sauce

1 tablespoon lime juice

Ground pepper, to taste

4 pounds chicken wings with wing tips removed, cut in half

Try Them Boneless!

For the boneless version of this classic appetizer, replace wings with 4 pounds of boneless, skinless tenders. Be prepared to eat with a fork! Serve as an appetizer as-is or over a bed of salad greens.

1. Add oil, hot sauce, and lime juice to a 4- or 6-quart slow cooker. Cook on high, about 15–20 minutes.

2. Add small amount of pepper to wings and place them on a broiler pan or baking sheet. Broil in the oven until lightly browned, about 5–6 minutes on each side.

3. Add chicken wings to slow cooker, and stir to coat with the sauce. Cover and cook on high for 3–4 hours.

PER SERVING | Calories: 372 | Fat: 28 g | Protein: 27 g | Sodium: 233 mg | Fiber: 0 g | Carbohydrates: 0 g

Lollipop Lamb Chops

This is an expensive appetizer, but it's worth every penny for a special occasion. Citrus zest adds a pungent flavor. The aromas of orange and lemon zest infuse everything from meats to veggies and dressings.

INGREDIENTS | SERVES 14

4 cloves garlic

4 tablespoons minced parsley

3 tablespoons rosemary

Grated zest of ½ lemon

3 tablespoons Dijon mustard

2 tablespoons avocado oil

Salt and pepper, to taste

14 baby rib lamb chops, trimmed, with long bones left on

1. Blend everything but the chops in a mini food processor or blender until combined.

2. Pour mixture into a large dish and add lamb chops, turning to coat both sides.

3. Broil or grill lamb chops over medium-high heat for 3 minutes per side.

PER SERVING | Calories: 268 | Fat: 13 g | Protein: 34 g | Sodium: 50 mg | Fiber: 0 g | Carbohydrates: 0 g

Crowd Pleaser

Baby lamb chops are the star of the show at parties and special occasions. Your guests will love these delicious finger foods. They are fun to eat like chicken wings but make less of a mess.

Stuffed Mushrooms (Crabmeat or Shrimp)

These can be made in advance and frozen. This is very good party fare, but be sure you make enough—they go quickly!

INGREDIENTS | SERVES 12

¼ pound cooked shrimp or crabmeat (canned or fresh)

1 cup almond meal

½ cup Homemade Mayonnaise (see Chapter 3)

Juice of ½ lemon

1 teaspoon fresh dill, or 1 teaspoon dried

Salt and pepper, to taste

12 white mushrooms, 1"–1½" across, stems removed

Buying Mushrooms

Buy only the whitest, crispest mushrooms. If you buy them from a grower, you'll see that they stay white and unblemished for at least three weeks. Old mushrooms are tan to brown with black/brown flecks.

1. In a large bowl, mix all the ingredients except the mushrooms.

2. At this point, you can stuff the mushrooms and refrigerate or freeze, or you can continue the recipe.

3. Preheat oven to 400°F. Place stuffed mushrooms on a baking sheet and bake for 15–20 minutes. Serve hot.

PER SERVING | Calories: 133 | Fat: 12 g | Protein: 5 g | Sodium: 74 mg | Fiber: 1 g | Carbohydrates: 3 g

Stuffed Mushrooms (Spicy Beef)

These disappear rapidly at a party—people love them! Just like the Stuffed Mushrooms (Crabmeat or Shrimp) (see previous recipe), you can make them in advance and either refrigerate or freeze.

INGREDIENTS | SERVES 12

2 tablespoons avocado oil

¼ pound ground sirloin (very lean)

2 shallots, minced

1 clove garlic, minced

Salt and pepper, to taste

1 teaspoon hot sauce

1 teaspoon minced fresh ginger

1 large egg

1 teaspoon Worcestershire or other steak sauce

12 white mushrooms, 1"–1½" across, stems removed

6 teaspoons almond meal

1. Preheat the oven to 400°F. Heat the oil over medium-high heat in a medium skillet and brown the sirloin, shallots, and garlic. Stir in the salt and pepper, hot sauce, ginger, egg, and Worcestershire sauce. Take off heat and set aside.

2. Set mushrooms on a baking sheet lined with parchment paper. Stuff mushrooms. Sprinkle with almond meal.

3. Bake for 30 minutes until tops are brown and mushrooms are sizzling.

PER SERVING | Calories: 54 | Fat: 4 g | Protein: 3 g | Sodium: 28 mg | Fiber: 0 g | Carbohydrates: 2 g

Stuffed Mushrooms (Bacon and Herbs)

This is a delicious appetizer for a brunch! You could also serve these on the side with eggs.

INGREDIENTS | SERVES 16

16 white mushrooms, 1"–1½" across, stems reserved and chopped

2 strips nitrate-free bacon, cut in small pieces

½ red onion, minced

¼ cup almond meal

Pinch nutmeg

2 teaspoons minced fresh parsley

2 teaspoons minced fresh sage

1 large egg

1. Preheat the oven to 350°F. Clean mushrooms and place caps on a baking sheet lined with parchment paper.

2. In a medium-size frying pan, sauté bacon, onion, and mushroom stems over medium-high heat until the bacon is crisp. Stir in almond meal, nutmeg, parsley, and sage. Take off heat, let cool slightly, and mix in the egg.

3. Spoon mixture into mushrooms. Bake for 20 minutes or until lightly browned and very hot.

PER SERVING | Calories: 33 | Fat: 3 g | Protein: 2 g | Sodium: 29 mg | Fiber: 0 g | Carbohydrates: 1 g

Clams Casino

This is great with tiny littleneck clams, which are sweet and tasty. Some are saltier than others, so between the combination of the clams and bacon, you do not need to add any salt at all.

INGREDIENTS | SERVES 4

16 littleneck clams, opened, juices reserved

4 tablespoons organic butter or ghee

1 small onion, finely minced

Juice of ½ fresh lemon

2 teaspoons chopped fresh parsley

½ teaspoon dried oregano

½ cup finely chopped roasted sweet red pepper

3 tablespoons almond meal

Freshly ground black pepper, to taste

3 slices nitrite-free bacon, cut into 1" pieces

1. Preheat oven to 400°F. Place the open clams on a baking pan.

2. In a saucepan over medium heat, add the butter, onion, lemon juice, herbs, and red pepper. Mix well when butter melts and sauté for about 4 minutes. Mix in almond meal and sprinkle with pepper. Moisten with reserved clam juice.

3. Divide the mixture among the clams.

4. Put a piece of bacon on top of each stuffed clam. Bake for 12 minutes, or until the bacon is crisp and the clams are bubbling.

PER SERVING | Calories: 296 | Fat: 24 g | Protein: 12 g | Sodium: 180 mg | Fiber: 4 g | Carbohydrates: 11 g

Deviled Eggs with Capers

If deviled eggs aren't spicy, they aren't devilish enough! This recipe can be adapted if you want less heat.

INGREDIENTS | SERVES 12

6 hard-boiled eggs, shelled and cut in half

½ avocado, mashed

1 teaspoon hot sauce

1 teaspoon celery salt

1 teaspoon onion powder

1 teaspoon garlic powder

1 chili pepper, finely minced, or to taste

2 tablespoons extra-small capers

Garnish of paprika or chopped chives

1. Scoop out egg yolks and place in food processor along with avocado, hot sauce, celery salt, onion powder, garlic powder, chili pepper, and capers.

2. Blend until smooth and spoon into the hollows in the egg whites.

3. Garnish with paprika or chives and cover loosely with foil. Refrigerate for at least 3 hours before serving.

PER SERVING | Calories: 52 | Fat: 4 g | Protein: 3 g | Sodium: 278 mg | Fiber: 1 g | Carbohydrates: 2 g

Brine-Packed Capers

Capers are actually caper berries that have been pickled. You can get them packed in salt, but they are better when packed in brine. You can get larger ones or very, very small ones—the tiny ones are tastier.

Paleo Chips

Most Paleolithic diet enthusiasts say they miss tortilla chips the most.
This is a close substitute and goes well with guacamole and salsa.

INGREDIENTS | SERVES 3

1½ cups almond flour

1 large egg

1 tablespoon minced garlic

1 tablespoon organic, no-salt-added tomato paste

1 jalapeño pepper, seeded and chopped

1 teaspoon chili powder

½ teaspoon onion powder

Complex Carbohydrates and the Paleolithic Diet

The most difficult part of the transition from a Neolithic diet to a Paleolithic diet is letting go of high-carbohydrate snack foods such as chips and pretzels. Those comfort foods are associated with gatherings, parties, and celebrations. It will take a while to detox your body from such foods, but once you make the switch, you will not look back. The great way your body feels a couple of weeks into the plan more than makes up for the withdrawal from complex carbohydrates and refined sugar.

1. Preheat oven to 350°F.

2. Combine all ingredients in food processor and blend completely.

3. Spread evenly on a baking sheet covered with parchment paper.

4. Bake for 10 minutes.

5. Remove from the oven and cut into squares.

6. Place back in the oven and continue baking for 5–10 minutes or until crunchy.

PER SERVING | Calories: 357 | Fat: 30 g | Protein: 15 g | Sodium: 76 mg | Fiber: 7 g | Carbohydrates: 15 g

Roasted Parsnip Chips

The parsnip is a root vegetable related to the carrot.
It has a sweet taste and a lower glycemic load than a potato.

INGREDIENTS | SERVES 6

6 parsnips
3 tablespoons avocado oil
⅛ teaspoon nutmeg
1 teaspoon cinnamon

1. Preheat oven to 400°F. Line a baking sheet with parchment paper.

2. Peel parsnips and cut at an angle to make long oval shapes.

3. In bowl, combine parsnips, oil, and spices. Mix well.

4. Spread parsnips out on baking sheet in a single layer. Cook 30 minutes. Remove from oven.

5. Turn on broiler and broil 5 minutes to make crispier chips.

PER SERVING | Calories: 160 | Fat: 7 g | Protein: 1.5 g | Sodium: 14 mg | Fiber: 6.5 g | Carbohydrates: 24 g

Sardines in Red Pepper Cups

These cups can be put together in a few minutes and are ideal snacks for transporting.
Additionally, this recipe is a great source of omega-3.

INGREDIENTS | SERVES 1

1 (3.75-ounce) can no-salt-added, boneless, skinless sardines
1 red pepper
Juice of 1 lemon
Black pepper, to taste

1. Open and drain container of sardines.

2. Cut red pepper in half, remove ribs and seeds, and fill with sardines.

3. Sprinkle with lemon juice and pepper. Serve.

PER SERVING | Calories: 187 | Fat: 8.5 g | Protein: 19 g | Sodium: 377 mg | Fiber: 2 g | Carbohydrates: 8 g

Shrimp Cocktail

Shrimp is another flavorful, low-fat shellfish that is a nice addition to the Paleolithic lifestyle.

INGREDIENTS | SERVES 4

6 tablespoons grated horseradish root

1 tablespoon raw honey

1 (6-ounce) can organic, no-salt-added tomato paste

Juice of 1 lemon

½ teaspoon red pepper flakes

1 pound jumbo cooked shrimp, peeled

In a small bowl, blend the horseradish, honey, tomato paste, lemon juice, and red pepper flakes. Serve immediately with jumbo shrimp.

PER SERVING | Calories: 152 | Fat: 2 g | Protein: 19 g | Sodium: 238 mg | Fiber: 3 g | Carbohydrates: 16 g

Shrimp Facts

Shrimp is a great protein source. A single (4-ounce) serving of shrimp contains 24 grams of protein with less than 1 gram of fat. It contains a high level of selenium, vitamin D, and vitamin B_{12}. Selenium has been linked with cancer-fighting properties and is utilized in DNA repair.

Roasted Spicy Pumpkin Seeds

This spicy seed recipe is sure to be a family favorite.
They are quick to prepare and easy to grab for on-the-go snacks.

INGREDIENTS | SERVES 6

3 cups raw pumpkin seeds
½ cup almond oil
½ teaspoon garlic powder
Freshly ground black pepper, to taste

Pumpkin Seed Benefits

Pumpkin seeds have great health benefits. They contain L-tryptophan, a compound found to naturally fight depression, and they are high in zinc, a mineral that protects against osteoporosis.

1. Preheat oven to 300°F.

2. In a medium-size bowl, mix together the pumpkin seeds, oil, garlic powder, and black pepper until the pumpkin seeds are evenly coated.

3. Spread in an even layer on a baking sheet.

4. Bake for 1 hour and 15 minutes, stirring every 10–15 minutes until toasted.

PER SERVING | Calories: 532 | Fat: 50 g | Protein: 17 g | Sodium: 13 mg | Fiber: 3 g | Carbohydrates: 12 g

Hot and Spicy Nuts

Serve these at a cocktail party as an alternative to plain salted nuts. They are
also delicious in trail mix.

INGREDIENTS | YIELDS 2½ CUPS

2½ cups skin-on almonds or mixed nuts
1 teaspoon almond oil
½ teaspoon ground jalapeño
½ teaspoon garlic powder
½ teaspoon cayenne pepper
½ teaspoon ground chipotle
½ teaspoon paprika

1. Place the nuts into a 2- or 4-quart slow cooker. Drizzle with the oil and stir. Add the spices, and then stir again to distribute the seasonings evenly.

2. Cover the slow cooker, and cook on low for 1 hour. Then uncover and cook on low for 15 minutes or until the nuts look dry.

PER SERVING (½ CUP) | Calories: 487 | Fat: 44 g | Protein: 17 g | Sodium: 1 mg | Fiber: 8 g | Carbohydrates: 14 g

Stuffed Grape Leaves

Although there are many versions of grape leaves served across the Mediterranean, these grape leaves are inspired by Greece.

INGREDIENTS | SERVES 30

16 ounces jarred grape leaves (about 60 leaves)

2 teaspoons bacon grease

¾ pound ground beef, chicken, or pork

1 shallot, minced

¼ cup minced dill

½ cup lemon juice, divided

2 tablespoons minced parsley

1 tablespoon dried mint

1 tablespoon ground fennel

¼ teaspoon freshly ground black pepper

2 cups water

1. Prepare the grape leaves according to package instructions. Set aside.

2. Heat bacon grease in a large frying pan over medium-high heat. Sauté the meat and shallot for 8–10 minutes, or until the meat is thoroughly cooked. Drain off any excess fat. Scrape into a bowl and add the dill, ¼ cup of the lemon juice, parsley, mint, fennel, and pepper. Stir to incorporate all ingredients.

3. Place a leaf, stem-side up, with the top of the leaf pointing away from you, on a clean work surface. Place 1 teaspoon of filling in the middle of the leaf. Fold the bottom toward the middle and then fold in the sides. Roll it toward the top to seal. Repeat until all leaves are used.

4. Place the rolled grape leaves in two or three layers in a 4-quart slow cooker. Pour in the water and remaining lemon juice. Cover and cook on low for 4–6 hours. Serve warm or cold.

PER SERVING | Calories: 41 | Fat: 2 g | Protein: 4 g | Sodium: 23 mg | Fiber: 2 g | Carbohydrates: 3 g

Slow-Cooked Almonds with a Kick

These crunchy, heart-healthy snacks are hard to resist.

INGREDIENTS | SERVES 24

6 cups skin-on almonds

4 tablespoons coconut oil

3 cloves garlic, minced

2–3 teaspoons coarsely ground black pepper

1. Heat a 4-quart slow cooker on high for 15 minutes. Add the almonds.

2. Drizzle oil over almonds and stir. Sprinkle with garlic and pepper and stir.

3. Cover and cook on low for 2 hours. Stir every 30 minutes.

4. Turn heat up to high and cook uncovered for 30 minutes, stirring every 15 minutes.

5. Turn heat to low and serve warm, or remove from heat and allow to cool.

PER SERVING | Calories: 138 | Fat: 12 g | Protein: 5 g | Sodium: 0.5 mg | Fiber: 3 g | Carbohydrates: 5 g

Eggplant Relish

Serve with grilled or raw veggies for dipping.

INGREDIENTS | SERVES 6

1 large eggplant, pierced all over with a fork

2 tablespoons extra-virgin olive oil

½ cup finely chopped tomato

¼ cup finely chopped onion

¼ cup almond yogurt

3 cloves garlic, minced

½ teaspoon dried oregano

1–2 tablespoons lemon juice

Pepper, to taste

1. Place pierced eggplant in a 4-quart slow cooker, cover, and cook on low until tender, 4–5 hours. Cool to room temperature.

2. Cut eggplant in half and remove eggplant pulp (including seeds) from the peel with a spoon. Mash eggplant pulp and mix with oil, tomato, onion, almond yogurt, garlic, and dried oregano. Season with lemon juice and pepper and serve.

PER SERVING | Calories: 49 | Fat: 5 g | Protein: 0 g | Sodium: 2 mg | Fiber: 0 g | Carbohydrates: 2 g

Spiced Hazelnuts

This fiery favorite can liven up any appetizer menu.

INGREDIENTS | SERVES 24

6 cups hazelnuts

3 tablespoons almond oil

3 tablespoons crushed dried rosemary

1 tablespoon raw honey

¾ teaspoon cayenne pepper

½ teaspoon garlic powder

1. Heat a 2- or 4-quart slow cooker on high for 15 minutes; add hazelnuts. Drizzle oil over hazelnuts and toss; add remaining ingredients and toss.

2. Cover and cook on low for 2 hours, stirring every hour. Turn heat to high, uncover, and cook 30 minutes, stirring after 15 minutes.

3. Turn heat to low to keep warm for serving or remove from slow cooker.

PER SERVING | Calories: 200 | Fat: 19 g | Protein: 4 g | Sodium: 0 mg | Fiber: 3 g | Carbohydrates: 6 g

Appetizer Meatballs

Combine the cooked meatballs in a slow cooker with your favorite tomato sauce or Jalapeño-Tomatillo Sauce (see Chapter 3) to enhance the flavor of these versatile meatballs.

INGREDIENTS | YIELDS 24 MEATBALLS

1 pound ground beef

1 large egg

2 tablespoons dried minced onion

1 teaspoon garlic powder

½ teaspoon pepper

1. Add all the ingredients to a large mixing bowl and combine with your clean hands. Shape the resulting mixture into approximately 24 small meatballs.

2. Add meatballs to a 2- or 4-quart slow cooker, cover, and cook on high until meatballs are cooked through, about 4 hours.

3. Turn heat to low and keep warm before serving.

PER SERVING (1 MEATBALL) | Calories: 49 | Fat: 3 g | Protein: 5 g | Sodium: 27 mg | Fiber: 0 g | Carbohydrates: 1 g

Slow-Cooked Paleo Party Mix

Grab it while it's hot, because it won't last long once the guests arrive!

INGREDIENTS | SERVES 24

4 tablespoons walnut oil

3 tablespoons lime juice

2 teaspoons garlic powder

2 teaspoons onion powder

1 cup raw almonds

1 cup raw pecans

1 cup raw walnut pieces

2 cups raw shelled pumpkin seeds

1 cup raw shelled sunflower seeds

1. Add oil to a 2-quart slow cooker. Then add the lime juice, garlic powder, and onion powder and stir all together.

2. Next, add the nuts and seeds. Stir well until all are evenly coated. Cover and cook on low for 5–6 hours, stirring occasionally.

3. Uncover slow cooker, stir, and cook another 45–60 minutes, to dry the nuts and seeds.

4. Cool and store in an airtight container.

PER SERVING | Calories: 207 | Fat: 19 g | Protein: 7 g | Sodium: 2 mg | Fiber: 3 g | Carbohydrates: 5 g

Spinach Dip

Serve with vegetables for dipping or Paleo-friendly crisps!

INGREDIENTS | SERVES 8

1 (10-ounce) package frozen spinach, thawed and undrained

1 small onion, finely chopped

1 stalk celery, thickly sliced

2 cloves garlic

2 tablespoons almond oil

½ teaspoon dried basil

½ teaspoon dried thyme

⅛ teaspoon ground nutmeg

Pepper, to taste

2 large eggs

1. In a food processor, process the spinach, onion, celery, garlic, oil, basil, thyme, and nutmeg until finely chopped.

2. Season to taste with pepper. Add eggs and process until smooth.

3. Spoon the mixture into greased, 1-quart soufflé dish, and place the dish inside a 6-quart slow cooker.

4. Cover and cook on low about 4 hours.

PER SERVING | Calories: 63 | Fat: 5 g | Protein: 3 g | Sodium: 48 mg | Fiber: 1 g | Carbohydrates: 3 g

Hot Cinnamon-Chili Walnuts

These seasoned walnuts are a sweet-and-spicy hit with chili powder, cinnamon, and honey.

INGREDIENTS | SERVES 6

1½ cups walnuts

¼ cup raw honey

2 teaspoons cinnamon

1½ teaspoons chili powder

2 teaspoons coconut oil

1. Combine all the ingredients and place in a greased 2½-quart slow cooker.

2. Cover slow cooker and vent lid with a chopstick or the handle of a wooden spoon. Cook on high for 2 hours or on low for 4 hours.

3. Pour walnut mixture out onto a baking sheet lined with parchment paper. Allow to cool and dry and then transfer to an airtight container. Store in the pantry for up to 2 weeks.

PER SERVING | Calories: 238 | Fat: 19 g | Protein: 5 g | Sodium: 8 mg | Fiber: 3 g | Carbohydrates: 16 g

Roasted Pistachios

Raw pistachios are available at Trader Joe's (www.traderjoes.com) and health food stores. Roasting your own lets you avoid salt on the nuts, which makes them a snack that perfectly matches your Paleo palate.

INGREDIENTS | SERVES 16

1 pound raw pistachios
2 tablespoons almond oil

Putting Roasted Pistachios to Work

You can make 8 servings of a delicious coleslaw alternative by mixing together 3 very thinly sliced heads of fennel; ½ cup roasted, chopped pistachios; 3 tablespoons almond oil; 2 tablespoons freshly squeezed lemon juice; and 1 teaspoon finely grated lemon zest. Add freshly ground black pepper and additional lemon juice if desired. Serve immediately or cover and refrigerate up to 1 day.

1. Add the nuts and oil to a 2-quart slow cooker. Stir to combine. Cover and cook on low for 1 hour.

2. Stir the mixture again. Cover and cook for 2 more hours, stirring the mixture again after 1 hour. Cool and store in an airtight container.

PER SERVING | Calories: 172 | Fat: 14 g | Protein: 6 g | Sodium: 0 mg | Fiber: 3 g | Carbohydrates: 8 g

Asparagus and Avocado Lettuce Wraps

This recipe is a great side dish for any main course, or add protein to make a complete meal. You can spice these wraps up with a few drops of your favorite hot sauce.

INGREDIENTS | SERVES 4

24 asparagus spears, trimmed

1 ripe avocado, pitted and peeled

1 tablespoon freshly squeezed lime juice

1 clove garlic, minced

2 cups chopped tomato

2 tablespoons chopped red onion

3–4 whole romaine lettuce leaves

⅓ cup fresh cilantro leaves, chopped

Health Benefits of Asparagus

Asparagus is an often undervalued vegetable in the kitchen. This healthy stalk weighs in at 60 percent RDA of folic acid. Additionally, it is high in vitamins A, B6, and C, as well as potassium. Asparagus is a great vegetable to eat if you're trying to lose weight. It has a diuretic effect and helps to release excess water from the body.

1. In a medium-size saucepan over high heat, bring 2" water to a boil.

2. Place the asparagus in a steamer basket, cover, and steam until just tender. Be careful not to overcook. The asparagus should still have a bit of crunch after about 5 minutes of steaming.

3. Remove asparagus and immediately rinse in cold water. Drain thoroughly.

4. In a small bowl, mash the avocado, lime juice, and garlic into a coarse purée.

5. In another bowl, stir together the tomatoes and onions.

6. Lay the lettuce leaves flat and spread avocado mixture equally among the lettuce leaves, then add asparagus and tomato-onion mixture.

7. Top with a dash of fresh cilantro leaves.

8. Fold in both sides and the bottom of each lettuce leaf.

PER SERVING | Calories: 75 | Fat: 5.5 g | Protein: 2.5 g | Sodium: 4.5 mg | Fiber: 4.5 g | Carbohydrates: 6.5 g

CHAPTER 3

Sauces and Spreads

Party Guacamole
58

Slow-Cooked Salsa
58

Rocking Salsa
59

Fresh Pepper Salsa
59

Melon Salsa
60

Salsa Verde
60

Aioli
61

Fresh Tomato Drizzle
62

Homemade
Mayonnaise
63

Wasabi Mayonnaise
63

Chipotle
Mayonnaise
64

Homemade Ketchup
64

Walnut-Parsley
Pesto
65

Red Pepper Coulis
65

Serrano-Mint Sauce
66

Habanero-Basil
Sauce
66

Mint Chimichurri
Sauce
67

Jalapeño-Tomatillo
Sauce
67

Fruity Balsamic
Barbecue Sauce
68

Lemon-Dill Sauce
68

Raspberry Coulis
69

Fennel and Caper
Sauce
69

Summer Berry Sauce
70

Artichoke Sauce
70

Mango Chutney
71

Apple Chutney
71

Plum Sauce
72

Tomato and Chicken
Sausage Sauce
72

Chipotle Tomato
Sauce
73

Bolognese Sauce
74

Sun-Dried Tomato
Sauce
74

Spinach Marinara
Sauce
75

Ground Turkey
Tomato Sauce
76

Cranberry Sauce
77

Cran-Apple Sauce
77

Rosemary-
Mushroom Sauce
78

Red Pepper Relish
78

Party Guacamole

Guacamole is a party favorite that is also quite healthy.

INGREDIENTS | SERVES 6

4 ripe avocados

2 vine-ripe tomatoes, diced

½ cup diced green onions

1 tablespoon seeded, diced jalapeño peppers

2 cloves garlic, minced

Juice of 1 lime

¾ teaspoon sea salt

½ teaspoon freshly ground black pepper

1. Scoop out the flesh of the avocados and place in a small bowl. Mash the avocado with a fork.

2. Add the tomatoes, onions, jalapeños, and garlic. Mix together.

3. Squeeze on fresh lime juice and mix.

4. Stir in salt and black pepper and serve immediately.

PER SERVING | Calories: 230 | Fat: 20 g | Protein: 3 g | Sodium: 308 mg | Fiber: 10 g | Carbohydrates: 15 g

Slow-Cooked Salsa

This may be the easiest salsa recipe ever, and it tastes so much fresher than jarred salsa.

INGREDIENTS | SERVES 10

4 cups halved grape tomatoes

1 small onion, thinly sliced

2 jalapeño peppers, diced

⅛ teaspoon salt

1. Place all ingredients into a 2-quart slow cooker. Stir. Cook on low for 5 hours.

2. Stir and lightly smash the tomatoes before serving, if desired.

PER SERVING | Calories: 4 | Fat: 0 g | Protein: 0 g | Sodium: 0.5 mg | Fiber: 1 g | Carbohydrates: 1 g

Rocking Salsa

*This salsa is sure to be a winner at any party. Serve with Paleo Chips
(see recipe in Chapter 2) for a great appetizer before dinner.*

INGREDIENTS | SERVES 4

½ cup chopped fresh cilantro

1½ cups chopped tomatoes

¼ cup sun-dried tomatoes

½ cup olive oil

2 teaspoons freshly squeezed lime juice

1 teaspoon minced ginger

1½ teaspoons minced garlic

1 teaspoon minced jalapeño pepper

Combine all ingredients in a food processor and pulse quickly to blend. Be careful not to over-pulse and completely liquefy this salsa. It should have a slight chunky texture.

PER SERVING | Calories: 254 | Fat: 27 g | Protein: 1 g | Sodium: 5 mg | Fiber: 1 g | Carbohydrates: 3 g

Fresh Pepper Salsa

*Tomatoes are a great source of the antioxidant vitamin C. You can also get creative and make your salsa
with other vegetables, fruits, and spices.*

INGREDIENTS | YIELDS 1 PINT

1 yellow bell pepper

1 orange bell pepper

2 poblano chilies

2 Anaheim chilies

2 small jalapeño peppers

2 cloves garlic

¼ red onion

Juice of ½ lime

Freshly ground black pepper, to taste

1 tablespoon avocado oil

Chopped cilantro (optional)

1. Place all ingredients except the oil and cilantro (if using) in a food processor and pulse until desired chunkiness results. Taste and adjust for saltiness and heat.

2. In a medium-size pot, heat oil until slightly smoking. Add blended pepper mixture. Cook on high for 8–10 minutes, stirring occasionally. Sprinkle some chopped cilantro on top, if desired. Serve hot, cold, or at room temperature with tortilla chips, as a garnish for fish or poultry, or in your favorite burrito.

PER SERVING (¼ CUP) | Calories: 40 | Fat: 2 g | Protein: 1 g | Sodium: 3 mg | Fiber: 1 g | Carbohydrates: 5 g

Melon Salsa

This sweet melon salsa is a fun alternative to traditional vegetable-based salsas.

INGREDIENTS | SERVES 4

3 tomatoes, seeded and finely diced
½ honeydew melon, peeled and finely diced
1 cantaloupe, peeled and finely diced
1 cup minced red onion
½ jalapeño pepper, seeded and minced
½ cup chopped fresh cilantro
Juice of 1 large lime

1. In a large serving bowl, combine all ingredients and mix well.

2. Chill for 4 hours and serve.

PER SERVING | Calories: 144 | Fat: 1 g | Protein: 4.5 g | Sodium: 59 mg | Fiber: 4.5 g | Carbohydrates: 32 g

Melons

Melon has a very low sugar content. One fruit serving of cantaloupe is half a melon. This is a good choice when you're watching calories or counting fruit servings per day.

Salsa Verde

Tomatillos, a relative of the tomato, are in peak season in the summer and early autumn.

INGREDIENTS | YIELDS 3 CUPS

1½ pounds fresh tomatillos
2 jalapeño peppers
½ cup chopped fresh cilantro
1 onion, chopped
Juice of 1 lime
2 teaspoons salt

1. Preheat oven to 400°F. Remove husks from the tomatillos, rinse in warm water, and place on a baking sheet with the jalapeños. Place jalapeños and tomatillos in the oven to roast until slightly charred, about 10 minutes.

2. Place tomatillos, jalapeños, cilantro, onion, lime juice, and salt in a blender. Purée until salsa is well-blended.

PER SERVING (¼ CUP) | Calories: 23 | Fat: 1 g | Protein: 1 g | Sodium: 394 mg | Fiber: 1 g | Carbohydrates: 5 g

Aioli

Aioli is a basic French mayonnaise used throughout the Mediterranean. It's loaded with garlic and can include a variety of different herbs. You can also add tomatoes and spices.

INGREDIENTS | YIELDS 1 CUP

2 pasteurized eggs, at room temperature

1 teaspoon lemon juice

1 teaspoon white wine vinegar

½ teaspoon Dijon mustard

4 cloves garlic, or to taste

¾ cup avocado oil

Choice of ½ teaspoon oregano, tarragon, or rosemary

Salt and pepper, to taste

1. Combine the eggs, lemon juice, vinegar, mustard, and garlic in a blender.

2. Add the oil a little at a time and continue to blend. When the mixture is creamy, taste. Add herb of choice and salt and pepper. Pulse to blend. Store in the refrigerator or serve.

PER SERVING (1 TABLESPOON) | Calories: 99 | Fat: 11 g | Protein: 1 g | Sodium: 10 g | Fiber: 0 g | Carbohydrates: 0 g

Storing Aioli

Aioli will keep in the refrigerator for a day or two, but it's best made and used the same day.

Fresh Tomato Drizzle

This is perfect over shrimp, drizzled onto avocados, or even used as a sauce for hot or cold chicken or fish. It tastes summery!

INGREDIENTS | YIELDS 2 CUPS

1 pint cherry tomatoes

4 cloves roasted garlic

2 shallots

2 jalapeño peppers, cored and seeded

¼ cup stemmed, loosely packed fresh basil

¼ cup red wine vinegar or balsamic vinegar

½ cup almond oil

½ teaspoon celery salt

2 teaspoons Worcestershire sauce

Freshly ground black pepper, to taste

½ teaspoon cayenne pepper, or to taste

Purée all ingredients in a blender. Taste and add more celery salt and pepper if desired. This dressing improves with age—try making it a day or two in advance.

PER SERVING (2 TABLESPOONS) | Calories: 78 | Fat: 7 g | Protein: 0 g | Sodium: 82 mg | Fiber: 0 g | Carbohydrates: 2 g

Balsamic Vinegar

There are various types of Italian vinegar, but perhaps the most famous is balsamic vinegar. Balsamic vinegar is made from reduced wine and aged in special wood barrels for years. Each year's barrels are made of a different type of wood—the vinegar absorbs the flavor of the wood. Authentic balsamic vinegar ages for a minimum of ten and up to thirty years.

Homemade Mayonnaise

This Paleo-friendly mayonnaise is great on beef, turkey, or chicken burgers.

INGREDIENTS | SERVES 8

2 large eggs
2 tablespoons lemon juice
1 teaspoon dry mustard
2 cups avocado oil

1. Combine eggs, lemon juice, and dry mustard in a food processor and pulse until blended.

2. Drizzle oil into egg mixture slowly and continue to pulse until completely blended.

PER SERVING | Calories: 500 | Fat: 56 g | Protein: 2 g | Sodium: 26 mg | Fiber: 0 g | Carbohydrates: 0 g

Wasabi Mayonnaise

Traditional wasabi paste is made with real mayonnaise. This version is Paleo-friendly and can be used with sushi or other types of proteins.

INGREDIENTS | SERVES 8

2 large eggs
2 tablespoons lemon juice
1 teaspoon dry mustard
2 tablespoons wasabi powder
1½ cups avocado oil

1. Combine eggs, lemon juice, dry mustard, and wasabi powder in a food processor and pulse until blended.

2. Drizzle oil into egg mixture slowly and continue to pulse until completely blended.

PER SERVING | Calories: 382 | Fat: 42 g | Protein: 2 g | Sodium: 16 mg | Fiber: 0 g | Carbohydrates: 1 g

Eating Raw Proteins

There has been some debate as to whether or not you should eat protein raw. There are certain vitamins that are diminished in the cooking process, like C, B_6, and B_9, but others, like egg protein, are more digestible.

Chipotle Mayonnaise

This dressing will add a nice flavor to most meat, poultry, and fish dishes.

INGREDIENTS | SERVES 8

2 large eggs
2 tablespoons lemon juice
1 teaspoon dry mustard
2 tablespoons minced chipotle peppers
1½ cups avocado oil

1. Combine eggs, lemon juice, dry mustard, and chipotle peppers in food processor and pulse until blended.

2. Drizzle oil into egg mixture slowly and continue to pulse until completely blended.

PER SERVING | Calories: 379 | Fat: 42 g | Protein: 1.5 g | Sodium: 16 mg | Fiber: 0 g | Carbohydrates: 0 g

Homemade Ketchup

Ketchups are traditionally high in sugar, and sugar-free versions are usually substituted with a chemical sweetener. If you make your own, you'll know exactly what ingredients are in your specially-made ketchup!

INGREDIENTS | SERVES 5

1 (15-ounce) can no-salt-added tomato sauce
2 teaspoons water
½ teaspoon onion powder
¾ cup raw honey
⅓ cup lime juice
¼ teaspoon cinnamon
⅛ teaspoon ground cloves
Pinch ground allspice
Pinch nutmeg
Pinch freshly ground black pepper
⅔ teaspoon sweet paprika

1. Combine all the ingredients in a 2½-quart slow cooker. Cover and cook on low, stirring occasionally, for 2–4 hours or until ketchup reaches desired consistency.

2. Turn off the slow cooker and allow mixture to cool, then transfer to a covered container (such as a recycled ketchup bottle). Store in the refrigerator for up to a month.

PER SERVING (½ CUP) | Calories: 156 | Fat: 0 g | Protein: 0 g | Sodium: 2 mg | Fiber: 0 g | Carbohydrates: 42 g

Ketchup with a Kick

If you like zesty ketchup, you can add red pepper flakes or salt-free chili powder along with, or instead of, the cinnamon and other seasonings. Another alternative is to use hot paprika rather than sweet paprika.

Walnut-Parsley Pesto

Walnuts add a significant blast of omega-3 fatty acids to this delicious pesto.

INGREDIENTS | SERVES 4

½ cup walnuts

8 cloves garlic

1 bunch parsley, roughly chopped

¼ cup walnut oil

Freshly ground black pepper, to taste

1. Chop the walnuts in a food processor or blender. Add the garlic and process to form a paste. Add the parsley; pulse into the walnut mixture.

2. While the blender is running, drizzle in the oil until the mixture is smooth. Add pepper to taste.

PER SERVING | Calories: 229 | Fat: 23 g | Protein: 3 g | Sodium: 6 mg | Fiber: 1 g | Carbohydrates: 4 g

Pesto for All

Pesto is a generic term for anything made by pounding the ingredients. Most people are familiar with traditional pesto, which is made with basil and pine nuts, but many prefer this variation with parsley and walnuts.

Red Pepper Coulis

Coulis can be made using any fruit or vegetable. To add more flavor, experiment with the addition of herbs and spices.

INGREDIENTS | SERVES 8

6 red peppers

1 tablespoon walnut oil

Freshly ground black pepper, to taste

1. Preheat oven to 375°F.

2. Toss the red peppers with the oil in a medium-size bowl. Place the peppers on a racked sheet pan and put in the oven for 15–20 minutes, until the skins begin to blister and the red peppers wilt.

3. Remove from oven and immediately place the red peppers in a glass or ceramic container with a top. Let sit for approximately 5 minutes, then peel off the skin. Stem, seed, and dice the peppers.

4. Place the red peppers in a blender and purée until smooth. Season with black pepper.

PER SERVING | Calories: 39 | Fat: 1.5 g | Protein: 0.5 g | Sodium: 1.5 mg | Fiber: 1.5 g | Carbohydrates: 6 g

Serrano-Mint Sauce

This mint sauce is great with fish, poultry, and steak. Use this in place of other condiments or as a salad dressing.

INGREDIENTS | SERVES 6

1 cup tightly packed mint leaves

2 serrano chili peppers, chopped

4 cloves garlic, chopped

1 (1") piece fresh ginger, peeled and chopped

¼ cup lime juice

2 tablespoons olive oil

Combine all ingredients into food processor and pulse to coarsely blend.

PER SERVING | Calories: 41 | Fat: 4.5 g | Protein: 0 g | Sodium: 0.5 mg | Fiber: 0 g | Carbohydrates: 0 g

Habanero-Basil Sauce

This sauce is very spicy and goes well with meats and poultry.

INGREDIENTS | SERVES 6

2 cups chopped basil leaves

3 habanero peppers, stemmed

2 cloves garlic

¼ cup lime juice

3 tablespoons olive oil

Combine all ingredients in food processor and pulse to coarsely blend.

PER SERVING | Calories: 66 | Fat: 7 g | Protein: 0.5 g | Sodium: 1 mg | Fiber: 1 g | Carbohydrates: 1 g

Mint Chimichurri Sauce

Instead of the traditional mint jelly, use this mint chimichurri sauce to make a lamb recipe extra special.

INGREDIENTS | YIELDS 2 CUPS

2 cups fresh parsley

2 cups fresh cilantro

1 cup fresh mint

¾ cup olive oil

3 tablespoons red wine vinegar

Juice of 1 lemon

3 cloves garlic, minced

1 large shallot, quartered

1 teaspoon salt

1 small jalapeño pepper, seeded and chopped

1. Wash herbs, remove stems, and chop leaves.

2. In a blender, combine oil, vinegar, lemon juice, garlic, shallot, salt, and jalapeño; blend ingredients together. Add parsley, cilantro, and mint to the blender in batches and blend until sauce is smooth.

PER SERVING (2 TABLESPOONS) | Calories: 98 | Fat: 10 g | Protein: 0 g | Sodium: 155 mg | Fiber: 1 g | Carbohydrates: 2 g

Jalapeño-Tomatillo Sauce

Serve this sauce over riced cauliflower or roasted root vegetables for a fiery southwestern dish.

INGREDIENTS | SERVES 4

1 teaspoon avocado oil

2 cloves garlic, minced

1 medium onion, sliced

7 large tomatillos, peeled and diced

2 jalapeño peppers, minced

½ cup water

1. Heat the oil in a medium-size frying pan over medium heat. Sauté the garlic, onion, tomatillos, and jalapeño peppers for 5–10 minutes, until softened.

2. Place the mixture in a 4-quart slow cooker. Add the water and stir. Cook on low for 8 hours.

PER SERVING | Calories: 14 | Fat: 1 g | Protein: 0 g | Sodium: 1 mg | Fiber: 0 g | Carbohydrates: 1 g

Fruity Balsamic Barbecue Sauce

Use this sauce in pulled pork, as a dipping sauce, over chicken or burgers, or even as a marinade.

INGREDIENTS | SERVES 20

¼ cup balsamic vinegar
2½ cups cubed mango
2 chipotle peppers in adobo, puréed
1 teaspoon raw honey

1. Place all ingredients in a 2-quart slow cooker. Stir. Cook on low for 6–8 hours.

2. Mash the sauce with a potato masher. Store in an airtight container for up to 2 weeks in the refrigerator.

PER SERVING | Calories: 19 | Fat: 0 g | Protein: 0 g | Sodium: 2 mg | Fiber: 0 g | Carbohydrates: 5 g

Lemon-Dill Sauce

Serve this delicious, tangy sauce over salmon, asparagus, or chicken.

INGREDIENTS | SERVES 4

2 cups chicken broth
½ cup lemon juice
½ cup chopped fresh dill
¼ teaspoon white pepper

Place all ingredients in a 2- or 4-quart slow cooker. Cook on high, uncovered, for 3 hours or until the sauce reduces by one-third.

PER SERVING | Calories: 51 | Fat: 2 g | Protein: 3 g | Sodium: 179 mg | Fiber: 0 g | Carbohydrates: 6 g

A Peek at Peppercorns

Black peppercorns are the mature fruit of the black pepper plant, which grows in tropical areas. Green peppercorns are the immature fruit of the black pepper plant. White peppercorns are mature black peppercorns with the black husks removed. Pink peppercorns are the dried berries of the Brazilian pepper plant.

Raspberry Coulis

A coulis is a thick sauce made from puréed fruits or vegetables. In this recipe, the slow-cooking causes the fruit to cook down enough that straining is unnecessary. This is delicious as both a breakfast fruit spread and a sweet dessert topping.

INGREDIENTS | SERVES 8

12 ounces fresh or frozen raspberries

1 teaspoon lemon juice

2 tablespoons raw honey

Place all the ingredients in a 2-quart slow cooker. Mash gently with a potato masher. Cook on low for 4 hours uncovered. Stir before serving.

PER SERVING | Calories: 16 | Fat: 0 g | Protein: 0 g | Sodium: 0 mg | Fiber: 0 g | Carbohydrates: 4 g

Taste, Taste, Taste

When using fresh berries, it is important to taste them prior to sweetening. One batch of berries might be tart while the next might be very sweet. Reduce or eliminate honey in this recipe if using very ripe, sweet berries.

Fennel and Caper Sauce

Try this sauce over boneless pork chops or boneless, skinless chicken breasts and grilled summer vegetables.

INGREDIENTS | SERVES 4

2 fennel bulbs with fronds, thinly sliced

2 tablespoons nonpareil capers

½ cup chicken broth

2 shallots, thinly sliced

2 cups diced fresh tomatoes

½ teaspoon freshly ground black pepper

⅓ cup fresh minced parsley

1. Place the fennel, capers, broth, shallots, tomatoes, and pepper in a 4-quart slow cooker.

2. Cook on low for 2 hours, and then add the parsley. Cook on high for an additional 15–30 minutes.

PER SERVING | Calories: 64 | Fat: 1 g | Protein: 3 g | Sodium: 108 mg | Fiber: 5 g | Carbohydrates: 13 g

Summer Berry Sauce

Drizzle this sauce over desserts and breakfast foods.

INGREDIENTS | SERVES 20

1 cup raspberries

1 cup blackberries

1 cup golden raspberries

½ cup water

½ teaspoon raw honey

Place all the ingredients in a 2-quart slow cooker. Lightly mash the berries with the back of a spoon or potato masher. Cover and cook on low for 2 hours, then uncover and cook on high for ½ hour.

PER SERVING | Calories: 10 | Fat: 0 g | Protein: 0 g | Sodium: 0 mg | Fiber: 1 g | Carbohydrates: 2 g

Artichoke Sauce

Slow-cooking artichoke hearts gives them a velvety texture.

INGREDIENTS | SERVES 4

1 teaspoon almond oil

8 ounces frozen artichoke hearts, defrosted

3 cloves garlic, minced

1 medium onion, minced

2 tablespoons capote capers

1 (28-ounce) can crushed tomatoes

1. Heat the oil in a nonstick frying pan over medium heat. Sauté the artichoke hearts, garlic, and onion for about 10–15 minutes, until the onion is translucent and most of the liquid has evaporated.

2. Put the mixture into a 4-quart slow cooker. Stir in the capers and crushed tomatoes.

3. Cook on high for 4 hours or on low for 8 hours.

PER SERVING | Calories: 24 | Fat: 1 g | Protein: 0 g | Sodium: 2 mg | Fiber: 1 g | Carbohydrates: 3 g

Cleaning Slow Cookers

Do not use very abrasive tools or cleansers on a slow-cooker insert. They may scratch the surface, allowing bacteria and food to soak in. Use a soft sponge and baking soda for stubborn stains.

Mango Chutney

This fruity, cool chutney is a nice accompaniment to spicy dishes. To peel a ripe mango, you can slide a spoon, bottom side up, under the skin to remove it easily, without damaging the fruit.

INGREDIENTS | SERVES 8

3 mangoes
1 red onion
½ bunch fresh cilantro
1 teaspoon fresh lime juice
½ teaspoon freshly grated lime zest
Freshly ground black pepper, to taste

Peel and dice the mangoes and onion. Chop the cilantro. Mix together all the ingredients in a medium-size bowl and adjust seasonings to taste.

PER SERVING | Calories: 56 | Fat: 0 g | Protein: 1 g | Sodium: 1.5 mg | Fiber: 1.5 g | Carbohydrates: 13 g

Apple Chutney

Try this as a side for pork dishes instead of applesauce. It is also wonderful with hearty winter squash.

INGREDIENTS | SERVES 4

2 cups ice water
1 tablespoon fresh lemon juice
3 Granny Smith apples
1 shallot
3 sprigs fresh mint
1 tablespoon freshly grated lemon zest
¼ cup white raisins
½ teaspoon cinnamon

1. Combine the water and lemon juice in a large mixing bowl. Core and dice the apples, leaving peels on, and place them in the lemon water.

2. Thinly slice the shallot and chop the mint.

3. Thoroughly drain the apples, then mix together all the ingredients in a medium-size bowl.

PER SERVING | Calories: 80 | Fat: 0 g | Protein: 0.5 g | Sodium: 2 mg | Fiber: 2.5 g | Carbohydrates: 21 g

Plum Sauce

Plum sauce is usually served with egg rolls, which are generally not Paleo-approved. But this delicious sauce is also wonderful brushed on chicken or pork ribs; doing so near the end of the grilling time will add a succulent glaze to the grilled meat.

INGREDIENTS | SERVES 16

8 cups pitted, halved plums (about 3 pounds)
1 small sweet onion, finely diced
1 cup water
1 teaspoon peeled, minced fresh ginger
1 clove garlic, minced
¾ cup raw honey
½ cup lemon juice
1 teaspoon ground coriander
½ teaspoon cinnamon
¼ teaspoon cayenne pepper
¼ teaspoon ground cloves

1. Add the plums, onion, water, ginger, and garlic to a 4-quart slow cooker. Cover and cook on low, stirring occasionally, for 4 hours or until plums and onion are tender.

2. Use an immersion blender to pulverize the contents of the slow cooker before straining it, or press the cooked plum mixture through a sieve.

3. Return the liquefied and strained plum mixture to the slow cooker and stir in honey, lemon juice, coriander, cinnamon, cayenne pepper, and cloves. Cover and cook on low, stirring occasionally, for 2 hours or until the sauce reaches the consistency of applesauce.

PER SERVING | Calories: 91 | Fat: 0 g | Protein: 1 g | Sodium: 3 mg | Fiber: 1 g | Carbohydrates: 24 g

Tomato and Chicken Sausage Sauce

Sausage is a delicious alternative to meatballs in this rich tomato sauce.

INGREDIENTS | SERVES 6

4 Italian chicken sausages, diced
2 tablespoons tomato paste
1 (28-ounce) can crushed tomatoes
3 cloves garlic, minced
1 large onion, minced
3 tablespoons minced basil
1 tablespoon minced Italian parsley
¼ teaspoon crushed rosemary
¼ teaspoon freshly ground black pepper

1. Quickly brown the sausage on both sides in a nonstick frying pan over medium-high heat, about 1 minute on each side. Drain any grease.

2. Add the sausage to a 4-quart slow cooker, along with the remaining ingredients. Stir.

3. Cook on low for 8 hours.

PER SERVING | Calories: 82 | Fat: 2 g | Protein: 13 g | Sodium: 88 mg | Fiber: 1 g | Carbohydrates: 3 g

Chipotle Tomato Sauce

Try this southwestern take on the classic Italian tomato sauce on spaghetti squash or as salsa on a southwestern dish of choice.

INGREDIENTS | SERVES 6

3 cloves garlic, minced

1 large onion, minced

1 (28-ounce) can crushed tomatoes

1 (14.5-ounce) can diced tomatoes

3 chipotle peppers in adobo, minced

1 teaspoon dried oregano

1 tablespoon fresh cilantro, minced

½ teaspoon freshly ground black pepper

Place all the ingredients in a 4-quart slow cooker. Cook on low for 8–10 hours. Stir before serving.

PER SERVING | Calories: 19 | Fat: 0 g | Protein: 1 g | Sodium: 3 mg | Fiber: 1 g | Carbohydrates: 4 g

Know Your Slow Cooker

When using a new or new-to-you slow cooker for the first time, pick a day when someone can be there to keep tabs on it. In general, older slow cookers cook at a higher temperature than newer models, but even new slow cookers can vary. It is a good idea to know the quirks of a particular slow cooker so food is not overcooked or undercooked. Tweak cooking times accordingly.

Bolognese Sauce

Also called Bolognese or ragù alla Bolognese, this recipe combines vegetables and meat to create the perfect sauce for pouring over just about any beef and/or veggie dish.

INGREDIENTS | SERVES 6

2 teaspoons avocado oil

½ pound lean, grass-fed ground beef

½ pound ground pork

1 large onion, minced

1 large carrot, minced

1 stalk celery, minced

3 ounces tomato paste

1 (28-ounce) can diced tomatoes

½ cup canned, unsweetened coconut milk

1 tablespoon Italian seasoning

¼ teaspoon ground black pepper

⅛ teaspoon nutmeg

1. Heat the oil in a nonstick frying pan over medium heat. Brown the ground beef and pork, about 5–10 minutes. Drain off any excess fat.

2. Add the meats and the remaining ingredients to a 4-quart slow cooker. Cook on low for 8–10 hours. Stir before serving.

PER SERVING | Calories: 174 | Fat: 14 g | Protein: 8 g | Sodium: 148 mg | Fiber: 1 g | Carbohydrates: 6 g

Sun-Dried Tomato Sauce

Sun-dried tomatoes are an excellent source of lycopene, a micronutrient shown to be associated with cardiovascular health benefits and disease prevention.

INGREDIENTS | SERVES 4

1½ cups chopped sun-dried tomatoes

1 (28-ounce) can tomatoes, chopped

1 (14.5-ounce) can tomatoes, chopped

1 medium onion, chopped

2 cloves garlic, minced

1 cup chopped celery

⅔ cup vegetable broth

1½ teaspoons basil

1 teaspoon dried fennel seed

½ teaspoon oregano

½ teaspoon pepper

8 ounces sliced mushrooms (optional)

Place all the ingredients in a 4- or 6-quart slow cooker, cover, and cook on low for 6–8 hours.

PER SERVING | Calories: 140 | Fat: 2 g | Protein: 7 g | Sodium: 1,050 mg | Fiber: 7 g | Carbohydrates: 30 g

Spinach Marinara Sauce

Powerfully flavored and nutrient-rich, this sauce goes well with chicken, beef, or turkey meatballs, or over a vegetable medley side dish or main course.

INGREDIENTS | SERVES 8

1 (28-ounce) can peeled, crushed tomatoes, with liquid

1 (10-ounce) package frozen, chopped spinach, thawed and drained

2 ⅔ (6-ounce) cans tomato paste (16 ounces)

1 (4.5-ounce) can sliced mushrooms, drained

1 medium onion, chopped

5 cloves garlic, minced

2 bay leaves

⅓ cup peeled and grated carrot

¼ cup avocado oil

2½ tablespoons red pepper flakes

2 tablespoons lemon juice

2 tablespoons dried oregano

2 tablespoons dried basil

1. In a 4- or 6-quart slow cooker, combine all the ingredients, cover, and cook on high for 4 hours.

2. Stir, reduce heat to low, and cook for 1–2 more hours.

PER SERVING | Calories: 154 | Fat: 8 g | Protein: 5 g | Sodium: 482 mg | Fiber: 6 g | Carbohydrates: 21 g

Ground Turkey Tomato Sauce

This sauce is packed full of fresh, natural flavor. It's an excellent complement to just about any Italian dish.

INGREDIENTS | SERVES 6

2 tablespoons avocado oil
1 pound ground turkey
1 (14.5-ounce) can stewed tomatoes
1 (6-ounce) can tomato paste
½ teaspoon dried thyme
1 teaspoon dried basil
½ teaspoon oregano
½–1 teaspoon raw honey (optional)
1 yellow onion, chopped
1 bell pepper, chopped
2 cloves garlic, crushed
1 bay leaf
¼ cup water
4 ounces chopped or sliced mushrooms, fresh or canned, drained

1. Heat the oil in a frying pan over medium heat. Add the ground turkey and cook for 5–7 minutes until brown.

2. While browning turkey, place stewed tomatoes, tomato paste, thyme, basil, oregano, and honey in a 4- or 6-quart slow cooker. Stir well and turn slow cooker to low heat.

3. Transfer browned turkey to slow cooker with slotted spoon. In pan with ground-turkey drippings, sauté onion, pepper, garlic, and bay leaf for 3–5 minutes until softened.

4. Add the sautéed vegetables, water, and chopped mushrooms to the slow cooker. Cover and cook on low 4–6 hours. Thin with a little water if necessary.

PER SERVING | Calories: 211 | Fat: 13 g | Protein: 15 g | Sodium: 389 mg | Fiber: 2 g | Carbohydrates: 9 g

Cranberry Sauce

Serve this sweet-tart cranberry sauce with a holiday meal.
You can also use it as a spread or pour it over your favorite dessert.

INGREDIENTS | SERVES 10

12 ounces fresh cranberries
½ cup freshly squeezed orange juice
½ cup water
½ teaspoon orange zest
½ teaspoon raw honey

Place all ingredients into a 1½- or 2-quart slow cooker. Cook on high for 2½ hours. Stir before serving.

PER SERVING | Calories: 22 | Fat: 0 g | Protein: 0 g | Sodium: 1 mg | Fiber: 2 g | Carbohydrates: 6 g

Cran-Apple Sauce

This sauce is simple, sweet, and loaded with antioxidants like vitamin C.

INGREDIENTS | SERVES 6

1 cup fresh cranberries
8 apples, peeled, cored, and chopped
½ cup raw honey
1 cinnamon stick, halved
6 whole cloves

1. Combine cranberries, apples, and honey in a 4- or 6-quart slow cooker.

2. Place cinnamon stick and cloves in center of a 6" square of cheesecloth. Pull up sides and tie to form a pouch. Place in slow cooker.

3. Cover and cook on low for 4–5 hours or until cranberries and apples are very soft.

PER SERVING (½ CUP) | Calories: 197 | Fat: 0 g | Protein: 1 g | Sodium: 1 mg | Fiber: 4 g | Carbohydrates: 53 g

Rosemary-Mushroom Sauce

This sauce can be used as a marinade as well as a sauce to enhance the flavor and texture of many beef and chicken dishes.

INGREDIENTS | SERVES 4

8 ounces fresh mushrooms, sliced
1 large onion, thinly sliced
1 teaspoon avocado oil
1 tablespoon crushed rosemary
3 cups chicken broth

1. In a frying pan over medium heat, sauté the mushrooms and onions in oil for about 5 minutes, until onions are soft.

2. Place onions and mushrooms in a 4-quart slow cooker. Add the rosemary and broth and stir.

3. Cook on low for 6–8 hours or on high for 3 hours.

PER SERVING | Calories: 133 | Fat: 4 g | Protein: 8 g | Sodium: 65 mg | Fiber: 5 g | Carbohydrates: 15 g

Red Pepper Relish

This sauce has a little kick, spicing up the flavor of just about any entrée or side.

INGREDIENTS | SERVES 8

4 large red bell peppers, stemmed, seeded, and cut into thin strips
2 small Vidalia onions, thinly sliced
6 tablespoons lemon juice
¼ cup raw honey
½ teaspoon dried thyme
½ teaspoon red pepper flakes
½ teaspoon black pepper

1. Combine all the ingredients in a 1½-quart slow cooker and mix well.

2. Cover and cook on low for 4 hours.

PER SERVING | Calories: 61 | Fat: 0 g | Protein: 1 g | Sodium: 6 mg | Fiber: 2 g | Carbohydrates: 15 g

CHAPTER 4

Salads and Dressings

French Dressing
80

Italian Dressing
80

Balsamic Vinaigrette
and Marinade
81

Curry Salad Dressing
82

Asian Dressing
82

Lemon-Dill Dressing
83

Zesty Pecan Chicken
and Grape Salad
84

Mackerel with Tomato
and Cucumber Salad
85

Avocado Chicken Salad
86

Crisp Avocado Salad
86

Apple Coleslaw
87

Avocado and Shrimp
Salad
88

Orange Salad
89

Greek Salad
89

Chicken Salad
90

Mediterranean Tomato
Salad
91

Minty Blueberry Melon
Salad
91

Rainbow Fruit Salad
92

Salmon-Spinach Salad
92

Blood Orange Salad
with Shrimp and Baby
Spinach
93

Five-Spice Crabmeat
Salad
94

Turkey Club Salad with
Bacon, Lettuce, and
Tomato
95

Grilled Tuna Salad with
Asian Vegetables and
Spicy Dressing
96

Filet Mignon and Red
Onion Salad
97

Fresh Tuna Salad à la
Niçoise
98

Arugula and
Fennel Salad with
Pomegranate
99

Shaved Fennel Salad
with Orange Sections
and Toasted Hazelnuts
100

Fire-Kissed Cantaloupe
Salad
100

Curried Chicken Salad
101

Broccoli, Pine Nut, and
Apple Salad
102

Red Pepper and Fennel
Salad
103

Floret Salad
104

Crunchy Fruit Salad
105

French Dressing

This is a great dressing on a crisp green salad.
You can also use it as a marinade for beef, chicken, or pork.

INGREDIENTS | YIELDS 1 CUP

⅓ cup red wine vinegar

½ teaspoon Worcestershire sauce

1 clove garlic, chopped

2 tablespoons chopped fresh parsley

1 teaspoon dried thyme

1 teaspoon dried rosemary

¼ teaspoon raw honey

⅔ cup extra-virgin olive oil

Place all ingredients except the oil in a blender. With the blender running on a medium setting, slowly pour the oil into the jar. Blend until very smooth. Serve immediately on salad or cover and store in the refrigerator for up to 7 days.

PER SERVING (2 TABLESPOONS) | Calories: 77 | Fat: 9 g | Protein: 0 g | Sodium: 3 mg | Fiber: 0 g | Carbohydrates: 1 g

Italian Dressing

Try doubling this recipe and storing in a glass jar.
It will keep for several days and is much better than supermarket dressings.

INGREDIENTS | YIELDS 1 CUP

⅓ cup balsamic vinegar

½ teaspoon dry mustard

1 teaspoon lemon juice

2 cloves garlic, chopped

1 teaspoon dried oregano or 1 tablespoon fresh oregano leaves

½ teaspoon salt

½ teaspoon ground black pepper

½ cup extra-virgin olive oil

Place all ingredients except the oil in a blender. With the blender running on a medium setting, slowly pour the oil into the jar. Blend until very smooth. Serve immediately on salad or cover and store in the refrigerator for up to 7 days.

PER SERVING (1 TABLESPOON) | Calories: 63 | Fat: 7 g | Protein: 0 g | Sodium: 74 mg | Fiber: 0 g | Carbohydrates: 0 g

Balsamic Vinaigrette and Marinade

Because balsamic vinegar is very sweet, it needs a slightly sour counterpoint. In this case, it is lemon juice. It also needs a bit of zip, like pepper or mustard. Use this recipe as a dressing or a marinade.

INGREDIENTS | YIELDS 1 CUP

2 cloves garlic, minced

2 shallots, minced

⅓ cup balsamic vinegar

Juice of ½ lemon

½ teaspoon salt

½ teaspoon freshly ground pepper

½ teaspoon Dijon mustard

½ cup avocado oil

Place all ingredients except the oil in a blender. With the blender running on a medium setting, slowly pour the oil into the jar. Blend until very smooth. Cover and store in the refrigerator for up to 7 days.

PER SERVING (2 TABLESPOONS) | Calories: 76 | Fat: 7 g | Protein: 0 g | Sodium: 3 mg | Fiber: 0 g | Carbohydrates: 4 g

The Condiment of Kings

Mustard is one of the oldest condiments, having been used for over 3,000 years. The first mustards were made from crushed black or brown mustard seeds mixed with vinegar. In 1856, Jean Naigeon of Dijon, France, created Dijon mustard by mixing crushed mustard seeds with sour juice made from unripe grapes.

Curry Salad Dressing

This dressing goes well on any salad and has a nice flavor from the curry powder.

INGREDIENTS | SERVES 1

Juice of 1 lime

1 teaspoon curry powder

½ teaspoon ground black pepper

1 teaspoon dried basil

3 tablespoons olive oil

Place all ingredients except the oil in a blender. With the blender running on a medium setting, slowly pour the oil into the jar. Blend until very smooth. Serve immediately on salad or cover and store in the refrigerator for up to 7 days.

PER SERVING | Calories: 370 | Fat: 41 g | Protein: 0.5 g | Sodium: 3 mg | Fiber: 1 g | Carbohydrates: 2 g

Curry Powder Power

Curry powder is a mixture of spices commonly used in South Asian cooking. While it does not correlate directly to any particular kind of curry, it is popular in Europe and North America to add an Indian flare to dishes. It can contain any number of spices but nearly always includes turmeric, which gives it its distinctive yellow color.

Asian Dressing

Asian dressing is perfect with poultry. When you crave the taste of Chinese food, add this dressing to any plain dish to spice things up a bit.

INGREDIENTS | SERVES 4

2 tablespoons sesame oil

2 tablespoons coconut aminos

½ teaspoon ground black pepper

1 teaspoon dried thyme

2 tablespoons olive oil

Place all ingredients except the oil in a blender. With the blender running on a medium setting, slowly pour the oil into the jar. Blend until very smooth. Serve immediately on salad or cover and store in the refrigerator for up to 7 days.

PER SERVING | Calories: 135 | Fat: 15 g | Protein: 0 g | Sodium: 1 mg | Fiber: 0 g | Carbohydrates: 1 g

Lemon-Dill Dressing

This traditional dressing is best on fish recipes.

INGREDIENTS | SERVES 2

Juice of 1 lemon
1 teaspoon fresh dill
½ teaspoon ground black pepper
2 tablespoons olive oil

Place all ingredients except the oil in a blender. With the blender running on a medium setting, slowly pour the oil into the jar. Blend until very smooth. Serve immediately on salad or cover and store in the refrigerator for up to 7 days.

PER SERVING | Calories: 120 | Fat: 14 g | Protein: 0 g | Sodium: 0.5 g | Fiber: 0 g | Carbohydrates: 0 g

Oils

Many salad dressing recipes call for olive oil, but you should feel free to experiment with various Paleo-friendly oils. Each oil has a different flavor and, more important, a different fat profile. Flaxseed oil is higher in omega-3 fatty acid than others. Walnut oil has a lower omega-6 to omega-3 ratio compared with others. Udo's Oil is a nice blend of oils with various omega-3s, 6s, and 9s. These oils together have a nice flavor and have the best to offer in a fat profile.

Zesty Pecan Chicken and Grape Salad

Coating your chicken with nuts adds a crispy skin that keeps the meat moist and tender.

INGREDIENTS | SERVES 6

¼ cup toasted chopped pecans

1 teaspoon chili powder

¼ cup avocado oil

1½ pounds boneless, skinless chicken breasts

1½ cups white grapes

6 cups salad greens

Toasting Nuts for Fresher Flavor and Crispness

To bring out the natural flavor of the nuts, heat them on the stovetop or in the oven for a few minutes. For the stovetop, spread nuts in a dry frying pan, and heat over a medium flame until their natural oils come to the surface. For the oven, spread the nuts in a single layer on a baking sheet, and toast for 5–10 minutes at 350°F, until the oils are visible. Cool nuts before serving.

1. Preheat oven to 400°F.

2. In a blender, mix the pecans and chili powder. Pour in the oil while the blender is running. When the mixture is thoroughly combined, pour it into a shallow bowl.

3. Coat the chicken with the pecan mixture and place on racked baking dish; roast for 40–50 minutes, until the chicken is thoroughly cooked. Remove from oven, let cool for 5 minutes, and thinly slice.

4. Slice the grapes and tear the greens into bite-size pieces. To serve, fan the chicken over the greens and sprinkle with sliced grapes.

PER SERVING | Calories: 220 | Fat: 13 g | Protein: 21 g | Sodium: 11 mg | Fiber: 1 g | Carbohydrates: 5.5 g

Mackerel with Tomato and Cucumber Salad

According to the USDA National Nutrient Database for Standard Reference, mackerel contains 2.3 grams of omega-3 for every 100 grams of fish. That makes mackerel the fish with the most essential fatty acids (EFA).

INGREDIENTS | SERVES 4

15 ounces mackerel fillets, drained

1 clove garlic, crushed

1½ tablespoons coconut oil

1 tablespoon chopped fresh basil

½ teaspoon ground black pepper

10 cherry tomatoes, halved

½ cucumber, peeled and diced

1 small onion, chopped

2 cups mixed lettuce greens

1. Place mackerel in a medium-size bowl with garlic and coconut oil.

2. Add basil and pepper to mackerel mixture, turn fish to coat evenly, and transfer to a medium-size frying pan. Sauté over medium heat for 5–8 minutes on each side, or until brown.

3. Cut cooked mackerel into bite-size pieces and place in a clean bowl.

4. Stir in tomatoes, cucumber, onion, and lettuce and serve.

PER SERVING | Calories: 235 | Fat: 16 g | Protein: 16 g | Sodium: 82 mg | Fiber: 1 g | Carbohydrates: 3.5 g

Avocado Chicken Salad

This recipe makes a great party salad.
You can serve it in lettuce cups for a meal or in small cups with spoons as an appetizer.

INGREDIENTS | SERVES 3

3 avocados, pitted and peeled

2 boneless, skinless chicken breasts, cooked and shredded

½ red onion, chopped

1 large tomato, chopped

¼ cup chopped cilantro

Juice of 1 large lime

1. In a medium-size bowl, mash avocados. Add chicken and mix well.

2. Add onion, tomato, cilantro, and lime juice to the avocado and chicken mixture. Mix well and serve.

PER SERVING | Calories: 340 | Fat: 23 g | Protein: 26 g | Sodium: 10 mg | Fiber: 10 g | Carbohydrates: 13 g

Crisp Avocado Salad

This recipe works well as a side dish to spicy entrées.

INGREDIENTS | SERVES 4

3 cups iceberg lettuce, shredded

2 cups chopped avocado

½ cup sliced red onion

1 (3-ounce) can sliced black olives, drained

1 tablespoon lime juice

2 tablespoons toasted pine nuts

Toss lettuce, avocado, onion, and olives together in a large salad bowl. Sprinkle salad with lime juice. Toss well to coat. Sprinkle with pine nuts and serve.

PER SERVING | Calories: 189 | Fat: 17 g | Protein: 3 g | Sodium: 72 mg | Fiber: 6 g | Carbohydrates: 10 g

Apple Coleslaw

This coleslaw recipe is a refreshing and sweet alternative to the traditional coleslaw with mayonnaise. Additionally, the sesame seeds give it a nice, nutty flavor.

INGREDIENTS | SERVES 4

2 cups packaged coleslaw mix

1 unpeeled tart apple, chopped

½ cup chopped celery

½ cup chopped green pepper

¼ cup extra-virgin olive oil

2 tablespoons lemon juice

½ cup halved seedless grapes

½ cup toasted pecan pieces

1. In a medium bowl, combine the coleslaw mix, apple, celery, and green pepper.

2. In a separate small bowl, whisk together olive oil and lemon juice. Stir in grapes and nuts. Pour over coleslaw and toss to coat.

PER SERVING | Calories: 262 | Fat: 24 g | Protein: 2 g | Sodium: 21 mg | Fiber: 3 g | Carbohydrates: 14 g

Seeds versus Nuts

Nuts have a higher omega-6 to omega-3 ratio. Seeds, on the other hand, have a different profile. Seeds have much lower saturated fat content and are more easily digested by individuals with intestinal issues.

Avocado and Shrimp Salad

Creamy avocado and refreshing citrus bring out the sweetness of shrimp.
This is a salad you will want to have again and again.

INGREDIENTS | SERVES 4

24 raw medium shrimp

2 tablespoons avocado oil

4 green onions, sliced

2 garlic cloves, finely minced

2 tablespoons dry white wine or chicken broth

Salt and pepper, to taste

1 red grapefruit, cut in half

8 ounces butter lettuce, washed and torn into bite-size pieces

1 ripe avocado, sliced

1. Peel and devein the shrimp.

2. In a frying pan set over medium-high heat, add the oil. Add shrimp and half of the green onions. Cook, stirring frequently, until shrimp are half-cooked. Add garlic and white wine or broth, cook for an additional minute, then add salt and pepper.

3. Add juice of one grapefruit half to the pan; cook for 2–3 minutes. Cut the peel off the remaining grapefruit half and cut fruit into bite-size pieces.

4. Place lettuce, avocado slices, and remaining green onions on salad plates for serving. Transfer cooked shrimp to plates.

5. Drizzle sauce from pan over top and garnish with remaining grapefruit pieces.

PER SERVING | Calories: 200 | Fat: 13 g | Protein: 10 g | Sodium: 62 mg | Fiber: 5 g | Carbohydrates: 13 g

Orange Salad

This is a healthful salad that makes a visual impact.

INGREDIENTS | SERVES 4

3 cups cubed butternut squash, drizzled with olive oil and roasted

2 carrots, peeled and shredded

2 cups peeled and diced papaya

2 tablespoons shredded fresh ginger

Juice of 1 lime

1 tablespoon raw honey, or to taste

1 tablespoon olive oil

Freshly ground black pepper

1. Combine the squash, carrots, and papaya in a large salad bowl. Set aside.

2. In a separate bowl, whisk together the ginger, lime juice, honey, olive oil, and pepper until well combined. Toss the dressing with the salad ingredients and serve.

PER SERVING | Calories: 160 | Fat: 4 g | Protein: 1 g | Sodium: 32 mg | Fiber: 7 g | Carbohydrates: 28 g

Greek Salad

Olives are a rich source of oleic acid, a heart-healthy monounsaturated fat. While various types of olives are commonly used in Mediterranean dishes, Greek salads often feature Kalamata olives.

INGREDIENTS | SERVES 4

4 cups chopped romaine lettuce

1 large tomato, seeded and chopped

1 small cucumber, sliced

1 green bell pepper, seeded and cut into rings

¼ cup red wine vinegar

Juice of 1 lemon

1 tablespoon Italian seasoning

Salt and pepper, to taste

¼ cup extra-virgin olive oil

2 teaspoons capers

16 Kalamata olives

1. Place lettuce, tomato, cucumber, and bell pepper in a large bowl.

2. To make dressing, whisk vinegar, lemon juice, Italian seasoning, and salt and pepper in a small bowl. Mix in olive oil.

3. Coat vegetables with dressing.

4. Place salad on plates. Top salad plates with capers and olives.

PER SERVING | Calories: 222 | Fat: 14 g | Protein: 3 g | Sodium: 59 mg | Fiber: 4 g | Carbohydrates: 25 g

Chicken Salad

This salad is the perfect lunch made with extra chicken from last night's dinner.

INGREDIENTS | SERVES 4

1 head romaine lettuce

¼ cup red wine vinegar

2 cloves garlic, minced

2 tablespoons Dijon mustard

1 teaspoon dried rosemary

Salt and pepper, to taste

¼ cup olive oil

¼ cup diced carrot

1 medium red bell pepper, seeded and minced

¼ cup sliced radish

2 cups shredded cooked chicken breast

Not Your Typical Chicken Salad

Using herbs and vegetables brightens up the typical deli-style chicken salad. Adding carrot, radish, bell pepper, and herbs not only spruces up the color on your plate, it also adds crunch and increases the amount of essential vitamins and fiber.

1. Wash romaine lettuce, remove core, and chop leaves into 1" pieces.

2. Combine vinegar, garlic, mustard, rosemary, and salt and pepper in small bowl. Whisk olive oil into vinegar mixture.

3. Place romaine lettuce, carrot, bell pepper, radish, and chicken in a large bowl. Pour dressing over salad and toss to coat.

PER SERVING | Calories: 281 | Fat: 17 g | Protein: 24 g | Sodium: 164 mg | Fiber: 5 g | Carbohydrates: 9 g

Mediterranean Tomato Salad

Use juicy tomatoes for this recipe, such as heirloom or beefsteak.
You can substitute orange bell pepper for the yellow if needed.

INGREDIENTS | SERVES 4

2 cups sliced tomatoes

1 cup peeled, chopped cucumber

⅓ cup diced yellow bell pepper

¼ cup sliced radish

¼ cup flat-leaf parsley, chopped

1 garlic clove, finely minced

1 tablespoon lemon juice

3 tablespoons extra-virgin olive oil

Salt and pepper, to taste

2 cups baby spinach leaves, torn

1. Toss tomatoes, cucumber, bell pepper, radish, and parsley together in a large salad bowl.

2. Sprinkle garlic, lemon juice, and oil over tomato mixture. Toss to coat. Add salt and pepper to taste. Split spinach between four plates and top with tomato mixture. Serve immediately.

PER SERVING | Calories: 131 | Fat: 10 g | Protein: 2.5 g | Sodium: 71 mg | Fiber: 2.5 g | Carbohydrates: 7 g

Minty Blueberry Melon Salad

Seedless watermelons can sometimes have small white seeds scattered among the flesh.
Use a fork to remove any noticeable seeds from the cubed watermelon before making the salad.

INGREDIENTS | SERVES 4

1½ cups cubed cantaloupe (1" cubes)

1 cup cubed seedless watermelon (1" cubes)

¾ cup blueberries

1 cup halved green grapes

1 tablespoon minced mint leaves

1 teaspoon minced flat-leaf parsley

1. Gently toss the cantaloupe, watermelon, blueberries, and grapes together in a large salad bowl.

2. Add mint and parsley and toss to mix. Serve immediately or chill in fridge for up to 2 hours.

PER SERVING | Calories: 65 | Fat: 0.5 g | Protein: 1.5 g | Sodium: 12 mg | Fiber: 1.5 g | Carbohydrates: 16 g

Rainbow Fruit Salad

You can't go wrong with this salad—it's juicy, fresh, naturally low in fat and sodium, and cholesterol-free. Enjoy it as a salad or as a dessert.

INGREDIENTS | SERVES 12

1 large mango, peeled and diced

2 cups fresh blueberries

1 cup sliced bananas

2 cups halved fresh strawberries

2 cups seedless grapes

1 cup unpeeled, sliced nectarines

½ cup peeled, sliced kiwi fruit

⅓ cup freshly squeezed orange juice

2 tablespoons lemon juice

1½ tablespoons raw honey

¼ teaspoon ground ginger

⅛ teaspoon ground nutmeg

1. Gently toss mango, blueberries, bananas, strawberries, grapes, nectarines, and kiwi together in a large mixing bowl.

2. In a separate bowl, whisk together orange juice, lemon juice, honey, ginger, and nutmeg.

3. Chill fruit until needed, up to 3 hours. Just before serving, pour honey-orange sauce over fruit and toss gently to coat.

PER SERVING | Calories: 83 | Fat: 0.5 g | Protein: 1.5 g | Sodium: 2 mg | Fiber: 3 g | Carbohydrates: 21 g

Salmon-Spinach Salad

This salad makes perfect use of leftover salmon. Salmon will only remain good in the fridge for two days, so make sure you find a use for it quickly!

INGREDIENTS | SERVES 1

1 (5-ounce) salmon fillet, cooked

1 cup spinach leaves

½ cup red grapes

¼ cup shredded carrots

1 tablespoon sliced almonds

1 tablespoon fresh raspberries

Combine ingredients in a bowl and enjoy.

PER SERVING | Calories: 314 | Fat: 15 g | Protein: 33 g | Sodium: 108 mg | Fiber: 3 g | Carbohydrates: 15 g

Blood Orange Salad with Shrimp and Baby Spinach

For an elegant supper or luncheon salad, this is a crowd-pleaser.
The deep red flesh of the blood oranges contrasted with the saturated green of spinach
and the bright pink shrimp make for a dramatic presentation!

INGREDIENTS | SERVES 4

6 cups baby spinach

2 blood oranges

1¼ pounds shrimp, cleaned, cooked, and chilled

2 tablespoons fresh lemon juice

¼ cup extra-virgin olive oil

¼ teaspoon dry mustard

¼ cup stemmed, loosely packed parsley

Fresh Spinach—Not Lettuce

When you can, substitute fresh baby spinach for less nutritious iceberg lettuce. White or pale green lettuce can be used as an accent but has less nutritional substance than such greens as spinach, escarole, and watercress.

1. Divide the spinach among four serving plates.

2. Peel the oranges. Slice them crosswise, about ¼" thick, picking out any seeds. Arrange on top of the spinach. Arrange the shrimp around the oranges.

3. Place the rest of the ingredients in a blender and purée until the dressing is a bright green. Pour over the salads. Serve chilled.

PER SERVING | Calories: 286 | Fat: 16 g | Protein: 24 g | Sodium: 194 mg | Fiber: 3 g | Carbohydrates: 14 g

Five-Spice Crabmeat Salad

This seafood salad makes a wonderful main course for lunch or supper. Mild and delicious, napa or Chinese cabbage keeps well in the refrigerator and adds an excellent crunch in salads.

INGREDIENTS | SERVES 4

2 cups shredded napa cabbage

1 pound fresh lump crabmeat (any kind)

1 cup Homemade Mayonnaise (see Chapter 3)

2 tablespoons champagne or white wine vinegar

2 tablespoons lemon juice

1 tablespoon sesame seed oil

¼ teaspoon Chinese five-spice powder

Salt and pepper, to taste

1. In a large serving bowl, toss the cabbage and crabmeat.

2. In a separate bowl, whisk together the rest of the ingredients, add to the cabbage-crab mixture, and toss to coat. Serve chilled.

PER SERVING | Calories: 528 | Fat: 48 g | Protein: 22 g | Sodium: 1,255 mg | Fiber: 0 g | Carbohydrates: 3 g

Exploring Vinegar

Champagne vinegar is made from the same champagne used for drinking. It is aged in oak barrels, and because it is made from light, sparkling wine, it has a bright, crisp taste that is delicious in vinaigrettes.

Turkey Club Salad with Bacon, Lettuce, and Tomato

This is a satisfying lunch salad, delicious and easy to make.

INGREDIENTS | SERVES 4

1 pound cooked turkey breast

4 strips nitrite-free bacon

1 pint cherry tomatoes, halved

1 ripe avocado, peeled and diced

½ cup Homemade Mayonnaise (see Chapter 3)

½ cup French Dressing (see recipe in this chapter)

2 cups shredded lettuce

Thickly dice turkey breast. Fry bacon until crisp and crumble into a large serving bowl. Mix all ingredients except the lettuce in the bowl. Serve over lettuce.

PER SERVING | Calories: 568 | Fat: 49 g | Protein: 21 g | Sodium: 1,680 mg | Fiber: 4 g | Carbohydrates: 13 g

Salad Dressings

Did you ever study the labels of commercial salad dressings? There are chemicals and preservatives in these dressings that you may not want to ingest. Instead, make your own dressing and store it in a empty, clean olive jar. You'll know everything in it is healthy!

Grilled Tuna Salad with Asian Vegetables and Spicy Dressing

The fish is hot, the vegetables are spicy, and the greens are chilled!
This is an exotic salad that is deceptively easy to make.

INGREDIENTS | SERVES 4

3 tablespoons sesame oil

½ cup olive oil

2 cloves garlic, minced

1 teaspoon minced fresh ginger

2 teaspoons sherry vinegar

1 tablespoon coconut aminos

2–3 cups shredded napa cabbage

1 red onion, cut in wedges

2 Japanese eggplants, cut in half lengthwise

4 (¼-pound) tuna steaks

A Quick Meal

Tuna is a large fish that is part of the mackerel family. It has a unique circulatory system that allows it to retain a higher body temperature than the cool water it inhabits. This provides tuna with an extra burst of energy that allows it to reach short-distance swimming speeds of over 40 miles per hour!

1. In a bowl, whisk together the sesame oil, olive oil, garlic, ginger, sherry vinegar, and coconut aminos. Divide evenly in two bowls and set aside.

2. Place the cabbage on serving plates. Brush the onion, eggplants, and tuna with the dressing from one bowl, being careful not to contaminate the dressing with a brush that has touched the fish.

3. Grill the vegetables and tuna for 3–4 minutes per side over medium-high heat. Arrange the vegetables and fish over the cabbage. Drizzle with the reserved dressing from the second bowl.

PER SERVING | Calories: 598 | Fat: 47 g | Protein: 34 g | Sodium: 432 mg | Fiber: 3 g | Carbohydrates: 11 g

Filet Mignon and Red Onion Salad

There are few things that taste better cold than filet mignon!

INGREDIENTS | SERVES 4

1¼ pounds well-trimmed whole filet mignon

Salt and pepper, to taste

½ cup French Dressing (see recipe in this chapter)

1 red onion, thinly sliced

2 tablespoons capers

16 black olives, pitted and sliced

Bed of chopped romaine lettuce

Know Your Beef

Filet mignon is the small part of a beef tenderloin and is considered the most delectable cut of beef because of its melt-in-your-mouth texture. Save yourself some money by preparing this at home instead of dining out!

1. Preheat oven to 400°F. Place the filet mignon on a baking pan. Sprinkle it with salt and pepper. Roast for 15 minutes. Rest the meat for 10 minutes before slicing.

2. Slice the filet mignon and place in a bowl with the French Dressing, onion, capers, and olives. Toss gently to coat.

3. Spread the lettuce on a serving platter. Arrange the filet mignon mixture over the top. Serve at room temperature or chilled.

PER SERVING | Calories: 501 | Fat: 34 g | Protein: 41 g | Sodium: 620 mg | Fiber: 1 g | Carbohydrates: 6 g

Fresh Tuna Salad à la Niçoise

The niçoise salad originates from Nice, a French city on the Mediterranean Sea. This salad is popular in France, like the Cobb salad is enjoyed in the United States.

INGREDIENTS | SERVES 2

¼ pound asparagus, trimmed and cut into 1" lengths

2 (4-ounce) tuna steaks

2 tablespoons avocado oil

Salt and pepper, to taste

1 head butter lettuce

1½ tablespoons capers

¼ cup niçoise olives

½ cup cherry tomatoes

2 tablespoons Italian Dressing (see recipe in this chapter)

2 hard-boiled eggs, peeled and quartered

Timesaving Tip

If you are tight on time and money, try substituting the tuna steaks with a large can of wild-caught tuna. Canned albacore usually contains more omega-3 fatty acids than chunk light tuna. The salad will still taste authentic without spending extra cash and time grilling the fish.

1. Cook asparagus in a pot of boiling water, uncovered, until crisp-tender, about 4 minutes, then transfer immediately to a bowl of ice water to stop cooking. Drain asparagus and pat dry.

2. Brush tuna with oil and season with salt and pepper as desired. Grill on lightly oiled rack or grill pan, uncovered, turning over once, until browned on the outside and pink in the center, 6–8 minutes total. Slice tuna into ¼"-thick pieces.

3. Wash lettuce and tear into bite-size pieces; place in large bowl. Add asparagus, capers, olives, and tomatoes to bowl; coat with Italian Dressing.

4. Divide salad onto two plates. Top with tuna and egg quarters.

PER SERVING | Calories: 430 | Fat: 29 g | Protein: 8 g | Sodium: 1,057 mg | Fiber: 4 g | Carbohydrates: 35 g

Arugula and Fennel Salad with Pomegranate

Pomegranates pack a high dose of health-promoting antioxidants. They are in peak season October through January and may not be easy to find at other times of the year. Cranberries can be substituted in this recipe if pomegranates are not available.

INGREDIENTS | SERVES 4

2 large navel oranges
1 pomegranate
4 cups arugula
1 cup thinly sliced fennel
4 tablespoons olive oil
Salt and pepper, to taste

Fennel Facts

Fennel, a crunchy and slightly sweet vegetable, is a popular Mediterranean ingredient. Fennel has a white or greenish-white bulb and long stalks with feathery green leaves stemming from the top. Fennel is closely related to cilantro, dill, carrots, and parsley.

1. Cut the tops and bottoms off of the oranges and then cut the remaining peel away. Slice each orange into 10–12 small pieces.

2. Remove seeds from the pomegranate.

3. Place arugula, orange pieces, pomegranate seeds, and fennel slices into a large bowl.

4. Coat the salad with olive oil and season with salt and pepper as desired.

PER SERVING | Calories: 224 | Fat: 15 g | Protein: 3 g | Sodium: 20 g | Fiber: 5 g | Carbohydrates: 24 g

Shaved Fennel Salad with Orange Sections and Toasted Hazelnuts

Tangelos, mandarin oranges, or any easily sectioned citrus will work wonderfully with this recipe.

INGREDIENTS | SERVES 6

3 bulbs fennel

6 large oranges

1 teaspoon finely chopped hazelnuts

⅓ cup fresh orange juice

2 tablespoons almond oil

1 tablespoon fresh orange zest

1. Finely slice the fennel bulbs. Remove the peel and pith from the oranges. With a small paring knife, remove each section of the oranges and slice away membrane.

2. Form a mound of shaved fennel on each serving plate and arrange the oranges on top. Sprinkle with nuts, then drizzle with the orange juice and oil. Finish with a sprinkle of zest.

PER SERVING | Calories: 172 | Fat: 5 g | Protein: 3 g | Sodium: 61 mg | Fiber: 7 g | Carbohydrates: 32 g

Fire-Kissed Cantaloupe Salad

*Garnish this light and spicy salad with fresh cilantro or a slice of mango.
Serve it as a side to any filling meat dish.*

INGREDIENTS | SERVES 4

½ medium mango, peeled, diced, and puréed in a blender

1 tablespoon walnut oil

⅛ teaspoon chili powder

⅛ teaspoon sweet paprika

⅛ teaspoon ground red pepper

3 cups cubed cantaloupe

½ cup diced red onion

1. Whisk mango purée, oil, chili powder, paprika, and red pepper together in a small bowl. Whisk until mixture is emulsified.

2. Add cantaloupe and red onion to a large mixing bowl. Pour dressing over salad. Toss well to mix and coat. Cover salad and let chill in refrigerator for 15 minutes. Remove bowl from refrigerator, toss salad gently, and serve.

PER SERVING | Calories: 291 | Fat: 27 g | Protein: 1.5 g | Sodium: 41 mg | Fiber: 1.5 g | Carbohydrates: 11 g

Curried Chicken Salad

The recipe makes two servings, but you can double or triple the amounts.
You can also change the spices around for more variety.

INGREDIENTS | SERVES 2

2 tablespoons almond oil

8 ounces chicken breast, cubed

1 stalk celery, sliced

1 small onion, diced

½ English cucumber, diced

½ cup chopped almonds

2 apples, cored, peeled, and chopped

½ teaspoon curry powder

4 cups baby romaine lettuce

1. In frying pan, heat oil over medium-high heat and cook chicken, celery, and onion thoroughly 5–10 minutes. Set aside to cool.

2. In mixing bowl, combine cucumber, almonds, apples, and curry powder with the cooled chicken mixture.

3. Serve over bed of baby romaine lettuce.

PER SERVING | Calories: 431 | Fat: 27 g | Protein: 27 g | Sodium: 31 mg | Fiber: 8 g | Carbohydrates: 28 g

Cage Free

Cage-free, barn-roaming chickens are an important component of the Paleolithic diet. Chickens raised in commercial chicken farms are fed a corn-based diet with low omega-3 fatty acid content. Additionally, they are kept in coops where they get little exercise and are fed antibiotics to maintain their health. All things injected into your meat sources will filter up through your food.

Broccoli, Pine Nut, and Apple Salad

This quick little salad will tide you over until your next meal. The broccoli and apple taste great together, and the toasted pine nuts add a little bit of crunch.

INGREDIENTS | SERVES 2

4 tablespoons almond oil
¾ cup pine nuts
2 cups broccoli florets
2 cups diced green apples
Juice of 1 lemon

1. Heat oil in a small frying pan over medium-high heat and sauté the pine nuts until golden brown.

2. Mix broccoli and apples in a medium-size bowl. Add the pine nuts and toss.

3. Squeeze lemon juice over salad and serve.

PER SERVING | Calories: 621 | Fat: 53 g | Protein: 15 g | Sodium: 34 mg | Fiber: 7 g | Carbohydrates: 31 g

Red Pepper and Fennel Salad

Fennel has a fantastic licorice flavor that blends nicely with nuts. The red pepper adds a flash of color and a bit of sweetness to the mix.

INGREDIENTS | SERVES 2

⅓ cup pine nuts, toasted

3 tablespoons sesame seeds, toasted

2 tablespoons avocado oil

1 medium red bell pepper, seeded and halved

6 leaves romaine lettuce, shredded

½ bulb fennel, diced

1 tablespoon walnut oil

Juice from 1 lime

Black pepper, to taste

Walnut Oil

Walnut oil cannot withstand high heat, so it's best to add it to food that has already been cooked or is served raw, such as a salad. If you choose to cook with it, use a lower flame to avoid burning the oil.

1. Preheat broiler.

2. In a medium-size frying pan, sauté pine nuts and sesame seeds in avocado oil over medium heat for 5 minutes.

3. Grill pepper under the broiler about 3 minutes per side until the skin is blackened, and the flesh has softened slightly.

4. Place pepper halves in a paper bag to cool slightly. When cool enough to handle, remove skin and slice into strips.

5. Combine red pepper slices, lettuce, and fennel in a salad bowl.

6. Add walnut oil, lime juice, and black pepper to taste. Mix well with salad bowl contents. Add nut mixture and serve.

PER SERVING | Calories: 456 | Fat: 43 g | Protein: 7 g | Sodium: 37 mg | Fiber: 6 g | Carbohydrates: 17 g

Floret Salad

Broccoli is one of the most nutrient-dense green vegetables. Try this floret salad to maximize on taste while boosting your health simultaneously.

INGREDIENTS | SERVES 2

⅔ cup fresh cauliflower florets

⅔ cup fresh broccoli florets

2 tablespoons chopped red onion

8 ounces uncured, nitrate-free bacon, cooked and chopped

5 teaspoons raw honey

¼ cup walnut oil

2 tablespoons sliced almonds

1. In a medium-size bowl, combine cauliflower, broccoli, red onion, and bacon.

2. In a small bowl, whisk honey and walnut oil.

3. Combine honey mixture with florets and toss.

4. Top with almonds just before serving.

PER SERVING | Calories: 864 | Fat: 80 g | Protein: 16 g | Sodium: 954 mg | Fiber: 2 g | Carbohydrates: 21 g

Broccoli: Superfood

Broccoli is one of the healthiest vegetables you can eat. Ounce for ounce, broccoli has more vitamin C than an orange and as much calcium as a glass of milk. Broccoli is packed with fiber to promote digestive health and it is quite rich in vitamin A.

Crunchy Fruit Salad

When you're in the mood for a sweet treat, this crunchy salad will fulfill that sugar craving and replenish glycogen storage after workouts.

INGREDIENTS | SERVES 2

½ fresh pineapple, peeled, cored, and cubed

1 medium fresh papaya, cubed

1 medium ripe banana, sliced

½ cup halved seedless grapes

1 tablespoon raw honey

¼ cup chopped pecans

¼ cup unsweetened coconut flakes

Combine all ingredients, toss, and serve.

PER SERVING | Calories: 412 | Fat: 14 g | Protein: 5 g | Sodium: 11 mg | Fiber: 10 g | Carbohydrates: 77 g

Seasonal Fruits

It is always best to eat foods that are native to your area and in season. If you eat fruits that are imported, they have traveled long distances and their freshness factor cannot be guaranteed. Your hunter-gatherer ancestors only had foods that were in season at the time of the hunt. They did not have the luxury of importing fruits from a neighboring area. Your body is made to change with the seasons.

CHAPTER 5

Stocks, Soups, and Stews

Basic Vegetable Stock
108

Brown Stock
109

Pork Broth
110

Turkey Stock
110

Fish Stock
111

Seafood Stock
112

Basic Chicken Soup
113

Mushroom Stock
114

Beef and Vegetable
Stew
114

Bouillabaisse
115

Curried Cauliflower
Soup
115

Caveman's Chili
116

No-Bean Chili
117

Paleo "Cream" of
Mushroom Soup
118

Paleo "Cream" of
Broccoli Soup
119

Mushroom and Onion
Soup
119

Chicken and
Mushroom Stew
120

Mediterranean
Seafood Soup
121

Pumpkin Soup
122

Pumpkin Bisque
123

Pork and Apple Stew
124

Caveman's Cabbage
Soup
125

Simple Tomato Soup
126

Acorn Squash Autumn
Bisque
126

Butternut Squash Soup
127

Pumpkin Turkey Chili
127

Cincinnati Chili
128

Lone Star State Chili
129

Texas Firehouse Chili
130

Chicken Chili Verde
131

Pumpkin and Ginger
Soup
132

Tomato Vegetable Soup
132

Zucchini Soup
133

Cream of Cauliflower
Soup
134

Gazpacho
135

Scallion Chive Soup
136

Carrot-Lemon Soup
137

Chicken Chowder
138

Spicy Bison Stew
138

Southwestern Soup
139

Rosemary-Thyme Stew
140

Chicken Bolognese
141

Simple Ground Turkey
and Vegetable Soup
142

Stuffed Pepper Soup
142

Lamb Stew
143

Basic Vegetable Stock

This broth is low in sodium and high in disease-fighting phytochemicals.
Try adding mushrooms for additional flavor.

INGREDIENTS | YIELDS 1 GALLON

2 pounds yellow onions

1 pound carrots

1 pound celery

1 bunch fresh parsley stems

1½ gallons water

4 fresh thyme stems

2 bay leaves (fresh or dried)

10–20 peppercorns

Homemade Stocks

Your homemade stocks give a special quality to all the dishes you add them to. Not only will the flavor of homemade stocks be better than that of store-bought varieties, but you will have added your own personal touch to the meal. Always cook them uncovered, as covering will cause them to become cloudy.

1. Peel and roughly chop the onions and carrots. Roughly chop the celery (stalks only; no leaves) and fresh parsley stems.

2. Put the vegetables, parsley, and water in a stockpot over medium heat; bring to a simmer and cook, uncovered, for 1½ hours.

3. Add the herbs and peppercorns and continue to simmer, uncovered, for 45 minutes. Adjust seasonings to taste.

4. Remove from heat and cool by submerging the pot in a bath of ice water. Transfer stock to freezer-safe containers and freeze until ready to use.

PER SERVING (1 CUP) | Calories: 22 | Fat: 0 g | Protein: 0 g | Sodium: 31 mg | Fiber: 0 g | Carbohydrates: 5.3 g

Brown Stock

When you add ¼ cup of this concentrated stock to a slow-cooked beef dish, you'll get the same succulent flavor as if you first seared the meat in a hot frying pan before adding it to the slow cooker. The stock also gives a delicious flavor boost to slow-cooked tomato sauce or tomato gravy.

INGREDIENTS | YIELDS 4 CUPS

2 large carrots, scrubbed
2 stalks celery
1½ pounds bone-in chuck roast
1½ pounds cracked beef bones
1 large onion, quartered
Freshly ground black pepper, to taste
4½ cups water

1. Preheat the oven to 450°F. Cut the carrots and celery into large pieces. Put them, along with the meat, bones, and onion into a roasting pan. Season with pepper. Put the pan on the middle rack in the oven and roast, turning the meat and vegetables occasionally, for 45 minutes or until evenly browned.

2. Transfer the roasted meat, bones, and vegetables to a 4- or 6-quart slow cooker. Add the water to the roasting pan; scrape any browned bits clinging to the pan and then pour the water into the slow cooker. Cover and cook on low for 8 hours. (It may be necessary to skim accumulated fat and scum from the top of the pan juices; check the broth after 4 hours and again after 6 hours to see if that's needed.)

3. Use a slotted spoon to remove the roast and beef bones. Reserve the roast and the meat removed from the bones for another use; discard the bones.

4. Once the broth has cooled enough to handle, strain it; discard the cooked vegetables. Refrigerate the broth overnight. Remove and discard the hardened fat. The resulting concentrated broth can be kept for 1 or 2 days in the refrigerator, or frozen for up to 3 months.

PER SERVING (1 CUP) | Calories: 33 | Fat: 0 g | Protein: 1 g | Sodium: 50 mg | Fiber: 2 g | Carbohydrates: 8 g

Pork Broth

Pork broth is seldom called for in recipes, but it can add layers of flavor when mixed with chicken broth in vegetable soups.

INGREDIENTS | YIELDS 4 CUPS

1 (3-pound) bone-in pork butt roast

1 large onion, quartered

12 baby carrots

2 stalks celery, cut in half

4½ cups water

Pork Roast Dinner

To make concentrated broth and a pork roast dinner at the same time, increase the amount of carrots, decrease the water to 2½ cups, and add 4 peeled, medium-size sweet potatoes (cut in half) on top. Cook on low for 6 hours.

1. Add all the ingredients to a 4-quart slow cooker. Cover and cook on low for 6 hours or until the pork is tender and pulls away from the bone.

2. Strain; discard the celery and onion. Reserve the pork roast and carrots for another use. Once cooled, cover and refrigerate the broth overnight. Remove and discard the hardened fat. The broth can be kept for 1 or 2 days in the refrigerator, or frozen up to 3 months.

PER SERVING (1 CUP) | Calories: 29 | Fat: 0 g | Protein: 1 g | Sodium: 49 mg | Fiber: 2 g | Carbohydrates: 7 g

Turkey Stock

Popular during the holidays, this is the perfect way to put your leftover turkey to good use. This can also be used as a substitute in recipes calling for chicken stock.

INGREDIENTS | YIELDS 16 CUPS

10 black peppercorns

6 sprigs parsley

4 medium carrots, thickly sliced

4 stalks celery, thickly sliced

4 quarts water

2 medium onions, thickly sliced

2 leeks (white parts only), thickly sliced

1 turkey carcass, cut up

1 cup water

1½ teaspoons dried thyme

Pepper, to taste

1. Combine all the ingredients except pepper in a 6-quart slow cooker. Cover and cook on low for 6–8 hours.

2. Strain the stock through a double-layer of cheesecloth, discarding the solids. Season with pepper to taste.

3. Refrigerate 3–5 hours, until chilled. Remove fat from surface of stock.

4. Freeze or refrigerate the stock and use within 1 week or freeze for up to 3 months.

PER SERVING (1 CUP) | Calories: 154 | Fat: 2 g | Protein: 28 g | Sodium: 104 mg | Fiber: 1 g | Carbohydrates: 4 g

Fish Stock

Use this fish stock in any fish or seafood dish instead of water or chicken stock.

INGREDIENTS | YIELDS 3 QUARTS

3 quarts water

2 large onions, quartered

Head and bones from 3 fish, any type

2 stalks celery, chopped

2 tablespoons peppercorns

1 bunch parsley

1. Place all the ingredients in a 4-quart slow cooker. Cook for 8–10 hours.

2. Remove all the solids. Transfer to another container. Refrigerate overnight.

3. The next day, skim off any foam that has floated to the top. Refrigerate and use within 1 week, or freeze for up to 3 months.

PER SERVING (1 CUP) | Calories: 33 | Fat: 0 g | Protein: 1 g | Sodium: 29 mg | Fiber: 1 g | Carbohydrates: 5 g

Seafood Stock

This recipe calls for the shells only because the amount of time it takes to slow-cook the stock would result in seafood that would be too tough to eat.

INGREDIENTS | YIELDS 4 CUPS

2 pounds large or jumbo shrimp, crab, or lobster shells

1 large onion, thinly sliced

1 tablespoon fresh lemon juice

4 cups water

Fish or Seafood Stock in a Hurry

For each cup of seafood or fish stock called for in a recipe, you can substitute ¼ cup of bottled clam juice and ¾ cup of water. Just keep in mind that the clam juice is very salty, so adjust any recipe in which you use it accordingly

1. Add the seafood shells, onion, lemon juice, and water to a 4-quart slow cooker. Cover and cook on low for 4–8 hours.

2. Strain through a fine sieve or wire-mesh strainer. Discard the shells and onions. Refrigerate in a covered container and use within 2 days or freeze for up to 3 months.

PER SERVING (1 CUP) | Calories: 253 | Fat: 4 g | Protein: 46 g | Sodium: 341 mg | Fiber: 1 g | Carbohydrates: 6 g

Basic Chicken Soup

The major advantage of this soup is that it will be much lower in sodium than canned chicken soups. The only limit is your imagination. Each time you make it, substitute different vegetables and seasonings to tantalize your taste buds.

INGREDIENTS | SERVES 6

1 (5- to 6-pound) whole chicken (including giblets)
2 medium carrots
2 stalks celery
4 large yellow onions
¼ bunch parsley
12 cups water
Freshly ground black pepper, to taste
Kosher salt, to taste

1. Clean, trim, and quarter the chicken. Peel and chop all the vegetables. Chop parsley leaves.

2. Place the chicken and giblets in a stockpot, add the water, and bring to a boil. Reduce heat to a simmer and skim off all foam.

3. Add all the vegetables and parsley, season with salt and pepper, and simmer uncovered for about 3 hours.

4. Remove the chicken and giblets from the stockpot; discard giblets. Remove the meat from the bones, discard the bones, and return the meat to the soup. Serve.

PER SERVING | Calories: 183 | Fat: 8 g | Protein: 16 g | Sodium: 84 mg | Fiber: 1.5 g | Carbohydrates: 5.5 g

Don't Cry over Cut Onions

The sulfur in onions can cause the tears to flow. To avoid teary eyes, peel onions under cold water to wash away the volatile sulfur compounds. Onions are worth it, since they have anti-inflammatory effects on the joints.

Mushroom Stock

Shiitake mushrooms add a rich, bold flavor and also provide a variety of beneficial phytonutrients. Be careful not to overcook this stock.

INGREDIENTS | YIELDS 2 QUARTS

1 quart water

12 ounces white mushrooms

6 sprigs parsley (with leaves)

1 large onion, sliced

1 leek (white part only), sliced

1 stalk celery, sliced

2 ounces dried shiitake mushrooms

1 tablespoon minced garlic

1½ teaspoons black peppercorns

¾ teaspoon dried sage

¾ teaspoon dried thyme

Freshly ground black pepper, to taste

1. Combine all the ingredients except ground pepper in a 6-quart slow cooker; cover and cook on low for 6–8 hours.

2. Strain, discarding solids; season to taste with pepper. Serve immediately, refrigerate and use within 1–2 weeks, or freeze.

PER SERVING (1 CUP) | Calories: 18 | Fat: 0 g | Protein: 1 g | Sodium: 11 mg | Fiber: 1 g | Carbohydrates: 4 g

Beef and Vegetable Stew

Fresh herbs brighten this traditional hearty stew. This recipe could be prepared with a variety of seasonal herbs, so experiment for yourself!

INGREDIENTS | SERVES 4

2 teaspoons almond oil

1 large onion, diced

2 parsnips, diced

2 large carrots, peeled and diced

2 stalks celery, diced

3 cloves garlic, minced

1 tablespoon minced fresh tarragon

2 tablespoons minced fresh rosemary

1 pound lean beef top round roast, cut into 1" cubes

1½ cups water

1 bulb fennel, diced

1 tablespoon minced parsley

1. Heat the oil in a large frying pan over medium-high heat. Sauté the onion, parsnips, carrots, celery, garlic, tarragon, rosemary, and beef for 5–10 minutes, until the ingredients begin to soften and brown. Drain off any excess fat.

2. Place the mixture in a 4-quart slow cooker. Pour in the water. Stir. Cook on low for 8–9 hours.

3. Add the fennel. Cover and cook on high for an additional ½ hour. Stir in the parsley before serving.

PER SERVING | Calories: 227 | Fat: 7 g | Protein: 27 g | Sodium: 145 mg | Fiber: 4 g | Carbohydrates: 13 g

Bouillabaisse

With one bite, this slightly simplified version of the Provençal fish stew will convert anyone who is skeptical about cooking seafood in the slow cooker into a believer.

INGREDIENTS | SERVES 8

1 bulb fennel, sliced

2 leeks, sliced

2 large carrots, peeled and cut into coins

2 shallots, minced

5 cloves garlic, minced

2 tablespoons minced fresh basil

1 tablespoon orange zest

1 tablespoon lemon zest

1 bay leaf

1 (14.5-ounce) can diced tomatoes

2 quarts water or Fish Stock (see recipe in this chapter)

1 pound cubed hake or catfish

8 ounces medium peeled shrimp

1 pound mussels, scrubbed and rinsed

1. Place the vegetables, garlic, basil, zests, bay leaf, tomatoes, and water or stock in a 6-quart slow cooker. Stir. Cook on low for 8 hours.

2. Add the seafood. Cook on high for 20 minutes. Stir prior to serving. Discard any mussels that do not open.

PER SERVING | Calories: 251 | Fat: 3.5 g | Protein: 27 g | Sodium: 384 mg | Fiber: 8 g | Carbohydrates: 31 g

Curried Cauliflower Soup

Orange cauliflower is an excellent variety to use in this recipe. It has 25 percent more vitamin A than white cauliflower and lends an attractive color to the soup.

INGREDIENTS | SERVES 4

1 pound cauliflower florets

2½ cups water

1 medium onion, minced

2 cloves garlic, minced

3 teaspoons curry powder

¼ teaspoon cumin

1. Place all the ingredients in a 4-quart slow cooker. Stir. Cook on low for 8 hours.

2. Using an immersion blender or standard blender (in batches), blend until smooth.

PER SERVING | Calories: 46 | Fat: 1 g | Protein: 3 g | Sodium: 40 mg | Fiber: 3 g | Carbohydrates: 10 g

Caveman's Chili

This chili is medium on the heat-o-meter. If you are looking for five-alarm chili, add more chipotles or a chopped jalapeño or two for some kick!

INGREDIENTS | SERVES 8

2 tablespoons coconut oil

1 medium onion, chopped

1 stalk celery, chopped

1 green bell pepper, seeded and chopped

1 red bell pepper, seeded and chopped

1 parsnip, peeled and diced

4 cloves garlic, minced

1 pound grass-fed ground beef

2 tablespoons chopped chipotles in adobo

1 tablespoon cumin

1 tablespoon dried oregano

1 tablespoon chili powder

1½ teaspoons salt

1 (28-ounce) can diced tomatoes

3 cups Brown Stock (see recipe in this chapter) or organic beef stock

1. Heat coconut oil in a large pot over medium heat.

2. Stir-fry onion, celery, peppers, parsnip, and garlic in oil for 10 minutes. Add ground beef and cook until no longer pink (about 7 minutes).

3. Stir in chipotles, cumin, oregano, chili powder, and salt. Add tomatoes and stock. Reduce heat to low and simmer, uncovered, for 45 minutes.

PER SERVING | Calories: 186 | Fat: 10 g | Protein: 14 g | Sodium: 1,430 mg | Fiber: 3 g | Carbohydrates: 12 g

Sauté the Meat When Making Chili

Even though it is not aesthetically necessary to brown the meat when making chili, sautéing meat before adding it to the slow cooker allows you to drain off any extra fat. Not only is it healthier to cook with less fat, your chili will be unappetizingly greasy if there is too much fat present in the meat during cooking.

No-Bean Chili

For a variation, try this with lean beef sirloin instead of pork.

INGREDIENTS | SERVES 6

1 tablespoon avocado oil

1 pound boneless pork tenderloin, cubed

1 large onion, diced

3 poblano chilies, diced

2 cloves garlic, minced

1 teaspoon cumin

1 teaspoon dried oregano

1 cup chicken broth

1 (15-ounce) can crushed tomatoes

2 teaspoons cayenne pepper

1. In a large nonstick frying pan, heat the oil over medium heat. Add the pork, onion, chilies, and garlic. Sauté 7–10 minutes, until the pork is no longer visibly pink on any side. Drain off any fats or oils and discard them.

2. Pour the pork mixture into a 4-quart slow cooker. Add the remaining ingredients. Stir.

3. Cook on low for 8–9 hours.

PER SERVING | Calories: 157 | Fat: 5 g | Protein: 19 g | Sodium: 64 mg | Fiber: 2 g | Carbohydrates: 5 g

Using Herbs

As a general rule, 1 tablespoon minced fresh herbs equals 1 teaspoon dried herbs. Fresh herbs can be frozen for future use. Discard dried herbs after one year.

Paleo "Cream" of Mushroom Soup

This Paleo-approved "cream" of mushroom soup is a simple and light main dish. It's also a perfect Paleo-friendly base to use when a recipe calls for canned cream soup.

INGREDIENTS | SERVES 4

2 tablespoons avocado oil

2 tablespoons coconut butter

1 cup finely diced fresh mushrooms

4 tablespoons arrowroot powder

2 cups full-fat coconut milk

½ teaspoon pepper

Cream Soup Variations

You can make any number of homemade cream soups with this recipe. If you would rather have cream of celery soup, use 1 cup of finely diced celery instead of the mushrooms. For a cream of chicken soup, use 1 cup finely diced chicken and 2 teaspoons of poultry seasoning.

1. Heat the oil and coconut butter in a deep saucepan until sizzling. Add the diced mushrooms and cook until soft, approximately 4–5 minutes.

2. In a medium-size bowl, whisk the arrowroot powder into the coconut milk. Slowly add to the mushrooms. Cook on medium heat for 5–10 minutes, whisking constantly, until slightly thickened.

3. Carefully pour cream soup into a greased 2½-quart slow cooker. Add pepper and any additional seasonings you would like. Cook on high for 2 hours or on low for 4 hours.

PER SERVING | Calories: 312 | Fat: 31 g | Protein: 2 g | Sodium: 15 mg | Fiber: 0 g | Carbohydrates: 10 g

Paleo "Cream" of Broccoli Soup

This Paleo-approved "cream" soup serves as a light meal on its own or can be poured over a chicken or vegetable dish to enhance flavor and richness.

INGREDIENTS | SERVES 4

1 (12-ounce) bag frozen broccoli florets, thawed
1 small onion, diced
4 cups chicken broth
Freshly ground black pepper, to taste
1 cup full-fat coconut milk

1. Add the broccoli, onion, broth, and pepper to a 2- or 4-quart slow cooker; cover and cook on low for 4 hours.

2. Use an immersion blender to purée the soup. Stir in the coconut milk. Cover and cook on low, stirring occasionally, for 30 minutes or until the soup is heated through.

PER SERVING | Calories: 241 | Fat: 16 g | Protein: 8 g | Sodium: 1,070 mg | Fiber: 3 g | Carbohydrates: 19 g

Mushroom and Onion Soup

This soup serves as an excellent opening course for a rich beef or pork dish.

INGREDIENTS | SERVES 6

6½ cups Mushroom Stock (see recipe in this chapter)
3 cups thinly sliced onions
2 cups sliced fresh mushrooms
1½ cups thinly sliced leeks
½ cup chopped shallots or green onions
1 teaspoon raw honey (optional)
Pepper, to taste

1. Combine all the ingredients, except the pepper, in a 6-quart slow cooker. Cover and cook on low 6–8 hours.

2. Season with pepper to taste.

PER SERVING | Calories: 103 | Fat: 1 g | Protein: 5 g | Sodium: 729 mg | Fiber: 6 g | Carbohydrates: 22 g

Chicken and Mushroom Stew

This is a fragrant blend of sautéed chicken, vegetables, and herbs, best enjoyed on a late-autumn night alongside a rich poultry dish.

INGREDIENTS | SERVES 6

16–24 ounces boneless, skinless chicken, cut into 1" cubes, browned (in 1 tablespoon avocado oil)

8 ounces fresh mushrooms, sliced

1 medium onion, diced

3 cups diced zucchini

1 cup diced green pepper

4 garlic cloves, minced

1 tablespoon avocado oil

3 medium tomatoes, diced

1 (6-ounce) can tomato paste

¾ cup water

1 teaspoon each: dried thyme, oregano, marjoram, and basil

1. Add browned chicken to a 4- or 6-quart slow cooker.

2. In a frying pan over medium heat, sauté the mushrooms, onion, zucchini, green pepper, and garlic in oil for 5–10 minutes, until crisp-tender, and add to slow cooker.

3. Add the tomatoes, tomato paste, water, and seasonings to the slow cooker. Stir.

4. Cover and cook on low for 4 hours or until the vegetables are tender. Serve hot.

PER SERVING | Calories: 222 | Fat: 6 g | Protein: 28 g | Sodium: 320 mg | Fiber: 4 g | Carbohydrates: 15 g

Mediterranean Seafood Soup

This quick and easy soup will give you a taste of the Mediterranean.

INGREDIENTS | SERVES 2

2 tablespoons olive oil

½ cup chopped sweet onion

2 cloves garlic, chopped

½ bulb fennel, chopped

½ cup dry white wine or chicken broth

1 cup clam juice

2 cups chopped tomatoes

6 littleneck clams, scrubbed and rinsed

6 mussels, scrubbed and rinsed

8 raw jumbo shrimp, peeled and deveined

1 teaspoon dried basil, or 5 leaves fresh basil, torn

Salt and red pepper flakes, to taste

1. Heat the oil in a large frying pan over medium heat and add onion, garlic, and fennel. After 10 minutes, stir in the wine or broth and clam juice and add the tomatoes. Bring to a boil.

2. Drop clams into the boiling liquid. When clams start to open, add the mussels. When mussels start to open, add the shrimp, basil, and salt and pepper flakes. Serve when shrimp turns pink.

PER SERVING | Calories: 450 | Fat: 18 g | Protein: 48 g | Sodium: 578 mg | Fiber: 5 g | Carbohydrates: 19 g

Littleneck Clams

Littleneck clams are the smallest variety of hard-shell clams and can be found off the northeastern and northwestern coasts of the United States. They have a sweet taste and are delicious in soup, steamed and dipped in melted butter, battered and fried, or baked.

Pumpkin Soup

If you have a sweet tooth, you can add some more palm sugar to this recipe.

INGREDIENTS | SERVES 4

1 cup finely chopped Vidalia or other sweet onion

½" fresh ginger, peeled and minced

2 cups freshly squeezed orange juice

2 cups chicken broth

1 (13-ounce) can pumpkin (unflavored)

1 teaspoon organic coconut palm sugar

½ teaspoon cinnamon

¼ teaspoon ground nutmeg

¼ teaspoon ground cloves

½ cup organic heavy cream (optional)

Combine all the ingredients in a large soup pot, one by one, whisking after each addition. Cover and simmer for 10 minutes. If you decide to use the cream, add at the last minute.

PER SERVING | Calories: 102 (with heavy cream, add 100 calories) | Fat: 0 g | Protein: 4 g | Sodium: 532 mg | Fiber: 4 g | Carbohydrates: 24 g

Pumpkin Bisque

This simple soup is a perfect first course at a holiday meal or as a light lunch.

INGREDIENTS | SERVES 4

2 cups puréed pumpkin

4 cups water

1 cup unsweetened coconut milk

¼ teaspoon ground nutmeg

2 cloves garlic, minced

1 large onion, minced

Make Your Own Pumpkin Purée

Preheat the oven to 350°F. Slice a pie pumpkin or an "eating" pumpkin into wedges and remove the seeds. Place the wedges on a baking sheet and bake until the flesh is soft, about 40 minutes. Scoop out the flesh and allow it to cool before puréeing it in a blender.

1. Place all ingredients in a 4-quart slow cooker. Stir. Cook on low for 8 hours.

2. Use an immersion blender (or blend the bisque in batches in a standard blender) to blend until smooth. Serve hot.

PER SERVING | Calories: 85 | Fat: 7 g | Protein: 1 g | Sodium: 12 g | Fiber: 2 g | Carbohydrates: 6 g

Pork and Apple Stew

If you prefer a tart apple taste, you can substitute Granny Smith apples for the Golden Delicious. You can also add more apples if you wish. Apples and pork were made for each other!

INGREDIENTS | SERVES 8

1 (3-pound) boneless pork shoulder roast

Freshly ground black pepper, to taste

1 large sweet onion, diced

2 Golden Delicious apples, peeled, cored, and diced

2 pounds carrots, peeled and roughly chopped

2 stalks celery, finely diced

2 cups chicken broth

½ cup unsweetened applesauce

1 tablespoon cooking sherry (optional)

2 tablespoons pure maple syrup (optional)

½ teaspoon dried thyme

¼ teaspoon ground allspice

¼ teaspoon dried sage

2 large sweet potatoes, peeled and quartered

1. Trim the roast of any fat; discard the fat and cut the roast into bite-size pieces. Add the pork to a 4-quart slow cooker along with the remaining ingredients in the order given. (You want to rest the sweet-potato quarters on top of the mixture in the slow cooker.)

2. Cover and cook on low for 6 hours or until the pork is cooked through and tender.

PER SERVING | Calories: 363 | Fat: 13 g | Protein: 36 g | Sodium: 494 mg | Fiber: 5 g | Carbohydrates: 24 g

Herbs and Spices Test

If you're unsure about the herbs and spices suggested in a recipe, wait to add them until the end of the cooking time. Once the meat is cooked through, spoon out ¼ cup or so of the pan juices into a microwave-safe bowl. Add a pinch of each herb and spice (in proportion to how they're suggested in the recipe), microwave on high for 15–30 seconds, and then taste the broth to see if you like it. Season the dish accordingly.

Caveman's Cabbage Soup

Slow-cooking cabbage soup preserves the nutrients in the cabbage and other vegetables, versus other, higher-temperature methods of preparation that tend to destroy many of the nutrients. Add cooked sausage slices to the pot for a well-rounded meal.

INGREDIENTS | SERVES 14

1 small head cabbage

2 green onions

1 red bell pepper

1 bunch celery

1 cup baby carrots

4 cups chicken broth

4 cups water

3 cloves garlic, minced

¼ teaspoon red pepper flakes

¼ teaspoon dried basil

¼ teaspoon dried oregano

¼ teaspoon dried thyme

¼ teaspoon onion powder

1. Chop all vegetables and place them in a 6-quart slow cooker.

2. Pour in the broth and water.

3. Stir in garlic and spices. Cover and cook on low for 8–10 hours.

PER SERVING | Calories: 49 | Fat: 1 g | Protein: 2 g | Sodium: 314 mg | Fiber: 2 g | Carbohydrates: 8 g

Simple Tomato Soup

This simple, healthy, three-step soup is made with canned tomatoes, which are available year-round at affordable prices. You can also make this soup with about 4 pounds of chopped fresh tomatoes if you prefer.

INGREDIENTS | SERVES 8

1 small sweet onion, finely diced

¼ cup organic unsalted butter or ghee

3 (14.5-ounce) cans diced tomatoes

1 tablespoon raw honey

15 ounces chicken broth

½ teaspoon lemon juice

1. In a small glass or microwave-safe bowl, cook onions and butter in the microwave on high for 1 minute, until onions are softened.

2. Add onion mixture, tomatoes, honey, and chicken broth to a greased 4-quart slow cooker. Cook on high for 4 hours or on low for 8 hours.

3. Turn off slow cooker. Add lemon juice to the soup. Allow soup to cool for about 20 minutes and then blend using an immersion blender or in batches using a standard blender.

PER SERVING | Calories: 109 | Fat: 7 g | Protein: 2 g | Sodium: 442 mg | Fiber: 2 g | Carbohydrates: 12 g

Acorn Squash Autumn Bisque

The yellow-orange color of acorn squash comes from its rich vitamin A content. One cup of acorn squash provides more than 100 percent of the daily recommended amount of vitamin A.

INGREDIENTS | SERVES 6

2 cups chicken broth

2 medium-size acorn squash, peeled and cubed

½ cup chopped onion

½ teaspoon cinnamon

¼ teaspoon ground coriander

¼ teaspoon cumin

½ cup unsweetened coconut milk

1 tablespoon lemon juice

Pepper, to taste

1. Combine the broth, squash, onion, cinnamon, coriander, and cumin in a 4-quart slow cooker. Cover and cook on high for 3–4 hours.

2. Blend the squash mixture, coconut milk, and lemon juice in a food processor until smooth.

3. Season with pepper to taste.

PER SERVING | Calories: 54 | Fat: 4 g | Protein: 2 g | Sodium: 11 mg | Fiber: 1 g | Carbohydrates: 3 g

Butternut Squash Soup

This soup is a scrumptious treat on a cool fall day.
Warm family and friends with a delightful blend of aroma and flavor.

INGREDIENTS | SERVES 4

1 tablespoon almond oil

1 medium onion, chopped

1 pound butternut squash, peeled, seeded, and chopped

2 parsnips, peeled and diced

3 cloves garlic, minced

½ cup almond meal

32 ounces organic low-sodium chicken broth

½ teaspoon cinnamon

¼ teaspoon ground cloves

¼ teaspoon ground nutmeg

1. In a soup pot or Dutch oven, heat oil over medium-high heat. Sauté onion, squash, parsnips, and garlic in oil for 5 minutes.

2. Add almond meal and chicken broth and increase heat to high.

3. Bring to a boil, then turn to low and simmer for 45 minutes.

4. In batches, purée squash mixture in blender or food processor and return to pot or use an immersion blender.

5. Stir in cinnamon, cloves, and nutmeg.

PER SERVING | Calories: 282 | Fat: 13 g | Protein: 11 g | Sodium: 330 mg | Fiber: 6 g | Carbohydrates: 34 g

Pumpkin Turkey Chili

Pumpkin keeps for 6 months whole, or for years canned. Pumpkin is most often enjoyed in the fall, but it can actually be enjoyed year-round.

INGREDIENTS | SERVES 6

2 red bell peppers, chopped

1 medium-size onion, chopped

3–4 cloves garlic, chopped

1 pound ground turkey, browned

1 (14.5-ounce) can pure pumpkin purée

1 (14.5-ounce) can diced tomatoes

½ cup water

1½ tablespoons chili powder

½ teaspoon black pepper

¼ teaspoon cumin

1. In a frying pan over medium heat, sauté the peppers, onion, and garlic with the browned turkey for 5–7 minutes.

2. Transfer the turkey and veggies to a 4-quart slow cooker. Add the remaining ingredients.

3. Cover and cook on low for 5–6 hours.

PER SERVING | Calories: 140 | Fat: 7 g | Protein: 14 g | Sodium: 188 mg | Fiber: 2 g | Carbohydrates: 6 g

Cincinnati Chili

This unusual regional favorite has a spicy-sweet flavor that is wonderfully addictive! Serve over cooked spaghetti squash with any combination of the following toppings: diced raw onion; chopped green, red, yellow, or orange pepper; and shredded carrots.

INGREDIENTS | SERVES 8

1 pound ground beef

1 (15-ounce) can crushed tomatoes, undrained

2 cloves garlic, minced

1 large onion, diced

1 teaspoon cumin

1 teaspoon cacao powder

2 teaspoons chili powder

½ teaspoon ground cloves

1 tablespoon lemon juice

1 teaspoon allspice

½ teaspoon cayenne pepper

½ teaspoon cinnamon

1. In a nonstick frying pan, quickly sauté the beef over medium heat until it is no longer pink, about 5–6 minutes. Drain all fat and discard it.

2. Place beef and all the other ingredients in a 4-quart slow cooker and stir. Cook on low for 8–10 hours.

PER SERVING | Calories: 110 | Fat: 6 g | Protein: 12 g | Sodium: 45 mg | Fiber: 1 g | Carbohydrates: 3 g

Lone Star State Chili

Texans prefer their chili without beans, which makes this a perfect Paleo meal.
Serve it with a tossed salad.

INGREDIENTS | SERVES 8

1 stalk celery, finely chopped

1 large carrot, peeled and finely chopped

1 (3-pound) chuck roast, cubed

2 large yellow onions, diced

6 cloves garlic, minced

6 jalapeño peppers, seeded and diced

½ teaspoon freshly ground black pepper

4 tablespoons chili powder

1 teaspoon oregano

1 teaspoon cumin

1 teaspoon raw honey

1 (28-ounce) can diced tomatoes

1 cup beef broth

1. Add all of the ingredients to a 4- or 6-quart slow cooker, in the order given, and stir to combine. The liquid in your slow cooker should completely cover the meat and vegetables. If additional liquid is needed, add more crushed tomatoes or broth, or some water.

2. Cover and cook on low for 8 hours. Taste for seasoning, and add more chili powder if desired.

PER SERVING | Calories: 60 | Fat: 1 g | Protein: 2 g | Sodium: 289 mg | Fiber: 4 g | Carbohydrates: 13 g

Hot Pepper Precautions

Wear gloves or sandwich bags over your hands when you clean and dice hot peppers. It's important to avoid having the peppers come into contact with your skin or especially your eyes. As an added precaution, wash your hands (and under your fingernails) thoroughly with hot, soapy water after you remove the gloves or sandwich bags.

Texas Firehouse Chili

This no-bean chili is similar to dishes entered into firehouse chili cook-offs all over Texas.

INGREDIENTS | SERVES 4

1 pound cubed lean beef
2 tablespoons onion powder
1 tablespoon garlic powder
2 tablespoons chili powder
1 tablespoon paprika
½ teaspoon oregano
½ teaspoon freshly ground black pepper
½ teaspoon white pepper
½ teaspoon cayenne pepper
½ teaspoon minced chipotle pepper
8 ounces tomato sauce

1. Brown the beef for 5–7 minutes in a nonstick frying pan over medium heat. Drain off any excess grease.

2. Add the meat and all of the remaining ingredients to a 4-quart slow cooker. Cook on low for up to 10 hours.

PER SERVING | Calories: 212 | Fat: 8 g | Protein: 26 g | Sodium: 359 mg | Fiber: 2.5 g | Carbohydrates: 9 g

Chicken Chili Verde

Enjoy this spicy chili over a southwestern-themed vegetable medley.
Avocado slices work well as a festive garnish.

INGREDIENTS | SERVES 8

½ tablespoon avocado oil

2 pounds boneless, skinless chicken breast, cubed

2 (28-ounce) cans whole peeled tomatoes, undrained

1 (4-ounce) can diced green chili peppers, undrained

1 teaspoon thyme

1 teaspoon oregano

1 teaspoon basil

1 tablespoon chili powder

2 teaspoons cumin

1 tablespoon raw honey

1 large onion, minced

3 cloves garlic, minced

½ cup water

1. Heat oil in a frying pan over medium heat. Add the chicken. Cook, stirring frequently, until chicken is browned on all sides, about 1–2 minutes per side. Place browned chicken in a greased 4- or 6-quart slow cooker.

2. Add the remaining ingredients over the chicken in the slow cooker.

3. Cover and cook on high for 3 hours or on low for 6 hours.

PER SERVING | Calories: 195 | Fat: 4 g | Protein: 26 g | Sodium: 423 mg | Fiber: 3 g | Carbohydrates: 14 g

Pumpkin and Ginger Soup

Relieve some stress with a hot cup of this comforting, seasonal favorite.

INGREDIENTS | SERVES 6

2 pounds pumpkin, peeled, seeded, and cubed

3½ cups chicken broth

1 cup chopped onion

1 tablespoon chopped fresh ginger

1 teaspoon minced garlic

½ teaspoon ground cloves

Pepper, to taste

1. In a 4-quart slow cooker, combine all ingredients except the pepper. Cover and cook on high for 4–5 hours.

2. Place the soup in a food processor and blend until smooth.

3. Season to taste with pepper.

PER SERVING | Calories: 109 | Fat: 2 g | Protein: 5 g | Sodium: 614 mg | Fiber: 1 g | Carbohydrates: 19 g

Tomato Vegetable Soup

The array of garden vegetables in this soup produces a light and fresh flavor with a "fall-ish" feel.

INGREDIENTS | SERVES 6

1 (28-ounce) can Italian plum tomatoes, undrained

2¼ cups beef broth

1 medium onion, chopped

1 large stalk celery, sliced

1 medium carrot, sliced

1 red bell pepper, chopped

1 teaspoon lemon juice

¾ teaspoon garlic powder

Pinch red pepper flakes

Pepper, to taste

1. Combine all the ingredients except pepper in a 4- or 6-quart slow cooker. Cover and cook on high for 4–5 hours.

2. Process the soup in blender until smooth; season to taste with pepper. Serve warm.

PER SERVING | Calories: 50 | Fat: 1 g | Protein: 3 g | Sodium: 314 mg | Fiber: 3 g | Carbohydrates: 10 g

Zucchini Soup

This smooth and soothing blend of fresh herbs and spices is perfect for a cold, late-autumn day.

INGREDIENTS | SERVES 8

4 cups sliced zucchini

4 cups chicken broth

4 cloves garlic, minced

2 tablespoons lime juice

2 teaspoons curry powder

1 teaspoon dried marjoram

¼ teaspoon celery seeds

½ cup canned unsweetened coconut milk

Cayenne pepper, to taste

Pinch paprika

1. Combine all the ingredients, except the coconut milk, cayenne pepper, and paprika, in a 4- or 6-quart slow cooker, and cook on high for 3–4 hours.

2. Process the soup, with the coconut milk, in a blender until combined.

3. Season to taste with cayenne pepper. Serve warm and sprinkle with paprika.

PER SERVING | Calories: 92 | Fat: 5 g | Protein: 4 g | Sodium: 531 mg | Fiber: 1 g | Carbohydrates: 9 g

Cream of Cauliflower Soup

Cauliflower is a fantastic vegetable in Paleolithic diet recipes.
Blended cauliflower can be used as a thickener in recipes that normally call for potatoes
or root vegetables. Best of all, cauliflower won't spike your insulin levels.

INGREDIENTS | SERVES 4

1 large head cauliflower, chopped

3 stalks celery, chopped

1 carrot, chopped

2 cloves garlic, minced

1 onion, chopped

2 teaspoons cumin

½ teaspoon ground black pepper

1 tablespoon chopped fresh parsley

1 teaspoon chopped fresh dill, plus additional for garnish

4 slices nitrate-free bacon, cooked and crumbled

1. In a soup pot or Dutch oven, combine cauliflower, celery, carrot, garlic, onion, cumin, and pepper.

2. Add enough water to just cover ingredients in pot. Bring to a boil over high heat.

3. Reduce heat to low. Simmer about 8 minutes or until vegetables are tender.

4. Stir in parsley and dill. Garnish with bacon and additional dill before serving.

PER SERVING | Calories: 56 | Fat: 0.5 g | Protein: 3 g | Sodium: 83 mg | Fiber: 5 g | Carbohydrates: 10 g

Gazpacho

Gazpacho is best made the day before so that the flavors can penetrate all the vegetables. It should be served chilled.

INGREDIENTS | SERVES 6

1 (28-ounce) can no-salt-added, chopped tomatoes

1 green bell pepper, chopped

3 medium tomatoes, peeled and chopped

1 cucumber, peeled and chopped

1 small onion, chopped

2 tablespoons olive oil

½ teaspoon black pepper

½ teaspoon paprika

¼ teaspoon cayenne pepper

1 teaspoon chopped chives

2 teaspoons chopped parsley

½ clove garlic, minced

4½ teaspoons lemon juice

1. Blend canned tomatoes in blender until smooth. Pour into large bowl.

2. Add remaining ingredients to bowl.

3. Refrigerate at least 12 hours, then serve.

PER SERVING | Calories: 113 | Fat: 5 g | Protein: 3 g | Sodium: 297 mg | Fiber: 3.5 g | Carbohydrates: 15 g

Scallion Chive Soup

Chive is a member of the onion family. It adds a sweet, mildly oniony taste to recipes.

INGREDIENTS | SERVES 2

3 teaspoons almond oil

½ cup shredded zucchini

½ cup chopped shallots

1 clove garlic, minced

1 cup chopped scallions

½ cup chopped chives

2 cups no-salt-added chicken broth

½ cup water

Chive as Insect Repellant

Chive has such a strong scent that it can be used in gardens as an insect repellant. Garlic has also been known to be an effective defense against pests.

1. Heat oil in a soup pot or Dutch oven over medium-low heat. Cook zucchini, shallots, and garlic in oil for 3–5 minutes.

2. Add scallions and chives and cook for 2 minutes more.

3. Add chicken broth and water. Increase heat to high and bring to a boil.

4. Reduce heat to low and simmer for 5 minutes.

5. In batches, purée soup in blender or food processor, or use immersion blender to blend.

PER SERVING | Calories: 130 | Fat: 7 g | Protein: 6 g | Sodium: 568 mg | Fiber: 2.5 g | Carbohydrates: 12 g

Carrot-Lemon Soup

This is a great "anytime" soup, and can be served either hot or cold.

INGREDIENTS | SERVES 6

3 tablespoons almond oil

2 pounds carrots, peeled and diced

2 large yellow onions, peeled and diced

2 cloves garlic, minced

6 cups Basic Vegetable Stock (see recipe in this chapter) or low-sodium canned vegetable stock

1 teaspoon minced fresh ginger

Zest and juice of 1 lemon

Freshly ground black pepper, to taste

3 tablespoons, finely chopped parsley (for garnish)

1. Heat the oil over medium heat in a large stockpot and lightly sauté the carrots, onions, and garlic for 5 minutes.

2. Add the stock and simmer for approximately 1 hour. Add the ginger, lemon juice, and zest. Season with pepper.

3. Chill and serve with parsley as garnish.

PER SERVING | Calories: 153 | Fat: 7 g | Protein: 3 g | Sodium: 62 mg | Fiber: 5 g | Carbohydrates: 16 g

Lemon Know-How

The thought of lemons may make your cheeks pucker, but it's well worth the powerful dose of cold-fighting vitamin C. The average lemon contains approximately 3 tablespoons of juice. Allow lemons to come to room temperature before squeezing to maximize the amount of juice extracted.

Chicken Chowder

A warm, traditional taste of home, this makes a great first course to a hearty poultry dish on a cold winter's night.

INGREDIENTS | SERVES 5

1 pound boneless, skinless chicken thighs, cut up into chunks

1 (14.5-ounce) can diced tomatoes

1 (8-ounce) package fresh, sliced mushrooms

1 large red onion, minced

2 parsnips, peeled and diced

4–6 cloves garlic, minced

½ cup chicken broth

½ cup dry red wine (or additional chicken broth)

1 teaspoon dried oregano

1 teaspoon dried basil

1 teaspoon ground pepper

1. Place all ingredients in a 4-quart slow cooker.

2. Cover and cook on low for 6 hours, stirring occasionally.

PER SERVING | Calories: 162 | Fat: 4 g | Protein: 19 g | Sodium: 239 mg | Fiber: 1 g | Carbohydrates: 8 g

Spicy Bison Stew

Bison contains fewer calories, less fat, and more iron per serving than both beef and chicken!

INGREDIENTS | SERVES 4

2 small onions, sliced

6 large carrots, peeled and sliced

1 bell pepper, diced

3 stalks celery, diced

2 jalapeño peppers, diced

2 pounds bison meat, cut into 1" cubes

1 (28-ounce) can fire-roasted tomatoes

½ cup unsalted beef broth

Handful of fresh cilantro, chopped

1 tablespoon oregano

Pepper, to taste

1 tablespoon hot sauce

1. Place onions, carrots, bell pepper, celery, and jalapeño peppers in a 4- or 6-quart slow cooker. Add bison meat and all remaining ingredients.

2. Cover and cook on low for 6–8 hours. Serve hot.

PER SERVING | Calories: 330 | Fat: 4 g | Protein: 50 g | Sodium: 691 mg | Fiber: 7 g | Carbohydrates: 25 g

Southwestern Soup

This is a zesty and hearty creation with a perfect balance of herbs and seasonings.

INGREDIENTS | SERVES 4

1 pound pork tenderloin, cut into 1" pieces

1 cup chopped onion

1 green bell pepper, seeded and chopped

1 jalapeño pepper, seeded and minced

2 cloves garlic, minced

1 teaspoon chili powder

1 teaspoon cumin

¼ teaspoon freshly ground black pepper

5 cups chicken broth

1 (14.5-ounce) can diced tomatoes

1 cup diced avocado, for garnish

2 tablespoons chopped cilantro, for garnish

Lime wedges, for garnish

1. In the bottom of a 6-quart slow cooker, combine the pork, onion, bell pepper, jalapeño pepper, garlic, chili powder, cumin, and black pepper. Stir to combine.

2. Add broth and tomatoes. Cover and cook on low for 6–8 hours or on high for 3–4 hours.

3. When ready to serve, ladle soup into bowls and top with avocado and cilantro. Serve with lime wedges.

PER SERVING | Calories: 266 | Fat: 9 g | Protein: 29 g | Sodium: 237 mg | Fiber: 6 g | Carbohydrates: 18 g

Rosemary-Thyme Stew

Lots of rosemary and thyme give this surprisingly light stew a distinctive flavor.

INGREDIENTS | SERVES 4

1 teaspoon unsalted organic butter or ghee

1 large onion, diced

1 large carrot, peeled and diced

2 stalks celery, diced

2 cloves garlic, minced

3½ tablespoons minced fresh thyme

3 tablespoons minced fresh rosemary

1 pound boneless, skinless chicken breast, cut into 1" cubes

½ teaspoon freshly ground black pepper

1½ cups water or chicken broth

1 cup diced green, red, and yellow peppers

1. Heat the butter in a large frying pan over medium-high heat. Sauté the onion, carrot, celery, garlic, thyme, rosemary, and chicken for 5–7 minutes, until the chicken is white on all sides. Drain off any excess fat.

2. Put sautéed ingredients into a 4-quart slow cooker. Sprinkle with black pepper. Pour in the water or stock and stir. Cook on low for 8–9 hours.

3. Add the diced peppers. Cover and cook on high for an additional ½ hour. Stir before serving.

PER SERVING | Calories: 187 | Fat: 4 g | Protein: 26 g | Sodium: 173 mg | Fiber: 3 g | Carbohydrates: 10 g

Chicken Bolognese

This easy-to-make chicken stew is sure to please the entire family. Both kids and adults love this delicious recipe. Serve alone or pour the sauce over spaghetti squash or riced cauliflower.

INGREDIENTS | SERVES 4

1 pound ground chicken

4 boneless, skinless chicken breasts

1 (6-ounce) can tomato paste

1 (28-ounce) can no-salt-added, diced tomatoes

4 garlic cloves, chopped

4 large carrots, sliced

2 red bell peppers, diced

2 green bell peppers, diced

1 tablespoon dried thyme

2 tablespoons bacon grease

1 tablespoon chili powder

1. In a medium-size frying pan, cook ground chicken over medium heat until browned, about 5 minutes. Drain and place in a 4- or 6-quart slow cooker.

2. Wipe out the pan and place it over medium-high heat. Brown the chicken breasts (5 minutes per side). Add to slow cooker.

3. Combine all the remaining ingredients in the slow cooker. Cook on high for 5 hours.

4. Serve over your favorite steamed vegetable.

PER SERVING | Calories: 469 | Fat: 14 g | Protein: 56 g | Sodium: 960 mg | Fiber: 9 g | Carbohydrates: 32 g

Slow Cookers Are Lifesavers

Slow cookers are the greatest appliance for the Paleo enthusiast. These countertop cookers allow you to prep ahead of time and cook in bulk, which helps make weeknight cooking easier.

Simple Ground Turkey and Vegetable Soup

This soup is easy to throw together with pantry ingredients.

INGREDIENTS | SERVES 6

1 tablespoon avocado oil

1 pound ground turkey

1 medium onion, diced

2 cloves garlic, minced

1 (16-ounce) package frozen mixed vegetables

4 cups chicken broth

½ teaspoon pepper

1. In a large frying pan over medium heat, add oil and heat until sizzling. Cook ground turkey until browned, about 5–6 minutes, stirring to break up the meat. Add meat to a greased 4-quart slow cooker.

2. In the same frying pan, sauté onion and garlic until softened, about 3–5 minutes. Add to the slow cooker.

3. Add remaining ingredients to the slow cooker. Cover and cook on high for 4 hours or on low for 8 hours.

PER SERVING | Calories: 254 | Fat: 11 g | Protein: 19 g | Sodium: 804 mg | Fiber: 3 g | Carbohydrates: 20 g

Stuffed Pepper Soup

This recipe delivers all the flavor of stuffed peppers in a warm and satisfying soup.

INGREDIENTS | SERVES 6

1½ pounds ground beef, browned and drained

3 cups diced green bell pepper

2 cups peeled and diced butternut squash

1 (28-ounce) can diced peeled tomatoes

1 (28-ounce) can tomato sauce

¾ cup raw honey

Seasonings of choice (basil, thyme, oregano, onion flakes, etc.), to taste

1. Mix all the ingredients in a 4-quart slow cooker. Cover and cook on low for 3–4 hours or until the green peppers are cooked.

2. Turn heat to high and cook for 20–30 more minutes. Serve.

PER SERVING | Calories: 415 | Fat: 12 g | Protein: 26 g | Sodium: 951 mg | Fiber: 6 g | Carbohydrates: 56 g

Lamb Stew

This high-protein concoction is a guaranteed Paleo crowd-pleaser.

INGREDIENTS | SERVES 4

1½ pounds boneless lamb shoulder, fat trimmed

1 cup beef broth

6 medium carrots, cut into ¾" pieces

12 ounces turnips, cut into ¾" pieces

¾ cup chopped onion

½ tablespoon crushed garlic

¼ teaspoon thyme

¼ teaspoon rosemary, crumbled

½ teaspoon black pepper

1. Cut lamb into 1½" chunks.

2. Combine all the ingredients in a 4-quart slow cooker and cook on low for 8–10 hours.

3. Before serving, skim off and discard fat.

PER SERVING | Calories: 532 | Fat: 32 g | Protein: 32 g | Sodium: 227 mg | Fiber: 7 g | Carbohydrates: 29 g

CHAPTER 6

Beef, Pork, and Lamb

Paleo Meatballs and Sauce
146

Rosemary Rack of Lamb in Berries Sauce
147

Rustic Lamb Shanks
148

Grass-Fed Lamb Meatballs
149

Easy Leg of Lamb
149

Herbed Lamb Chops
150

Lamb with Garlic, Lemon, and Rosemary
151

Easy Slow-Cooker Pork Tenderloin
152

Roasted Pork Tenderloin
152

Pork Tenderloin with Nectarines
153

Paleo Pulled Pork
153

Mushroom Pork Medallions
154

Apples-and-Onions Pork Chops
155

Beef with Bell Peppers
155

Filet Mignon and Roasted Red Pepper Wraps
156

London Broil with Onions and Sweet Potato Sticks
157

Beef Tenderloin with Chimichurri
158

Corned Beef and Cabbage
158

Pot Roast with Vegetables and Gravy
159

Beef Brisket with Onions and Mushrooms
160

Ginger Beef and Napa Cabbage
161

Steak-and-Mushroom Kebabs
162

Beef and Broccoli Stir-Fry
163

Boeuf Bourguignon
164

Pot Roast with a Touch of Sweet
165

Sausage and Spicy Eggs
166

Tomato-Braised Pork
167

Honey-Mustard Pork Loin
167

Pork Tenderloin with Sweet and Savory Apples
168

Beef and Coconut Curry
169

Beef and Cabbage
169

Beef and Ginger Curry
170

Paleo Meatballs and Sauce

These meatballs are so close to traditional meatballs, you won't know the difference.

INGREDIENTS | SERVES 6

1 (16-ounce) can no-salt-added, diced tomatoes

1 (4-ounce) can no-salt-added, tomato paste

2 pounds grass-fed ground beef

1 cup chopped celery

1 cup chopped onion

1 cup chopped carrots

4 garlic cloves, finely chopped

3 eggs

½ cup almond flour

1 tablespoon oregano

1 teaspoon black pepper

¼ teaspoon chili powder

1. Pour canned tomatoes and tomato paste into 4- or 6-quart slow cooker.

2. Place all remaining ingredients in a large bowl and mix well with clean hands.

3. Roll resulting meat mixture into 2- to 3-ounce (large, rounded tablespoon-size) balls and add to slow cooker.

4. Cook on low for 5 hours minimum.

PER SERVING | Calories: 400 | Fat: 21 g | Protein: 38 g | Sodium: 419 mg | Fiber: 6 g | Carbohydrates: 16 g

Rosemary Rack of Lamb in Berries Sauce

This rack of lamb recipe is sure to be a winner at any holiday or dinner party.
The flavors are strong and the presentation a winner.

INGREDIENTS | SERVES 4

1 rack grass-fed lamb, on the bone
1 teaspoon freshly ground black pepper
2 cloves garlic, crushed and divided
1½ teaspoons dried thyme
2 sprigs fresh rosemary, divided
2 tablespoons olive oil
1 cup mixed berries
1 cup no-salt-added, organic beef stock

1. Place rack of lamb in a roasting pan with a rack. Sprinkle lamb with black pepper, 1 clove crushed garlic, thyme, and 1 sprig of fresh rosemary.

2. Place lamb in a 400°F oven. Roast for 13 minutes per pound or until internal temperature reaches 135°F. Remove from oven and set aside to rest.

3. Prepare sauce by combining remaining garlic, rosemary, olive oil, berries, and beef stock in a medium saucepan over low heat. Stir and cook for about 5 minutes.

4. Reduce sauce until thick (may take another 5 minutes) and pour over cooked lamb.

PER SERVING | Calories: 820 | Fat: 84 g | Protein: 9 g | Sodium: 157 mg | Fiber: 1 g | Carbohydrates: 7 g

Rustic Lamb Shanks

This is a French bistro and comfort meal that most people find delicious on a cool evening.

INGREDIENTS | SERVES 4

4 lamb shanks, well trimmed

1 teaspoon salt

½ teaspoon freshly ground black pepper

1 tablespoon olive oil

1 large yellow onion, chopped

4 garlic cloves, minced

2 large parsnips, peeled and cut into chunks

1 carrot, peeled and cut into chunks

2 tablespoons tomato paste

1 cup dry red wine or additional chicken broth

1 cup chicken broth

2 bay leaves

¼ cup fresh parsley, chopped

1. Sprinkle the lamb shanks with salt and pepper. In a Dutch oven over medium-high heat, brown in the olive oil, adding onion, garlic, parsnips, and carrot. Cook for 5 minutes. Stir in tomato paste, red wine, chicken broth, bay leaves, and parsley.

2. Cover the pot and simmer for 2 hours. Remove bay leaves before serving.

PER SERVING | Calories: 417 | Fat: 12 g | Protein: 31 g | Sodium: 1,505 mg | Fiber: 11 g | Carbohydrates: 44 g

Not Crazy about Lamb?

When people say they don't like lamb, it's usually the fat, not the lamb, they dislike. When you prepare roast lamb, stew, or shanks, be sure to remove all of the fat.

Grass-Fed Lamb Meatballs

Meatballs are always a kid favorite. These grass-fed lamb meatballs are high in good fats that contribute to their great taste and high health factor.

INGREDIENTS | SERVES 6

¼ cup pine nuts

4 tablespoons olive oil, divided

1½ pounds ground grass-fed lamb

¼ cup minced garlic

2 tablespoons cumin

1. In a frying pan over medium-high heat, sauté pine nuts in 2 tablespoons olive oil for 2 minutes until brown. Remove from pan and allow to cool.

2. In a large bowl, combine lamb, garlic, cumin, and pine nuts and form into meatballs.

3. Add remaining olive oil to pan and fry meatballs until cooked through, about 5–10 minutes, depending on size of meatballs.

PER SERVING | Calories: 148 | Fat: 13 g | Protein: 5 g | Sodium: 201 mg | Fiber: 2.5 g | Carbohydrates: 6.5 g

Easy Leg of Lamb

Although lamb can be an expensive cut of meat, you can often find it on sale during the holidays. Stock up on several cuts and freeze them when you find good prices.

INGREDIENTS | SERVES 6

1 (4-pound) bone-in leg of lamb

5 cloves garlic, cut into spears

2 tablespoons olive oil

1 tablespoon dried rosemary

½ teaspoon ground pepper

4 cups chicken broth

¼ cup dry red wine or additional chicken broth

1. Make small incisions evenly over the lamb. Place garlic spears into the incisions in the lamb.

2. Rub olive oil, rosemary, and pepper over the lamb. Place lamb into a greased 4- or 6-quart slow cooker.

3. Pour broth and wine around the leg of lamb. Cook on high for 4 hours or on low for 8 hours.

4. Serve the roast lamb in bowls. Ladle the sauce from the slow cooker over each serving.

PER SERVING | Calories: 74 | Fat: 5 g | Protein: 7 g | Sodium: 15 mg | Fiber: 1 g | Carbohydrates: 3 g

Herbed Lamb Chops

The simple herb rub used in this recipe would make a fun holiday gift to give to friends or family members who enjoy cooking! Include this recipe with a small jar of the rub.

INGREDIENTS | SERVES 4

1 medium onion, sliced
1 teaspoon dried oregano
½ teaspoon dried thyme
½ teaspoon garlic powder
⅛ teaspoon ground pepper
2 pounds (about 8) lamb loin chops
1 tablespoon olive oil

1. Place the onion on the bottom of a greased 4-quart slow cooker.

2. In a small bowl mix together oregano, thyme, garlic powder, and pepper. Rub herb mixture over the lamb chops.

3. Place herb-rubbed lamb chops over the sliced onions in the slow cooker. Drizzle olive oil over the lamb chops.

4. Cook on high for 3 hours or on low for 6 hours, until tender.

PER SERVING | Calories: 43 | Fat: 3 g | Protein: 0 g | Sodium: 2 mg | Fiber: 1 g | Carbohydrates: 3 g

Lamb with Garlic, Lemon, and Rosemary

You can use the spice rub in this recipe as a marinade by applying it to the leg of lamb and refrigerating for several hours (or up to one full day) before cooking.

INGREDIENTS | SERVES 4

4 cloves garlic, crushed

1 tablespoon fresh rosemary, chopped

1 tablespoon avocado oil

1 teaspoon ground pepper

1 (3-pound) leg of lamb

1 large lemon, cut into ¼" slices

½ cup chicken or beef stock

1. In a small bowl mix together garlic, rosemary, oil, and pepper. Rub this mixture onto the leg of lamb.

2. Place a few lemon slices in the bottom of a greased 4-quart slow cooker. Place spice-rubbed lamb on top of lemon slices.

3. Add remaining lemon slices on top of lamb. Pour stock around the lamb.

4. Cook on low heat for 8–10 hours or on high for 4–6 hours.

PER SERVING | Calories: 763 | Fat: 52 g | Protein: 62 g | Sodium: 194 mg | Fiber: 0 g | Carbohydrates: 2 g

Easy Slow-Cooker Pork Tenderloin

Slow-cooker meals are a great way to cook for your family. Large quantities can be thrown into the cooker hours in advance. Most leftovers can be easily frozen for future meals.

INGREDIENTS | SERVES 4

1 (1-pound) lean pork loin

1 (28-ounce) can no-salt-added diced tomatoes

3 medium zucchinis, diced

4 cups cauliflower florets

Chopped fresh basil, to taste

Garlic, to taste

1. Combine all ingredients in a slow cooker.

2. Cook on low for 6–7 hours.

PER SERVING | Calories: 165 | Fat: 6.5 g | Protein: 19 g | Sodium: 336 mg | Fiber: 4 g | Carbohydrates: 9.6 g

Low-Fat Meat Choice

Pork is a nice low-fat protein source. It is versatile for cooking and quite flavorful. This often-overlooked meat is a fantastic friend of the Paleo lifestyle.

Roasted Pork Tenderloin

When you are preparing for a large family gathering and find yourself with a bit more time than expected, this is the recipe to go for. It serves ten easily and will wow your guests with its flavorful punch.

INGREDIENTS | SERVES 10

2½ pounds pork loin

Juice of 1 large orange

3 tablespoons lime juice

2 tablespoons red wine

10 cloves garlic, minced

2 tablespoons dried rosemary

1 tablespoon ground black pepper

1. Combine all ingredients in a shallow dish or large zip-top plastic bag. Refrigerate and marinate pork for at least 2 hours.

2. Remove pork from marinade and bring to room temperature. Preheat oven to 350°F.

3. In a roasting pan, cook for 20–25 minutes, or until the internal temperature reaches 165°F. Allow the pork to rest for 5 minutes before carving.

PER SERVING | Calories: 218 | Fat: 9.5 g | Protein: 30 g | Sodium: 53 mg | Fiber: 0 g | Carbohydrates: 1 g

Pork Tenderloin with Nectarines

Pork combined with the flavor of ripe nectarines makes a lovely sweet and slightly tangy sauce. Serve sliced pork and sauce over steamed zucchini strips.

INGREDIENTS | SERVES 4

1¼ pounds pork tenderloin

1 tablespoon olive oil

4 ripe but firm nectarines, each cut into 4 wedges

2 tablespoons lemon juice

Ground black pepper to taste (optional)

1. Rub pork tenderloin with olive oil. Place in a greased 4-quart slow cooker.

2. Place nectarine wedges on top of and around the pork tenderloin. Drizzle lemon juice over the pork and fruit. Cook on high for 3–4 hours or on low for 6–8 hours, until pork is very tender.

3. Remove pork from slow cooker and slice before serving. If desired, add pepper, to taste.

PER SERVING | Calories: 246 | Fat: 7 g | Protein: 31 g | Sodium: 76 mg | Fiber: 2 g | Carbohydrates: 15 g

Paleo Pulled Pork

This pulled pork recipe has super flavors. Adjust the spices as needed to kick it up a notch or cool it down. Either way, this recipe is sure to please the entire family.

INGREDIENTS | SERVES 8

2½ pounds pork loin

1 large onion, chopped

1 (16-ounce) can organic, no-salt-added tomato paste

3 tablespoons olive oil

2 cups lemon juice

½ cup unsalted beef broth

4 cloves garlic

¼ teaspoon cayenne pepper

½ teaspoon paprika

2 teaspoons chipotle chili powder

1 teaspoon thyme

1 teaspoon cumin

1. Combine all ingredients in a slow cooker.

2. Cook on low for 5 hours or until meat is softened completely.

3. Once cooled, shred meat with fork and serve.

PER SERVING | Calories: 382 | Fat: 17 g | Protein: 40 g | Sodium: 138 mg | Fiber: 3.5 g | Carbohydrates: 18 g

Mushroom Pork Medallions

You would never guess this meal is Paleo-approved. It tastes so amazing, you will swear it was deep fried with flour.

INGREDIENTS | SERVES 2

1 pound pork tenderloin
1 tablespoon olive oil
1 small onion, sliced
¼ cup sliced fresh mushrooms
1 clove garlic, minced
2 teaspoons almond meal
½ cup beef broth
¼ teaspoon crushed dried rosemary
⅛ teaspoon ground black pepper

1. Slice tenderloin into ½"-thick medallions.

2. In a frying pan, heat olive oil over medium-high heat. Brown pork in oil for 2 minutes on each side.

3. Remove pork from frying pan and set aside.

4. In same frying pan, add onion, mushrooms, and garlic and sauté for 1 minute.

5. Stir in almond meal until blended.

6. Gradually stir in the broth, rosemary, and pepper. Bring to a boil; cook and stir for 1 minute or until thickened.

7. Lay pork medallions over mixture. Reduce heat; cover and simmer for 15 minutes or until meat juices run clear.

PER SERVING | Calories: 196 | Fat: 11 g | Protein: 16 g | Sodium: 325 mg | Fiber: 1 g | Carbohydrates: 3.5 g

Apples-and-Onions Pork Chops

Try Sonya apples in this sweet and savory dish; they are crisp and sweet.

INGREDIENTS | SERVES 4

4 crisp, sweet apples, peeled and cut into wedges

2 large onions, sliced

4 thick-cut boneless pork chops (1 pound total)

½ teaspoon cayenne pepper

½ teaspoon cinnamon

¼ teaspoon allspice

¼ teaspoon ground fennel

1. Place half of the apple wedges in the bottom of a 4-quart slow cooker along with half of the sliced onions.

2. Top with a single layer of pork chops. Sprinkle with spices, and top with the remaining apples and onions.

3. Cook on low for 8 hours.

PER SERVING | Calories: 267 | Fat: 6 g | Protein: 42 g | Sodium: 94 mg | Fiber: 2 g | Carbohydrates: 7 g

Slow Cooking with Boneless Pork

Not only is there less waste associated with boneless pork chops or roasts, there is often less fat attached to the meat. Even without much fat, boneless pork is well suited to slow cooking. All of the moisture stays in the dish, ensuring tender pork.

Beef with Bell Peppers

Choose a variety of red, yellow, orange, and green bell peppers to bring vibrant color to this one-pot dinner.

INGREDIENTS | SERVES 4

1 pound lean beef

4 bell peppers, seeded and chopped

3 cloves garlic, minced

Juice of 2 lemons

½ cup diced button mushrooms

4 stalks celery, chopped

3 large shallots, sliced

Salt and pepper, to taste

1. Preheat oven to 350°F.

2. Cut beef into cubes. Place all ingredients in a casserole dish and stir to combine. Bake for 30 minutes.

PER SERVING | Calories: 358 | Fat: 13 g | Protein: 31 g | Sodium: 111 mg | Fiber: 13 g | Carbohydrates: 31 g

Filet Mignon and Roasted Red Pepper Wraps

This meal is pure Paleo. Your taste buds will dance with the decadence of the filet and the mix of seasoning flavors and textures from the veggies.

INGREDIENTS | SERVES 2

4 large leaves romaine lettuce

1 tablespoon avocado oil

1 sweet onion, such as Vidalia, finely chopped

2 cloves garlic, minced

1 teaspoon salt

1 teaspoon freshly ground black pepper

1 (8-ounce) filet mignon, thinly sliced

1 teaspoon Worcestershire sauce

½ teaspoon hot sauce

2 ounces roasted red pepper, chopped

1. Lay the lettuce out on paper towels. Add the oil to the bottom of a medium-size frying pan set over medium heat. Sauté the onion and garlic for 1–2 minutes.

2. Sprinkle salt and pepper on the filet mignon. Add steak to the frying pan and sauté for about 3–4 minutes.

3. Scoop onions, garlic, and sliced filet mignon into each lettuce leaf. Sprinkle with Worcestershire sauce and hot sauce. Top with roasted red peppers. Wrap and serve.

PER SERVING | Calories: 415 | Fat: 31 g | Protein: 44 g | Sodium: 1,823 mg | Fiber: 9 g | Carbohydrates: 7 g

London Broil with Onions and Sweet Potato Sticks

This will give you a real energy boost! To get the maximum energy out of this recipe, eat slowly and enjoy a smaller portion.

INGREDIENTS | SERVES 2

1 tablespoon avocado oil

½ pound London broil, diced

1 teaspoon salt

½ teaspoon freshly ground black pepper

1 teaspoon steak seasoning

½ cup chopped sweet onion

½ teaspoon red pepper flakes, or to taste

1 teaspoon Worcestershire sauce

2 tablespoons salsa

2 large sweet red bell peppers, cored, seeded, and cut in half lengthwise

1 recipe Baked Sweet Potato Sticks (see Chapter 9)

1. Heat oil over medium heat in a frying pan. Season the steak with salt, pepper, and steak seasoning. Add seasoned steak and onions to the pan and sauté until the steak reaches the desired level of doneness. Use a meat thermometer to test the internal temperature of the meat. At 130°F, the steak will be medium-rare.

2. Sprinkle steak with red pepper flakes and Worcestershire sauce. Mix in salsa and stuff the red peppers with the mixture.

3. Serve with the Baked Sweet Potato Sticks on the side.

PER SERVING | Calories: 384 | Fat: 15 g | Protein: 38 g | Sodium: 1,454 mg | Fiber: 9 g | Carbohydrates: 26 g

What Is London Broil?

Surprisingly, London broil is not actually a cut of beef but a cooking method. Although many grocery stores and butchers may have a very lean piece of meat labeled London broil, it is likely to be a top round roast or top round steak.

Beef Tenderloin with Chimichurri

This is simple to make for an easy weeknight meal or perfect for a sophisticated gourmet dinner party.

INGREDIENTS | SERVES 2

1 cup parsley

3 cloves garlic

¼ cup capers, drained

2 tablespoons red wine vinegar

1 teaspoon Dijon mustard

2 tablespoons olive oil

Salt and pepper, to taste

2 (5-ounce) beef tenderloins

1. In a blender, blend together parsley, garlic, capers, vinegar, mustard, and oil. Season with salt and pepper as desired.

2. Grill steaks over medium-high heat until internal temperature reaches 145° (for medium-rare). Serve with chimichurri.

PER SERVING | Calories: 435 | Fat: 30 g | Protein: 37 g | Sodium: 634 mg | Fiber: 2 g | Carbohydrates: 4 g

Corned Beef and Cabbage

The slow cooker is the secret cooking technique of the busy home cook. It requires little attention, and the meat will come out tender and juicy.

INGREDIENTS | SERVES 10

3 pounds corned beef brisket

3 carrots, peeled and cut into 3" pieces

3 onions, quartered

1 cup water

½ small head cabbage, cut into wedges

1. Place beef, carrots, onions, and water in a slow cooker. Cover and cook on low for 8–10 hours.

2. Add cabbage to the slow cooker; be sure to submerge the cabbage in liquid. Turn the heat up to high, cover, and cook for 2–3 hours.

PER SERVING | Calories: 300 | Fat: 20 g | Protein: 21 g | Sodium: 1,374 mg | Fiber: 4 g | Carbohydrates: 7 g

Pot Roast with Vegetables and Gravy

As a family dinner, this can't be beat. The leftovers can be reheated and served over spaghetti squash or mashed cauliflower for a quick lunch or supper.

INGREDIENTS | SERVES 6

3 pounds beef bottom round roast, trimmed of fat

2 tablespoons avocado oil

4 medium-size sweet onions, chopped

4 cloves garlic, chopped

4 carrots, peeled and chopped

4 stalks celery, chopped

8 small bluenose turnips, peeled and chopped

1 (1") piece fresh ginger, peeled and minced

1 (13-ounce) beef broth

½ cup dry red wine (or additional beef broth)

1 teaspoon sea salt

1 teaspoon freshly ground black pepper

1 tablespoon coconut flour

1 tablespoon arrowroot powder

1. Brown the beef in oil in a large pot over medium-high heat. Remove the beef from the pot and set aside. To the same pot add the onions, garlic, carrots, celery, turnips, and ginger and cook, stirring until wilted. Return the beef to the pot and add the rest of the ingredients. Cover and cook over very low heat for 3 hours.

2. To serve, slice the beef across, not with, the grain. Serve surrounded by vegetables and place the gravy on the side or over the top.

PER SERVING | Calories: 590 | Fat: 24 g | Protein: 67 g | Sodium: 836 mg | Fiber: 5 g | Carbohydrates: 24 g

Beef Brisket with Onions and Mushrooms

This recipe makes a roast so packed with flavor it will melt in your mouth.

INGREDIENTS | SERVES 4

4 cloves garlic
1½ teaspoon salt, divided
4 tablespoons avocado oil, divided
2 teaspoons chopped fresh rosemary
1 pound beef brisket
1 teaspoon freshly ground black pepper
3 large onions, quartered
3 cups sliced white mushrooms
3 celery stalks, cut into large chunks
2 cups beef broth
1 (16-ounce) can whole tomatoes, chopped
2 bay leaves

Kitchen Gadgets

The mortar and pestle was originally used in pharmacies to crush ingredients together to make medicines. In the culinary world, the mortar and pestle is a very useful tool for crushing seeds and nuts and making guacamole, pesto, and garlic paste.

1. Preheat oven to 325°F.

2. Using a mortar and pestle or the back of a spoon and a bowl, mash together the garlic, ½ teaspoon salt, 2 tablespoons oil, and chopped rosemary leaves to make a paste.

3. Season the brisket with pepper and 1 teaspoon salt. Heat remaining oil in a large frying pan, place brisket in the pan, and sear over medium-high heat to make a dark crust on both sides. Place in a large roasting pan and spread the rosemary paste on the brisket. Place the onion, mushrooms, and celery in the pan around the brisket. Pour broth and tomatoes over the brisket and toss in the bay leaves.

4. Tightly cover the pan with foil and place in the oven. Bake for about 4 hours, basting with pan juices every 30 minutes, until the beef is very tender.

5. Let the brisket rest for 15 minutes before slicing it across the grain at a slight diagonal. Remove bay leaves before serving.

PER SERVING | Calories: 633 | Fat: 39 g | Protein: 25 g | Sodium: 2,206 mg | Fiber: 4 g | Carbohydrates: 26 g

Ginger Beef and Napa Cabbage

This stir-fry delivers the perfect balance of sweet, spicy, and savory.

INGREDIENTS | SERVES 4

3 tablespoons coconut aminos

2 cloves garlic, minced

1 tablespoon minced fresh ginger

1 teaspoon raw honey

½ teaspoon red pepper flakes

1 pound beef tenderloin or sirloin steak

1 cup beef broth

2 teaspoons arrowroot powder

2 tablespoons sesame oil

1 large onion, thinly sliced

½ head Napa cabbage, shredded

3 green onions, sliced

1. Combine coconut aminos, garlic, ginger, honey, and red pepper flakes in a small bowl. Slice beef into ¼"-thick strips. Toss beef in ginger-honey sauce. Cover, and place in refrigerator for at least 30 minutes to marinate.

2. Mix broth and arrowroot and set aside.

3. Heat half the oil in a large frying pan over medium heat. Add onion to the pan and cook for 5 minutes until tender and slightly brown. Remove from pan and set aside.

4. Heat remaining oil over medium-high heat. Add marinated beef and cabbage to the pan and stir-fry for 5 minutes or until beef is only slightly pink in the center and cabbage is tender. Add cooked onion and broth to the pan. Cook for about 2 minutes, until sauce boils. Reduce heat to low and allow sauce to thicken.

5. Garnish with green onion before serving.

PER SERVING | Calories: 446 | Fat: 32 g | Protein: 25 g | Sodium: 935 mg | Fiber: 1 g | Carbohydrates: 15 g

Steak-and-Mushroom Kebabs

These meaty, juicy kabobs are a hit at summer barbecues.
They can also be cooked indoors on a well-seasoned grill pan.

INGREDIENTS | SERVES 3

1 pound sirloin steak

3 tablespoons avocado oil

¼ cup balsamic vinegar

1 tablespoon Worcestershire sauce

½ teaspoon salt

2 cloves garlic, minced

Freshly ground black pepper, to taste

½ pound large white mushrooms

1. Cut steak into 1½" cubes.

2. Combine oil, vinegar, Worcestershire sauce, salt, garlic, and pepper to make a marinade.

3. Wash mushrooms and cut in half. Place steak and mushrooms in shallow bowl with marinade and place in refrigerator for 1–2 hours.

4. Place marinated mushrooms and steak cubes on separate wooden or metal skewers. Grill 4 minutes per side over medium-high heat for medium-rare steak. You may need additional cooking time for mushrooms. Serve.

PER SERVING | Calories: 321 | Fat: 17 g | Protein: 25 g | Sodium: 541 mg | Fiber: 0 g | Carbohydrates: 16 g

Beef and Broccoli Stir-Fry

With a little imagination, simple everyday ingredients can be transformed into an exotic Asian dish like this one.

INGREDIENTS | SERVES 4

¾ pound sirloin beef, sliced into ½"-thick pieces

1 teaspoon salt

½ teaspoon freshly ground black pepper

1½ tablespoons arrowroot powder or coconut flour

3 tablespoons sesame oil

1 teaspoon minced fresh ginger

½ pound broccoli florets

3 cloves garlic

¼ cup soy sauce

Juice of 1 large orange

¼ cup water

½ teaspoon red pepper flakes

1. Season beef with salt and pepper. Coat beef with arrowroot or coconut flour.

2. Heat 2 tablespoons of oil in a wok over medium-high heat, then stir-fry beef and ginger for 1–2 minutes. Transfer beef to a bowl, cover, and set aside.

3. Add remaining oil to the hot wok. Add broccoli and garlic and stir-fry for 3–4 minutes, until broccoli is tender. Take care not to burn garlic.

4. Pour soy sauce, orange juice, water, and red pepper flakes into the wok with the broccoli and bring to a boil. Return the cooked beef to the wok. Stir until sauce thickens, about 2–3 minutes.

PER SERVING | Calories: 290 | Fat: 18 g | Protein: 21 g | Sodium: 1,556 mg | Fiber: 3 g | Carbohydrates: 12 g

Boeuf Bourguignon

Boeuf Bourguignon is a well-known classic French beef stew.

INGREDIENTS | SERVES 8

2 pounds stewing beef, cut into ½" cubes

1½ teaspoons salt

1 teaspoon freshly ground black pepper

1 tablespoon avocado oil

3 cloves garlic, minced

3 onions, quartered

2 cups dry red wine or beef broth

¾ pound carrots, peeled and sliced

¾ pound white mushrooms, sliced

1 bunch fresh rosemary, chopped

1 bunch fresh thyme, chopped

Water, as needed

1. Season beef with salt and pepper.

2. Add oil to a large frying pan over medium heat. Place beef in the pan to brown on the outside, about 5 minutes per side. Add garlic and onions to the pan and cook until tender. Add red wine or broth, bring to a boil, and then simmer.

3. Add carrots, mushrooms, and herbs to the pan. Add a few cups of water, as needed, to increase volume of liquid and keep the stew's sauce from cooking down. Cook for 3 hours, occasionally stirring.

PER SERVING | Calories: 383 | Fat: 25 g | Protein: 21 g | Sodium: 536 mg | Fiber: 2 g | Carbohydrates: 14 g

Pot Roast with a Touch of Sweet

Serve this roast alongside a hearty portion of Mashed Cauliflower (see Chapter 9).

INGREDIENTS | SERVES 8

1 teaspoon freshly ground black pepper

1 teaspoon smoked paprika

1 teaspoon garlic powder

1 teaspoon onion powder

½ cup lime juice

½ cup tomato sauce

2 pounds beef chuck roast

1 large sweet onion, thickly sliced

1 teaspoon coconut or avocado oil

½ cup water

2 tablespoons dry red wine or beef broth

1. In a small bowl, combine the pepper, paprika, garlic powder, and onion powder.

2. In a separate bowl, combine the lime juice and tomato sauce. Set aside.

3. Season all sides of the roast with the prepared spice mixture.

4. Place onion slices on the bottom of a 4-quart slow cooker.

5. Warm the oil in a large frying pan over medium-high heat. Brown the roast on all sides in the frying pan, about 8 minutes on each side.

6. Place browned roast on top of the onions in the slow cooker. Turn heat to low, and add water and wine or broth to the frying pan.

7. Pour pan liquid over the roast, then the lime juice and sauce mixture on top. Cover and cook on low for 8 hours.

PER SERVING | Calories: 189 | Fat: 8 g | Protein: 80 g | Sodium: 153 mg | Fiber: 3 g | Carbohydrates: 6 g

Sausage and Spicy Eggs

This is a very pretty dish that is not only a delicious breakfast but is also good for lunch or a late supper. Be careful not to overly salt the dish—most sausage has quite a lot of salt in it, so taste first.

INGREDIENTS | SERVES 4

1 pound sweet Italian sausage

¼ cup water

1 tablespoon avocado or coconut oil

2 sweet red peppers, roasted and chopped

1 jalapeño pepper, seeded and minced

8 eggs

2 tablespoons chopped fresh parsley

1. Cut the sausage in ¼" coins. Place in a heavy frying pan with the water and oil. Bring to a boil, then turn down the heat to low to simmer.

2. When the sausages are brown (after about 10 minutes), remove them and place on a paper towel. Add the roasted red peppers and jalapeño pepper to the pan and sauté over medium heat for 5 minutes.

3. While the peppers sauté, beat the eggs vigorously. Add to the pan and gently fold over until puffed and moist.

4. Mix in the reserved sausage, garnish with parsley, and serve hot.

PER SERVING | Calories: 383 | Fat: 23 g | Protein: 35 g | Sodium: 1,516 mg | Fiber: 1 g | Carbohydrates: 8 g

Tomato-Braised Pork

*Here the pork is gently cooked in tomatoes to yield beautifully tender meat.
If you'd prefer oregano or thyme in place of the marjoram, consider using a bit less than
what the recipe calls for, as these herbs tend to have a stronger flavor.*

INGREDIENTS | SERVES 4

1 (28-ounce) can crushed tomatoes

3 tablespoons tomato paste

1 cup loosely packed fresh basil

½ teaspoon freshly ground black pepper

½ teaspoon marjoram

1¼ pounds boneless pork roast

1. Place the tomatoes, tomato paste, basil, pepper, and marjoram in a 4-quart slow cooker. Stir to create a uniform sauce. Add the pork.

2. Cook on low for 7–8 hours or until the pork easily falls apart when poked with a fork.

PER SERVING | Calories: 192 | Fat: 5 g | Protein: 32 g | Sodium: 166 mg | Fiber: 1 g | Carbohydrates: 3 g

Honey-Mustard Pork Loin

A mixture of mustard and honey keeps the pork from drying out during the long cooking time.

INGREDIENTS | SERVES 2

3 tablespoons Dijon mustard

1 tablespoon raw honey

½ pound pork tenderloin

1. In a small bowl, mix the mustard and honey. Spread the mixture on the pork tenderloin in an even layer.

2. Place pork in a 4- or 6-quart slow cooker. Cook on low for 6 hours.

PER SERVING | Calories: 170 | Fat: 3 g | Protein: 25 g | Sodium: 326 mg | Fiber: 1 g | Carbohydrates: 10 g

Pork Tenderloin with Sweet and Savory Apples

The tart apples sweeten over the long cooking time and nearly melt into the pork.

INGREDIENTS | SERVES 2

¼ teaspoon freshly ground black pepper

¾–1 pound boneless pork tenderloin

½ cup sliced onions

5 fresh sage leaves

2 cups peeled, diced Granny Smith apples

Pork Tenderloin Tip

Lean, boneless pork tenderloin is often sold in very large packages containing 2 or more tenderloins, with a combined weight that is frequently over 15 pounds. As a result, it can be very expensive. Buy pork tenderloin on sale, and cut the meat into meal-sized portions. Label and freeze the portions until they are needed.

1. Sprinkle pepper on the tenderloin. Place the onion slices on the bottom of a 1½- or 4- or 6-quart slow cooker. Add the tenderloin. Place the sage on top of the meat. Top with the diced apples.

2. Cover and cook on low for 8–10 hours.

PER SERVING | Calories: 261 | Fat: 5 g | Protein: 47 g | Sodium: 120 mg | Fiber: 1 g | Carbohydrates: 4 g

Beef and Coconut Curry

This Indian-inspired recipe has the perfect blend of beef and vegetables, and the finished product is both sweet and savory.

INGREDIENTS | SERVES 4

2 tablespoons coconut oil

2 pounds beef chuck roast, cut into 2" pieces

2 large onions, each cut into 8 wedges

4 cloves garlic, finely chopped

2 tablespoons finely chopped fresh ginger

12 ounces coconut milk

2 tablespoons raw honey

1 tablespoon curry powder

1 teaspoon cayenne pepper

1 pint cherry tomatoes

1. In a large frying pan, warm oil over medium-high heat. Brown beef on all sides, about 3 minutes per side. Transfer to a 4-quart slow cooker along with onions, garlic, and ginger.

2. In a large bowl, whisk together the coconut milk, honey, curry powder, and cayenne pepper, and pour over meat. Cover and cook on low until meat is fork-tender, about 4–5 hours.

3. Stir in cherry tomatoes and let them warm and soften in stew for 15–20 minutes.

PER SERVING | Calories: 315 | Fat: 25 g | Protein: 4 g | Sodium: 20 mg | Fiber: 3 g | Carbohydrates: 23 g

Beef and Cabbage

The longer cooking time helps the flavors develop. But because the meat is already cooked, this meal is done when the cabbage is tender. Serve over mashed turnip, cauliflower, or butternut squash.

INGREDIENTS | SERVES 4

1 pound cooked stew beef

1 small head cabbage, chopped

1 medium onion, diced

2 large carrots, peeled and thinly sliced

2 stalks celery, sliced in ½" pieces

1 clove garlic, minced

2 cups beef broth

1 (14.5-ounce) can diced tomatoes

¼ teaspoon raw honey

⅛ teaspoon freshly ground black pepper

1. Cut the cooked beef into bite-size pieces and add it to a 4-quart slow cooker along with the cabbage, onion, carrots, and celery. Stir to combine.

2. Add the garlic, broth, tomatoes, honey, and pepper to a bowl; mix well and pour over the beef. Cook on high for 1 hour or until the cabbage has begun to wilt.

3. Reduce heat to low and cook for 3–4 hours or until cabbage is very tender. Adjust seasonings if necessary.

PER SERVING | Calories: 354 | Fat: 8 g | Protein: 29 g | Sodium: 241 mg | Fiber: 12 g | Carbohydrates: 43 g

Beef and Ginger Curry

This hearty and spicy curry dish, typically served over rice, is just as tasty over a bed of Paleo-approved carrots and cauliflower.

INGREDIENTS | SERVES 4

1 pound stewing steak

1 tablespoon sesame oil

Pepper, to taste

2 cloves garlic, minced

1 teaspoon chopped fresh ginger

1 fresh green chili, diced

1 tablespoon curry powder

1 (14.5-ounce) can stewed tomatoes, chopped

1 large onion, quartered

8 ounces beef broth

1. In a large frying pan, brown the steak in the oil over medium-high heat for 5–10 minutes. Once browned, remove from pan, leaving juices. Season beef with pepper.

2. In the remaining juice from the steak, cook the garlic, ginger, and chili over medium heat for 2 minutes, stirring frequently.

3. Season with curry powder. Mix in the chopped tomatoes.

4. Place the onion on the bottom of a 2- or 4-quart slow cooker, and layer with browned beef.

5. Add mixture from pan to the slow cooker, and add the broth. Cover and cook on low for 6–8 hours.

PER SERVING | Calories: 82 | Fat: 4 g | Protein: 2 g | Sodium: 192 mg | Fiber: 4 g | Carbohydrates: 16 g

CHAPTER 7

Poultry

Pheasantly Pleasant
172

Ground Turkey Joes
172

Turkey Meatballs
173

Mango Duck Breast
174

Thyme-Roasted Turkey Breast
174

Poached Chicken
175

Foolproof Chicken
175

Hot Buffalo Chicken Bites
176

Chicken Piccata
177

Shredded Chicken Wraps
178

Chicken Enchiladas
179

Chicken with Sautéed Tomatoes and Pine Nuts
180

Pecan-Crusted Chicken
180

Spicy Chicken Sliders
181

No-Crust Chicken Potpie
181

Chicken with Eggplant
182

Chicken and Vegetable Frittata
183

Poached Chicken with Pears and Herbs
184

Grilled San Francisco–Style Chicken
184

Braised Chicken with Citrus
185

Lemon Chicken
185

Braised Chicken with Kale
186

Stewed Chicken with Vegetables
187

Baked Chicken Legs
188

Chicken Cacciatore
189

Thai Chicken Stew with Vegetables in Coconut Cream
190

Jerk Chicken
191

Tuscan Chicken
192

Coconut Mango Spiced Chicken
192

Ginger-Orange Chicken Breast
193

Pheasantly Pleasant

Wild game like pheasants move more frequently than the average chicken and therefore contain less saturated fat and calories per ounce.

INGREDIENTS | SERVES 6

2 pheasants, cut into small, 1–2" chunks

¼ cup almond flour, seasoned with a pinch of pepper

4 tablespoons avocado or coconut oil

4 tablespoons coconut butter

1 clove garlic

1 large onion, diced

1 cup dry white wine or additional chicken broth

1 tablespoon raw honey

1 (10.75-ounce) can chopped mushrooms

10 ounces chicken broth

1. Coat pheasant pieces in seasoned almond flour.

2. In a frying pan over medium heat, sauté the pheasant for 5–7 minutes in oil and butter. Transfer pheasant to a 4-quart slow cooker.

3. Mash garlic clove in frying pan juices, add onion, wine, honey, mushrooms, and broth. Heat to bubbling and simmer 5 minutes, then pour over pheasant in the slow cooker.

4. Cover and cook on low for 6–8 hours.

PER SERVING | Calories: 493 | Fat: 21 g | Protein: 58 g | Sodium: 381 mg | Fiber: 1 g | Carbohydrates: 10 g

Ground Turkey Joes

This easy, sweet-and-sour turkey dish comes together quickly and serves well over puréed cauliflower, mashed sweet potatoes, or turnips. If you prefer, you can also use ground chicken or ground beef as a substitute for the ground turkey.

INGREDIENTS | SERVES 4

2 teaspoons organic butter or ghee

1 pound lean ground turkey

½ cup finely chopped onion

½ cup finely chopped green pepper

1 teaspoon garlic powder

1 tablespoon prepared yellow mustard

¾ cup Homemade Ketchup (see Chapter 3)

3 tablespoons raw honey

¼ teaspoon lemon juice

½ teaspoon ground pepper

1. In a large frying pan, heat butter over medium-high heat. Brown ground turkey, onion, and green pepper for approximately 5–6 minutes. Drain off any grease.

2. Add turkey mixture to a greased 2½- or 4-quart slow cooker. Add garlic powder, mustard, ketchup, honey, lemon juice, and pepper.

3. Mix ingredients together and cook on low for 4 hours or on high for 2 hours.

PER SERVING | Calories: 270 | Fat: 12 g | Protein: 20 g | Sodium: 108 mg | Fiber: 1 g | Carbohydrates: 22 g

Turkey Meatballs

This is a fairly generic meatball recipe with some basic additions. You can substitute any type of ground meat you prefer: bison, beef, chicken, or pork. Flaxseed meal can replace the almond meal as well.

INGREDIENTS | SERVES 8

2 pounds (93% lean) ground turkey

1 cup almond meal

2 large eggs

5 scallions, chopped

1 red bell pepper, seeded and diced

2 cloves garlic, minced

1 tablespoon dried basil

1 tablespoon dried oregano

2 tablespoons avocado oil

1. Preheat oven to 400°F.

2. Combine all ingredients, except oil, in a large bowl. Mix well with clean hands.

3. Add oil to turkey mixture and mix well.

4. Form turkey mixture into 24 meatballs and place on 2 rimmed baking pans.

5. Bake for 20 minutes.

PER SERVING | Calories: 198 | Fat: 6 g | Protein: 29 g | Sodium: 21 mg | Fiber: 1.5 g | Carbohydrates: 13 g

Fat Content in Ground Meats

Although most people make sure to buy ground meat with the lowest fat content, it is more beneficial to buy fattier ground meat when it is from grass-fed or barn-roaming animals. This meat is lower in saturated fat than most commercial ground meat, and the fat profiles favor the omega-3 fatty acids to fight inflammation and heart disease in your body.

Mango Duck Breast

Slow cooked mangoes soften and create their own sauce in this easy duck dish.

INGREDIENTS | SERVES 4

2 boneless, skinless duck breasts
1 large mango, cubed
¼ cup duck or chicken stock
1 tablespoon ginger juice
1 tablespoon minced hot pepper
1 tablespoon minced shallot

Place all ingredients in a 4-quart slow cooker. Cook on low for 4 hours.

PER SERVING | Calories: 412 | Fat: 18 g | Protein: 55 g | Sodium: 225 mg | Fiber: 0 g | Carbohydrates: 3 g

Thyme-Roasted Turkey Breast

Slow-cooked turkey is so moist there's no basting required!

INGREDIENTS | SERVES 10

2 large onions, thinly sliced
1 (6–7-pound) turkey breast, skin on
½ cup minced thyme
½ tablespoon freshly ground black pepper
½ tablespoon dried parsley
½ tablespoon celery flakes
½ tablespoon mustard seed

1. Arrange the onion slices in a thin layer on the bottom of a 6- or 7-quart slow cooker.

2. Make a small slit in the skin of the turkey and spread the thyme between the skin and meat. Smooth the skin back onto the turkey.

3. In a small bowl, stir the pepper, parsley, celery flakes, and mustard seed. Rub the spice mixture onto the skin of the turkey.

4. Place the turkey in the slow cooker on top of the onion layer. Cook for 8 hours. Remove the skin and onions and discard them before serving the turkey.

PER SERVING | Calories: 341 | Fat: 2 g | Protein: 72 g | Sodium: 146 mg | Fiber: 1 g | Carbohydrates: 4 g

Poached Chicken

Use this moist, tender poached chicken in any recipe that calls for cooked chicken. It is especially good in salads and sandwiches.

INGREDIENTS | SERVES 8

4–5 pounds whole chicken or chicken parts
1 large carrot, peeled
1 stalk celery
1 medium onion, quartered
1 cup water

1. Place the chicken into an oval 6-quart slow cooker. Arrange the vegetables around the chicken. Add the water. Cook on low for 7–8 hours.

2. Remove the skin before eating.

PER SERVING | Calories: 310 | Fat: 8 g | Protein: 54 g | Sodium: 206 mg | Fiber: 1 g | Carbohydrates: 2 g

Foolproof Chicken

This is just about the simplest chicken recipe there is, and it's perfect for any occasion.

INGREDIENTS | SERVES 6

3 pounds boneless, skinless chicken breasts or thighs
24 ounces tomato sauce

Place chicken in a 4-quart slow cooker and add sauce. Cover and cook on low for 8 hours or on high for 4–5 hours. Once cooked, shred the chicken with a fork and enjoy.

PER SERVING | Calories: 282 | Fat: 6 g | Protein: 49 g | Sodium: 845 mg | Fiber: 2 g | Carbohydrates: 6 g

Hot Buffalo Chicken Bites

Love buffalo wings? Then you will love these chicken bites even more; they are made with juicy chicken breasts so you won't have to worry about bones. They are super easy and much less messy! Serve with celery and carrot sticks.

INGREDIENTS | SERVES 6

3 large boneless, skinless chicken breasts, cut into 2" strips

2 tablespoons almond flour

¼ cup melted coconut butter

3 cloves garlic, minced

⅓ cup hot sauce

Fresh Garlic versus Garlic Powder

In a pinch you can use 1½ teaspoons garlic powder in this recipe. The garlic flavor won't be quite as pungent and rich as it is when you use fresh garlic, but it will still be easy and enjoyable.

1. Place chicken strips in a greased 2½-quart slow cooker.

2. In a saucepan, whisk together the almond flour and melted coconut butter for 2–3 minutes to toast the flour.

3. Slowly whisk in the garlic and hot sauce. Pour sauce over chicken in the slow cooker.

4. Cover and cook on high for 3 hours or on low for 6 hours. Serve with celery and carrot sticks. If using a larger slow cooker, make sure to reduce cooking time by about half.

PER SERVING | Calories: 145 | Fat: 4 g | Protein: 24 g | Sodium: 461 mg | Fiber: 0 g | Carbohydrates: 1 g

Chicken Piccata

Chicken is a staple for the Paleolithic eater. This lunchtime treat is a pleasant departure from the ordinary.

INGREDIENTS | SERVES 4

1 cup unsalted chicken broth

½ cup lemon juice

4 boneless, skinless chicken breasts

3 tablespoons almond oil

1 cup chopped onion

1 clove garlic, minced

2 cups chopped fresh artichoke hearts

3 tablespoons capers

1 teaspoon pepper

Capers

Capers are salted and should be used only occasionally for a dish such as this one. This dish is still full of flavor without them and will be a delightful treat for your family.

1. Combine chicken broth, lemon juice, and chicken in shallow dish. Cover and marinate overnight in the refrigerator.

2. Heat oil in a medium-size frying pan over medium heat and cook onion and garlic until softened, about 2 minutes.

3. Remove chicken from marinade, reserving marinade. Add chicken to pan and brown each side, 5–10 minutes.

4. Add artichoke hearts, capers, pepper, and reserved marinade. Reduce heat and simmer until chicken is thoroughly cooked, approximately another 10 minutes.

PER SERVING | Calories: 269 | Fat: 13 g | Protein: 35 g | Sodium: 390 mg | Fiber: 1 g | Carbohydrates: 5 g

Shredded Chicken Wraps

These are a great way to get the feel of a wrap without the forbidden carbohydrates of a tortilla. You can easily substitute your favorite meat or fish for the chicken to vary your lunchtime menu.

INGREDIENTS | SERVES 8

2 cooked boneless, skinless chicken breasts (baked, poached, or broiled)

2 stalks celery, chopped

¼ cup chopped basil

2 tablespoons almond oil

2 tablespoons lemon juice

1 teaspoon minced garlic

Ground black pepper, to taste

1 teaspoon hot sauce

1 head radicchio or romaine lettuce

1. Shred chicken and place in a medium-size bowl.

2. Mix chicken with celery, basil, oil, lemon juice, garlic, pepper, and hot sauce.

3. Separate lettuce leaves and place on 8 plates.

4. Spoon chicken mixture onto lettuce leaves and roll up.

PER SERVING | Calories: 123 | Fat: 3.5 g | Protein: 9 g | Sodium: 14 mg | Fiber: 0.5 g | Carbohydrates: 1 g

Chicken Enchiladas

If you have been craving a Mexican feast, try this spicy Paleolithic alternative. This recipe has most of the taste of traditional enchiladas without the carbohydrates.

INGREDIENTS | SERVES 8

2 tablespoons avocado oil

2 pounds boneless, skinless chicken breast, cut in 1" cubes

4 cloves garlic, minced

½ cup finely chopped onion

2 cups chopped tomatoes

1 teaspoon cumin

1 teaspoon chili powder

½ cup fresh cilantro

Juice from 2 limes

1 (10-ounce) package frozen chopped spinach, thawed and drained

¼ cup sliced green olives

8 collard green leaves

1. Heat oil in a medium-size frying pan. Sauté chicken, garlic, and onion in the hot oil until thoroughly cooked, about 10 minutes.

2. Add tomatoes, cumin, chili powder, cilantro, and lime juice and simmer for 5 minutes.

3. Add spinach and simmer for 5 more minutes. Remove from heat. Stir in olives.

4. In a separate pan, quickly steam collard greens to soften, about 3 minutes.

5. Wrap chicken mixture in collard greens and serve.

PER SERVING | Calories: 200 | Fat: 7 g | Protein: 26 g | Sodium: 207 mg | Fiber: 3 g | Carbohydrates: 8 g

Chicken with Sautéed Tomatoes and Pine Nuts

Sautéed tomatoes and pine nuts add a nice, nutty flavor to an ordinary dish.
This topping can be added to fish or beef just as easily.

INGREDIENTS | SERVES 2

¼ cup avocado oil
1 cup halved cherry tomatoes
¼ cup chopped green chilies
¼ cup cilantro
½ cup pine nuts
2 boneless, skinless chicken breasts

1. Heat oil in a medium-size frying pan over medium-high heat. Sauté tomatoes, chilies, cilantro, and pine nuts until golden brown, about 5 minutes. Remove from pan and set aside.

2. In the same pan, cook chicken 5 minutes on each side.

3. Return tomato mixture to pan and cover. Simmer on low for 5 minutes until chicken is fully cooked.

PER SERVING | Calories: 595 | Fat: 45 g | Protein: 44 g | Sodium: 6.5 mg | Fiber: 2 g | Carbohydrates: 8 g

Pecan-Crusted Chicken

This pecan crust recipe is quite versatile. It works for fish as well as chicken,
and other nuts can be substituted for different flavors.

INGREDIENTS | SERVES 4

1 cup ground pecans
2 large eggs, beaten
4 boneless, skinless chicken breasts

1. Preheat oven to 350°F.

2. Place ground nuts in a shallow bowl and eggs in a separate shallow bowl.

3. Dip each chicken breast in egg and then in nuts. Place coated chicken breasts in a shallow baking dish.

4. Bake for 25 minutes.

PER SERVING | Calories: 377 | Fat: 24 g | Protein: 40 g | Sodium: 32 mg | Fiber: 3 g | Carbohydrates: 4 g

Spicy Chicken Sliders

You can substitute ground turkey or pork for the chicken.
Adjust the quantity of pepper flakes to control the spiciness.

INGREDIENTS | SERVES 4

1 pound ground chicken breast
¼ cup finely chopped yellow onion
¼ cup finely chopped red bell pepper
1 teaspoon minced garlic
¼ cup thinly sliced scallions
½ teaspoon red pepper flakes
½ teaspoon chili powder
½ teaspoon sea salt
Freshly ground black pepper, to taste

1. Clean and oil broiler rack. Preheat broiler to medium.

2. Combine all the ingredients in a medium-size bowl, mixing lightly. Form mixture into 8 small patties.

3. Broil the burgers for 3–4 minutes per side until firm through the center and the juices run clear. Transfer to a plate and tent with tinfoil to keep warm. Allow to rest 1–2 minutes before serving.

PER SERVING | Calories: 145 | Fat: 3 g | Protein: 27 g | Sodium: 20 mg | Fiber: 0 g | Carbohydrates: 1 g

No-Crust Chicken Potpie

This is a traditional comfort food converted to satisfy even the hardest-to-please Paleo palate.

INGREDIENTS | SERVES 4

2 teaspoons organic butter or ghee
10 ounces coconut milk
1 teaspoon dried parsley
1 teaspoon dried onion flakes
1 (16-ounce) package frozen cauliflower, broccoli, and carrot blend
1 pound boneless, skinless chicken breasts, cut into ½" cubes

1. Melt butter in a 4-quart slow cooker.

2. Add coconut milk, parsley, and onion flakes to the slow cooker.

3. Stir in the frozen vegetables and chicken pieces. Cover and cook on low for 8 hours. Mix well before serving.

PER SERVING | Calories: 310 | Fat: 20 g | Protein: 28 g | Sodium: 167 mg | Fiber: 3 g | Carbohydrates: 7 g

Chicken with Eggplant

Adding chicken to a typical Asian-inspired eggplant dish makes for a well-balanced dinner.

INGREDIENTS | SERVES 4

4 boneless, skinless chicken breasts

1 pound eggplant

2 tablespoons avocado oil

2 cloves garlic, minced

1 medium red bell pepper, finely chopped

½ cup water

¼ cup coconut aminos

¼ cup red wine vinegar

2 tablespoons raw honey

2 tablespoons sesame oil

¼ teaspoon red pepper flakes

1. Cut chicken breasts lengthwise into ½"-wide strips. Cut eggplant lengthwise into 1"-wide strips.

2. Heat avocado oil in a large frying pan over medium-high heat and cook chicken until well done. Transfer to a bowl and set aside.

3. Return pan to high heat and add eggplant, garlic, bell pepper, and water. Bring to a boil, then reduce heat to medium-low, cover pan, and cook until eggplant is very soft and liquid has evaporated, stirring occasionally.

4. In a small bowl, mix coconut aminos, vinegar, honey, and sesame oil. Add cooked chicken, coconut aminos mixture, and red pepper flakes to pan with cooked eggplant and bring to a boil. Reduce heat to medium and cook, occasionally stirring, for about 5 minutes. Serve.

PER SERVING | Calories: 463 | Fat: 20 g | Protein: 52 g | Sodium: 308 mg | Fiber: 5 g | Carbohydrates: 18 g

Chicken and Vegetable Frittata

Eggs and chicken make this satisfying meal both high in protein and a complete one-pot dish.

INGREDIENTS | SERVES 4

1 teaspoon organic butter or ghee
3 shallots, sliced
2 cloves garlic, minced
1 teaspoon salt
½ teaspoon freshly ground black pepper
8 ounces boneless, skinless chicken breast, diced
1 cup broccoli florets
1 cup sliced zucchini
1 cup sliced yellow squash
12 asparagus spears, chopped into 1" pieces
8 eggs

1. Preheat oven to 350°F. Melt butter in a small frying pan over medium heat and sauté shallots and garlic until soft, about 3 minutes. Be careful not to burn garlic.

2. Sprinkle salt and pepper over diced chicken breast as desired. Add chicken to pan with shallots and garlic and sauté until chicken is cooked, about 7 minutes.

3. Grease a round casserole dish. Place all vegetables and chicken with shallots into the greased dish.

4. Whisk eggs and pour over contents in the dish.

5. Bake at 350°F for 20–25 minutes, until eggs are set but not brown.

PER SERVING | Calories: 232 | Fat: 11 g | Protein: 25 g | Sodium: 790 mg | Fiber: 2 g | Carbohydrates: 8 g

Poached Chicken with Pears and Herbs

Any seasonal fresh fruit will make this dish very special. Pears go very well with all poultry.
Try this for a quick treat and double the recipe for company.

INGREDIENTS | SERVES 2

1 ripe pear, peeled, cored, and cut into chunks

2 shallots, minced

½ cup dry white wine or chicken broth

1 teaspoon dried rosemary or 1 tablespoon fresh

1 teaspoon dried thyme or 1 tablespoon fresh

1 teaspoon salt

½ teaspoon freshly ground black pepper

2½ pounds boneless, skinless chicken breasts

Prepare the poaching liquid by mixing pear, shallots, wine or broth, rosemary, and thyme and bringing to a boil in a medium saucepan. Salt and pepper the chicken and add to the pan. Simmer over low heat for 10 minutes. Serve with pears on top of each piece of chicken.

PER SERVING | Calories: 307 | Fat: 9 g | Protein: 41 g | Sodium: 917 mg | Fiber: 1 g | Carbohydrates: 15 g

Grilled San Francisco–Style Chicken

This is a quick chef's delight. It's excellent, and everyone at your table will ask
"What is in this?" (in a good way)!

INGREDIENTS | SERVES 4

1 tablespoon almond oil, plus more for grilling

1 tablespoon Dijon mustard

2 tablespoons raspberry white wine vinegar

1 small chicken (about 2½–3 pounds), cut in quarters

1 teaspoon celery salt

½ teaspoon freshly ground black pepper

1. Heat grill to 400°F. In a small bowl, mix 1 tablespoon oil, mustard, and vinegar. Sprinkle the chicken with celery salt and pepper.

2. Paint the skin side of the chicken with the mustard mixture. Rub a few drops of oil on the bone side.

3. Grill the chicken, bone side to flame, for 15 minutes. Reduce heat to 325°F; cover and cook for 15 minutes.

PER SERVING | Calories: 95 | Fat: 10 g | Protein: 40 g | Sodium: 893 mg | Fiber: 0 g | Carbohydrates: 7 g

Braised Chicken with Citrus

Chicken is wonderfully flavored by lemons, oranges, and grapefruits. Try using the sauce in this recipe over riced cauliflower or chilled in a salad.

INGREDIENTS | SERVES 2

¼ cup freshly squeezed orange juice

¼ cup freshly squeezed grapefruit juice

1 tablespoon raw honey

1 teaspoon dried summer savory

½ teaspoon lemon zest

1 teaspoon almond oil

½ pound boneless, skinless chicken breasts, cut in chunks

1 teaspoon salt

½ teaspoon freshly ground black pepper

Make poaching liquid with orange juice, grapefruit juice, honey, savory, zest, and oil. Sprinkle the chicken with salt and pepper. Poach for 10 minutes warm or chilled.

PER SERVING | Calories: 209 | Fat: 5 g | Protein: 24 g | Sodium: 1,310 mg | Fiber: 1 g | Carbohydrates: 16 g |

Lemon Chicken

This is a classic citrus chicken with fresh herbs that isn't too sour—it calls for the perfect amount of lemon!

INGREDIENTS | SERVES 6

⅓ cup lemon juice

2 tablespoons lemon zest

3 cloves garlic, minced

2 tablespoons chopped fresh thyme

2 tablespoons chopped fresh rosemary

2 tablespoons almond oil

1 teaspoon salt

1 teaspoon fresh ground black pepper

3 pounds bone-in chicken thighs

1. To make the marinade, combine lemon juice, lemon zest, garlic, thyme, rosemary, oil, salt, and pepper in a small bowl. Place chicken in a large bowl and pour marinade on top. Let marinate in the refrigerator for 2 hours.

2. Heat oven to 425°F. Place marinated chicken in one layer in a large baking dish. Spoon leftover marinade over top of chicken.

3. Bake until chicken is completely cooked through, about 50 minutes. The internal temperature will be 175°F.

PER SERVING | Calories: 254 | Fat: 19 g | Protein: 16 g | Sodium: 589 mg | Fiber: 0 g | Carbohydrates: 4 g

Braised Chicken with Kale

This dish is inspired by a traditional Tuscan kale and white bean soup.

INGREDIENTS | SERVES 4

1 pound boneless, skinless chicken breasts

1½ teaspoons salt, divided

1 teaspoon freshly ground black pepper, divided

2 tablespoons almond oil

½ onion, chopped

2 cloves garlic, minced

1 large bunch kale, chopped

1 teaspoon red pepper flakes

1 tablespoon fresh rosemary, chopped

1 (15-ounce) can diced tomatoes

1 (14.5-ounce) can chicken broth

1. Slice chicken breasts into small pieces. Season chicken with 1 teaspoon salt and ½ teaspoon pepper.

2. Heat oil in a large frying pan over medium-high heat and sauté onion and garlic for 3–4 minutes. Add chicken and cook an additional 4 minutes.

3. Add kale in batches to the pan with the chicken and cook until wilted, about 2 minutes. Season with red pepper flakes and rosemary.

4. Add tomatoes, broth, ½ teaspoon salt, and ½ teaspoon pepper to the pan; stir and simmer for 10–15 minutes.

PER SERVING | Calories: 252 | Fat: 11 g | Protein: 28 g | Sodium: 1,311 mg | Fiber: 2 g | Carbohydrates: 10 g

Emerald Kale

Kale, a member of the cabbage family, provides a ton of nutritional value but has very few calories. Kale is an excellent source of vitamins A, K, and C and is known for its health-promoting phytonutrients.

Stewed Chicken with Vegetables

This is a good old-fashioned way to prepare chicken for the family.

INGREDIENTS | SERVES 4

1 frying chicken, cut up

1 cup chicken stock

16 pearl onions

2 large carrots, peeled and cut into 1" pieces

2 stalks celery, cut in chunks

2 cloves garlic, smashed with the side of a knife

1 bulb fennel, trimmed and cut into chunks

4 small bluenose turnips, peeled and cut into chunks

1 teaspoon dried thyme, or 3 teaspoons fresh

1 teaspoon dried rosemary

2 bay leaves

3 cups chicken broth

Salt and pepper, to taste

In a large stew pot, mix all ingredients. Bring to a boil. Reduce heat to a simmer; cover and cook over very low heat for 50 minutes. Remove bay leaves.

PER SERVING | Calories: 348 | Fat: 9 g | Protein: 42 g | Sodium: 1,112 mg | Fiber: 4 g | Carbohydrates: 24 g

A Crown of Laurel

Bay leaves, also known as laurel, are originally from the Mediterranean. They have a strong, woody, and somewhat spicy flavor and are usually sold dried in jars in the spice section of the grocery store.

Baked Chicken Legs

This is so simple—an everyday baked chicken that requires no fuss or hassle.

INGREDIENTS | SERVES 6

6 bone-in chicken legs and thighs

2 tablespoons avocado oil, divided

2 tablespoons paprika

1½ tablespoons onion powder

1 teaspoon salt

1. Preheat oven to 400°F. Rinse and pat dry chicken. Coat the bottom of a large roasting pan with 1 tablespoon oil.

2. Coat chicken pieces lightly with remaining oil. Cover chicken evenly with paprika, onion powder, and salt. Place chicken pieces skin-side up in the pan.

3. Bake chicken at 400°F for 30 minutes, then lower the temperature to 350°F and cook for 10–15 minutes. The internal temperature of the chicken thighs should be 185°F.

PER SERVING | Calories: 355 | Fat: 25 g | Protein: 28 g | Sodium: 527 mg | Fiber: 1 g | Carbohydrates: 1 g

Chicken Cacciatore

This classic Italian dish, also called hunter's stew, is cooked slowly until the chicken is falling off the bone.

INGREDIENTS | SERVES 6

3 tablespoons avocado oil

1 whole chicken, cut up

1 cup chopped onion

1 cup chopped red bell pepper

3 cloves garlic, minced

2 (15-ounce) cans stewed tomatoes

¾ cup chicken broth

1 tablespoon Italian seasoning

1 teaspoon salt

½ teaspoon freshly ground black pepper

1 bay leaf

3 tablespoons capers

Timesaving Tip

A recipe like this that contains a good amount of liquid and a longer cooking time at a lower temperature is well suited for a slow cooker. The slow-cooker technique requires very little active cooking time.

1. Heat oil in a medium-size frying pan over medium-high heat. Brown chicken thoroughly, about 10 minutes. Remove chicken from pan. Add onion, red bell pepper, and garlic to the hot pan; sauté until onion is tender, about 10 minutes.

2. Stir in tomatoes, broth, Italian seasoning, salt, pepper, and bay leaf. Add chicken back into the pan with sauce and bring to a boil.

3. Reduce heat to low, cover, and simmer for 40–45 minutes. Stir in capers. Remove bay leaf from the sauce before serving.

PER SERVING | Calories: 249 | Fat: 11 g | Protein: 26 g | Sodium: 938 mg | Fiber: 3 g | Carbohydrates: 12 g

Thai Chicken Stew with Vegetables in Coconut Cream

Asian flavorings can provide so many minimal yet wonderful additions to rather ordinary foods. This vegetable-loaded chicken stew is spicy and tastes very rich.

INGREDIENTS | SERVES 4

2 cloves garlic, minced

1 (1" piece) fresh ginger, peeled and minced

2 tablespoons almond oil

2 carrots, shredded

1 cup canned unsweetened coconut cream

1 cup chicken broth

2 cups shredded Napa cabbage

4 boneless, skinless chicken breasts (about 5 ounces each), cut into bite-size pieces

¼ cup coconut aminos

2 tablespoons Asian fish sauce

1 teaspoon Thai chili paste (red or green) or hot sauce

1 tablespoon sesame oil

½ cup chopped scallions (green parts only)

¼ cup chopped cilantro

1. In a medium-size frying pan over medium-high heat, sauté the garlic and ginger in the almond oil for 1–2 minutes. Add the carrots, coconut cream, and chicken broth and simmer for 10 minutes. Add the cabbage, chicken, coconut aminos, and fish sauce.

2. Whisk in the chili paste. Stir in the sesame oil, scallions, and cilantro. Simmer for 20 minutes.

PER SERVING | Calories: 678 | Fat: 30 g | Protein: 54 g | Sodium: 1,317 mg | Fiber: 2 g | Carbohydrates: 48 g

Coconut Cream, Coconut Milk, Coconut Juice

Contrary to popular belief, coconut milk is not the liquid found inside a whole coconut (that is called coconut juice). It is made from mixing water with shredded coconut. This mixture is then squeezed through cheesecloth to filter out the coconut pieces. Coconut cream is the same as coconut milk but made with less water and more coconut.

Jerk Chicken

This is a milder take on this typically ultra-spicy Caribbean favorite.

INGREDIENTS | SERVES 8

2 pounds chicken pieces

1 small onion, chopped

2 green onions, chopped into large pieces

1 jalapeño pepper, seeded

3 cloves garlic

1 teaspoon black pepper

¾ teaspoon salt

½ teaspoon dried thyme

¼ teaspoon cayenne pepper

1 tablespoon coconut aminos

¼ cup lime juice

3 tablespoons avocado oil

Turn Up the Heat!

If you can handle more heat, crank up the spiciness by substituting the jalapeño pepper with 2 chopped habanero peppers with their seeds.

1. Wash chicken and pat dry. Place in a large glass baking dish.

2. In a food processor or blender, combine onion, green onion, jalapeño, and garlic. Pulse to chop, then add black pepper, salt, thyme, cayenne pepper, coconut aminos, lime juice, and oil. Process until smooth.

3. Pour mixture over chicken and stir well to coat evenly. Cover with plastic wrap and refrigerate for 12 hours or overnight.

4. Preheat oven to 425°F. Place chicken in one layer in a greased roasting pan. Bake for approximately 50 minutes.

PER SERVING | Calories: 187 | Fat: 9 g | Protein: 24 g | Sodium: 352 mg | Fiber: 0 g | Carbohydrates: 2 g

Tuscan Chicken

This simple dish is perfect served over grilled or oven-roasted asparagus.

INGREDIENTS | SERVES 4

1 pound boneless, skinless chicken breast tenderloins

1 cup chicken broth

4 cloves garlic, minced

1 shallot, minced

2 tablespoons lime juice

1 tablespoon lemon juice

1 tablespoon minced fresh rosemary

1. Place all the ingredients in a 4-quart slow cooker. Stir.

2. Cook on low for 4 hours or until the chicken is fully cooked.

PER SERVING | Calories: 141 | Fat: 3 g | Protein: 25 g | Sodium: 136 mg | Fiber: 0 g | Carbohydrates: 2 g

Coconut Mango Spiced Chicken

This simple, sweet, and spicy dish requires just four ingredients and is easily prepared in just a few minutes.

INGREDIENTS | SERVES 4

1 can unsweetened coconut milk

1 large, firm mango, peeled and cubed (save mango pit)

1 pound boneless, skinless chicken breasts or thighs, cubed

1 tablespoon dried paprika flakes

1. Pour coconut milk into a 4-quart slow cooker.

2. Place the cubes of mango in the slow cooker, along with the pit of the mango. Add the chicken and paprika flakes. Stir well.

3. Cook on high for 3 hours or on low for 5–6 hours.

PER SERVING | Calories: 133 | Fat: 3 g | Protein: 24 g | Sodium: 131 mg | Fiber: 1 g | Carbohydrates: 1 g

Ginger-Orange Chicken Breast

This recipe is great chilled, sliced, and served on a crispy green salad.

INGREDIENTS | SERVES 4

4 (5-ounce) boneless, skinless chicken breasts

2 tablespoons avocado oil

½ teaspoon seasoned salt

Freshly ground black pepper, to taste

2 cloves garlic, minced

2 tablespoons grated fresh ginger

2 teaspoons orange zest

½ cup freshly squeezed orange juice

1. Rinse the chicken under cold running water and pat dry with paper towels. Heat the oil in a small nonstick frying pan over medium-high heat. Season the chicken with salt and pepper. Brown the chicken in the oil, turning it once, about 8 minutes per side. Transfer the chicken to a plate and cover to keep warm.

2. Add the garlic to the pan and cook for about 1 minute, stirring frequently to prevent burning. Add the ginger, orange zest, and juice and bring to a simmer. Add the chicken and any reserved juices and heat through, about 4–5 minutes. Cut through the bottom of the chicken to make sure it is cooked. Adjust seasoning to taste. Serve hot with the sauce.

PER SERVING | Calories: 240 | Fat: 9.5 g | Protein: 34 g | Sodium: 138 mg | Fiber: 0 g | Carbohydrates: 3 g

CHAPTER 8

Fish and Seafood

Steamed King Crab Legs
196

Salmon Cakes
196

Salmon in Parchment with Baby Brussels Sprouts
197

Citrus-Baked Snapper
198

Fried Sardines
199

Haddock Fish Cakes
200

Fresh Tuna with Sweet Lemon Leek Salsa
201

Lime-Poached Flounder
202

Baked Coconut Shrimp
203

Pecan-Crusted Catfish
204

Almond-Crusted Salmon
204

Coconut Shrimp
205

Salmon with Leeks
206

Grilled Halibut Herb Salad
207

Shrimp Fra Diavolo
208

Ginger-Lime Salmon
209

Salmon with Lemon, Capers, and Rosemary
209

Romaine-Wrapped Halibut Steaks
210

Foiled Fish Fillets
211

Caveman's Catfish
211

Orange Tilapia
212

Mahi Mahi and Green Vegetable Medley
212

Shrimp Creole
213

Herbed Tilapia Stew
213

Scallop and Shrimp Jambalaya
214

Fish "Bake"
215

Cioppino
216

Almond-Stuffed Flounder
217

Poached Swordfish with Lemon-Parsley Sauce
218

Manhattan Scallop Chowder
219

Hatteras Clam Chowder
220

Mahi Mahi Wraps with Avocado and Fresh Cabbage
220

Steamed King Crab Legs

Shellfish is a healthy and flavorful protein source. It is naturally low in fat and has a nice, sweet taste. A great alternative to the usual poultry or beef dish.

INGREDIENTS | SERVES 4

2 tablespoons coconut oil
3 cloves garlic, crushed
1 (1") piece fresh ginger, crushed
1 stalk lemongrass, crushed
2 pounds Alaskan king crab legs
1 teaspoon ground black pepper

1. Heat the oil in a large pot over medium-high heat.

2. Add the garlic, ginger, and lemongrass; cook and stir until brown, about 5 minutes.

3. Add crab legs and pepper. Cover and cook, tossing occasionally, for 15 minutes.

PER SERVING | Calories: 208 | Fat: 8 g | Protein: 31 g | Sodium: 1,022 mg | Fiber: 0 g | Carbohydrates: 1 g

Salmon Cakes

These salmon cakes are a great party appetizer. Even non-Paleo dieters will rave about them.

INGREDIENTS | SERVES 10

3 pounds salmon, finely diced
5 egg whites
1 teaspoon dried dill
¼ teaspoon ground ginger
¼ teaspoon cayenne pepper
¼ cup black pepper
¼ cup freshly squeezed lemon juice
¼ cup sesame oil
2 tablespoons arrowroot powder
1 cup almond meal

1. Preheat broiler.

2. Mix salmon, egg whites, dill, ginger, cayenne, black pepper, lemon juice, oil, and arrowroot powder together in a large bowl.

3. Form about 20 small patties from the mixture.

4. Pour almond meal into a shallow dish.

5. Dredge patties in almond meal and place on an ungreased baking sheet.

6. Broil each side for 4 minutes.

PER SERVING | Calories: 327 | Fat: 20 g | Protein: 31 g | Sodium: 88 mg | Fiber: 2 g | Carbohydrates: 7 g

Super Omega

The more omega-3 fatty acid you ingest, the better chance you will have at fighting silent inflammation. It is also proven to significantly reduce your recovery time from workouts or endurance races. The more omega-3, the better for optimum health all around.

Salmon in Parchment with Baby Brussels Sprouts

Cooking the salmon in parchment paper works to keep the fish from drying out, a common problem when cooking fish in the oven. The paper also helps to contain flavors so they are not cooked off.

INGREDIENTS | SERVES 2

2 (4- to 5-ounce) salmon fillets or steaks

2 tablespoons finely chopped petite Brussels sprouts

2 cloves garlic, crushed

2 dashes lemon juice

1 tablespoon avocado oil

1. Preheat oven to 425°F.

2. Place each piece of salmon on a large (12") circle of parchment paper.

3. Cover each salmon piece with a spoonful of Brussels sprouts, a clove of crushed garlic, a dash of lemon juice, and a drizzle of oil.

4. Fold the paper over into a packet and seal the edges by crimping and folding like a pastry. Place on a baking sheet.

5. Bake for 15 minutes, or until fish flakes easily with a fork.

PER SERVING | Calories: 189 | Fat: 12 g | Protein: 17 g | Sodium: 39 mg | Fiber: 0.5 g | Carbohydrates: 1.5 g

Citrus-Baked Snapper

Snapper is a tasty fish that absorbs the flavors in this recipe quite nicely. If cleaning and scaling a fish is overwhelming for you, ask your grocer or fishmonger to do it for you.

INGREDIENTS | SERVES 4

1 (3-pound) whole red snapper, cleaned and scaled
3½ tablespoons grated fresh ginger
3 green onions, chopped
1 tomato, seeded and diced
¼ cup freshly squeezed orange juice
¼ cup freshly squeezed lime juice
¼ cup freshly squeezed lemon juice
3 thin slices lime
3 thin slices lemon

Snapper and Omega-3

Snapper is not the fish that comes to mind when you're thinking about omega-3, but this cold-water fish does have some beneficial DHA fatty acid packed inside. Those with elevated blood triglycerides will benefit greatly from even small amounts of EPA and DHA.

1. Preheat the oven to 350°F.

2. Make three slashes across each side of the fish using a sharp knife. This will keep the fish from curling as it cooks.

3. Place the fish in a shallow baking dish or roasting pan.

4. Cover each side of fish with ginger, green onions, and tomatoes.

5. Combine juices and drizzle over snapper.

6. Place lime and lemon slices on top of fish.

7. Cover with aluminum foil and bake until the flesh is opaque and can be flaked with a fork, about 20 minutes.

PER SERVING | Calories: 271 | Fat: 3.5 g | Protein: 53 g | Sodium: 166 mg | Fiber: 0.5 g | Carbohydrates: 4 g

Fried Sardines

There are not many fried items in a Paleolithic diet, because most fried dishes are made with flour. This is a healthier alternative to traditional frying. The alcohol in the wine is mostly cooked off, so you will not have to worry about the alcohol either.

INGREDIENTS | SERVES 6

1 cup almond flour

2 pounds boneless, skinless, no-salt-added sardines

¾ cup plus 1 tablespoon almond oil, divided

2 cloves garlic, chopped

1 cup dry white wine

1 cup apple cider vinegar

½ cup chopped mint leaves

Mercury in Fish

Sardines are a great source of omega-3 and lack the dangerous mercury that other cold-water fish higher up on the food chain have. On lower-level fish, mercury is not amplified and therefore does not pose as much of a risk for humans.

1. Pour almond flour into a shallow dish. Roll sardines in almond flour.

2. Heat ¾ cup oil in a large frying pan over medium-high heat.

3. When the oil is hot, fry the sardines until brown and crispy, approximately 5 minutes. Drain on paper towels and keep warm.

4. In another frying pan over medium heat, warm garlic in remaining oil. Cook for 1 minute.

5. Add the wine and vinegar. Simmer mixture, stirring occasionally, until the liquid has reduced by half, about 15 minutes.

6. Pour the sauce over the sardines, and sprinkle with fresh mint.

PER SERVING | Calories: 318 | Fat: 14 g | Protein: 31 g | Sodium: 575 mg | Fiber: 2.5 g | Carbohydrates: 18 g

Haddock Fish Cakes

This version of a familiar fish cake has the fresh flavor of haddock.
Serve this with a spicy sauce or a fresh spritz of lemon.

INGREDIENTS | SERVES 6

1 pound haddock
2 leeks
1 red pepper
2 egg whites
2 teaspoons Old Bay Seasoning
1 teaspoon sea salt
½ teaspoon freshly ground black pepper
1 tablespoon almond oil

1. Finely shred the raw fish with a fork. Dice the leeks and red pepper.

2. Combine all the ingredients, except the oil, in a medium-size bowl; mix well. Form the mixture into small oval patties.

3. Heat the oil in a medium-size frying pan over medium heat. Place the cakes in the pan and loosely cover with the lid; sauté the cakes for 4–6 minutes on each side. Drain on a rack covered with paper towels; serve immediately.

PER SERVING | Calories: 131 | Fat: 4 g | Protein: 17 g | Sodium: 470 mg | Fiber: 3 g | Carbohydrates: 8 g

Fresh Tuna with Sweet Lemon Leek Salsa

The tuna can be prepared the night before, refrigerated, then either reheated or served at room temperature.

INGREDIENTS | SERVES 6

Tuna

1½ pounds fresh tuna steaks (cut into 4-ounce portions)

¼–½ teaspoon almond oil

Freshly ground black pepper, to taste

Salsa

1 teaspoon almond oil

3 fresh leeks (light green and white parts only), thinly sliced

1 tablespoon fresh lemon juice

1 tablespoon raw honey

Tuna Packs a Punch

Tuna is truly a nutrient-dense food. This omega-3 fatty acid–rich food has anti-inflammation properties with heaps of other valuable disease-fighting nutrients as well. Health authorities are urging consumers to eat fish two times per week to reap the significant health benefits.

1. Preheat grill to medium-high.

2. Brush each portion of the tuna with the oil and drain on a rack. Season the tuna with pepper, then place the tuna on the grill; cook for 3 minutes. Shift the tuna steaks on the grill to form an X grill pattern on the fish; cook 3 more minutes.

3. Turn the steaks over and grill 3 more minutes, then change position again to create an X grill pattern. Cook to desired doneness.

4. For the salsa: Heat the oil in a medium-size frying pan on medium heat, then add the leeks and sauté for about 3 minutes, just until leeks are wilted. Add the lemon juice and honey. Plate each tuna portion with a spoonful of salsa.

PER SERVING | Calories: 171 | Fat: 5.5 g | Protein: 21 g | Sodium: 43 mg | Fiber: 1 g | Carbohydrates: 9.5 g

Lime-Poached Flounder

Lime brings out the delicate flavor of the fish and complements the zip of the cilantro.

INGREDIENTS | SERVES 6

¾ cup sliced leeks

¼ cup cilantro leaves (reserve the stems)

1½ pounds flounder fillets

1¾ cups fish stock

2 tablespoons fresh lime juice

½ teaspoon fresh lime zest

¼ teaspoon ground black pepper

1 cup shredded yellow onion

⅔ cup shredded carrots

⅔ cup shredded celery

2 tablespoons extra-virgin olive oil

1. Place the leek slices and cilantro stems (reserve the leaves) in a large skillet over medium-high heat, then lay the flounder on top.

2. Add the stock, lime juice, lime zest, and pepper. Bring just to a boil, reduce heat, and cover. Simmer for 7–10 minutes, until the flounder is thoroughly cooked. Remove from heat. Discard the liquid.

3. To serve, lay the shredded onions, carrots, and celery in separate strips on serving plates. Top with flounder, drizzle with the olive oil, and sprinkle with the reserved cilantro leaves.

PER SERVING | Calories: 150 | Fat: 6 g | Protein: 18 g | Sodium: 218 mg | Fiber: 1 g | Carbohydrates: 3.5 g

Using Frozen Fish

Don't fret if you do not have fresh fish available in your area. Using a quality fish frozen at sea is perfectly fine. In fact, sometimes the frozen fish is fresher than the fresh!

Baked Coconut Shrimp

This sweet, crunchy dish is a tropical treat. The whole family will love coconut shrimp!

INGREDIENTS | SERVES 8

⅓ cup almond flour
½ teaspoon ground red pepper
1 teaspoon salt
Juice of ½ lime
2 tablespoons raw honey
⅓ cup egg whites
¾ cup unsweetened coconut flakes
1½ pounds extra-large shrimp, shelled and cleaned with tails remaining

1. Preheat oven to 425ºF and line a baking sheet with parchment paper.

2. In a small bowl, combine almond flour, pepper, and salt.

3. In a separate bowl, mix lime juice and honey and stir. Continuously stirring, add egg whites to lime-honey mixture.

4. Place coconut in a thin layer on a flat dish. Dip each shrimp first into the almond-flour mixture, then in the egg-white mixture, and then roll in coconut.

5. Place on baking sheet. Bake 10–15 minutes or until coconut appears lightly toasted.

PER SERVING | Calories: 157 | Fat: 6 g | Protein: 19 g | Sodium: 438 mg | Fiber: 1 g | Carbohydrates: 6 g

Pecan-Crusted Catfish

Catfish and tilapia rank among the most popular fish in the United States today. They are relatively inexpensive and have a nice flavor. You can use either fish in this recipe.

INGREDIENTS | SERVES 4

½ cup almond meal
½ cup finely chopped pecans
¼ teaspoon ground black pepper
1½ pounds catfish
2 tablespoons coconut oil

1. In a shallow dish, mix almond meal, pecans, and pepper.

2. Dredge the catfish in the pecan mixture; coating well.

3. Add coconut oil to medium-size frying pan over medium-high heat.

4. Place catfish in pan and fry 3–5 minutes on each side. Serve.

PER SERVING | Calories: 331 | Fat: 21 g | Protein: 23 g | Sodium: 60 mg | Fiber: 2.5 g | Carbohydrates: 14 g

Almond-Crusted Salmon

Sushi-grade salmon is very high quality and is safe to eat mostly raw. Obtain this quality fish from a fish company that specializes in high-end fish.

INGREDIENTS | SERVES 4

1 cup crushed almonds
4 (4-ounce) sushi-grade salmon fillets
2 tablespoons coconut oil

1. Spread crushed almonds on a flat plate.

2. Place salmon on almonds and coat all sides.

3. Preheat frying pan over high heat and add coconut oil to coat pan.

4. Cook salmon quickly, 2–3 minutes per side.

PER SERVING | Calories: 355 | Fat: 26 g | Protein: 27 g | Sodium: 50 mg | Fiber: 3 g | Carbohydrates: 5 g

Coconut Shrimp

This is an irresistibly sweet way to enjoy a commonly served first-course dish.

INGREDIENTS | SERVES 6

3½ cups chicken broth

1 cup water

1 teaspoon ground coriander

1 teaspoon cumin

Cayenne pepper, to taste

Zest of 1 lime

⅓ cup lime juice

7 cloves garlic, minced

1 tablespoon minced fresh ginger

1 large onion, chopped

1 red bell pepper, diced

1 large carrot, peeled and shredded

½ cup unsweetened coconut flakes

1½ pounds large or jumbo shrimp, peeled and thawed if frozen

Toasted coconut, for garnish

1. Mix the chicken broth, water, coriander, cumin, cayenne pepper, lime zest, lime juice, garlic, and ginger in a 4- or 6-quart slow cooker.

2. Stir in the onion, bell pepper, carrot, and coconut.

3. Cover and cook on low for 3 hours.

4. Stir in the shrimp. Cover and cook another 30 minutes.

5. Serve garnished with toasted coconut.

PER SERVING | Calories: 235 | Fat: 7 g | Protein: 27 g | Sodium: 794 mg | Fiber: 2 g | Carbohydrates: 17 g

Salmon with Leeks

Salmon and leeks complement each other well. This recipe is a nice combination of the two.

INGREDIENTS | SERVES 4

4 leeks
2 tablespoons coconut butter
1 tablespoon raw honey
3 carrots, cut into matchsticks
2 pounds salmon fillets
2 teaspoons avocado oil
1 teaspoon ground black pepper

Leeks Are a Healthy Choice

Not only are leeks high in fiber but they also contain folic acid, calcium, potassium, and vitamin C. Leeks have been found to have anti-arthritic properties.

1. Preheat oven to 425°F.

2. Trim leeks and discard root end and outer leaves. Cut lengthwise.

3. Melt coconut butter in a large frying pan over medium-high heat, add leeks, and cook until soft, about 5 minutes.

4. Drizzle the leeks with honey and cook until they turn brown, 15–20 minutes.

5. Stir in carrots and cook until tender, about 10 minutes.

6. Line a baking sheet with parchment paper. Place salmon on baking sheet. Brush salmon with oil and sprinkle with black pepper.

7. Roast the salmon in oven until flesh is pink and flaky, about 6–8 minutes. Serve salmon topped with leek-and-carrot mixture.

PER SERVING | Calories: 423 | Fat: 19 g | Protein: 37 g | Sodium: 160 mg | Fiber: 4.5 g | Carbohydrates: 27 g

Grilled Halibut Herb Salad

*If you don't care for oranges or don't have any fresh ones handy, use drained capers
to garnish this entrée salad instead.*

INGREDIENTS | SERVES 2

2 (6-ounce) halibut fillets

4 teaspoons orange juice

3 tablespoons avocado oil

¼ teaspoon lemon pepper

¼ teaspoon garlic powder

¼ teaspoon sweet paprika

2 cups torn romaine lettuce

¼ cup chopped flat-leaf parsley

1 tablespoon chopped fresh basil

1 tablespoon sliced fresh chives

2 orange slices

1. Place a large grill pan over medium-high heat. Sprinkle each fillet side with 1 teaspoon of orange juice and lightly rub it in. Brush both sides of each fillet with oil. Sprinkle each side with a little lemon pepper, garlic powder, and paprika.

2. Add fillets to hot grill pan and cook for 5 minutes on each side. Remove fillets from pan as soon as they are cooked and place on a plate. Let fillets rest for 3 minutes, then slice each one widthwise into 2" slices.

3. Combine romaine, parsley, basil, and chives in a large salad bowl. Toss to mix. Split salad between two plates. Top each salad with a sliced fillet. Squeeze an orange slice over each salad, garnish with slice, and serve.

PER SERVING | Calories: 317 | Fat: 23 g | Protein: 24 g | Sodium: 179 mg | Fiber: 2 g | Carbohydrates: 5 g

Shrimp Fra Diavolo

Serve this spicy sauce over hot "Paleo pasta," that is, spaghetti squash. Spaghetti squash is an excellent substitute for pasta. When cooked in the oven for 40–50 minutes, the squash becomes soft enough to lightly separate with a fork, forming an angel hair–like "pasta."

INGREDIENTS | SERVES 4

1 teaspoon avocado oil

1 medium onion, diced

3 cloves garlic, minced

1 teaspoon red pepper flakes

1 (15-ounce) can diced fire-roasted tomatoes

1 tablespoon minced Italian parsley

½ teaspoon freshly ground black pepper

¾ pound medium-size shrimp, shelled

1. Heat the oil in a nonstick frying pan over medium-high heat. Sauté the onion, garlic, and red pepper flakes for 8–10 minutes, until the onion is soft and translucent.

2. Add the onion mixture, tomatoes, parsley, and black pepper to a 4-quart slow cooker. Stir. Cook on low for 2–3 hours.

3. Add the shrimp. Stir, cover, and cook on high for 15 minutes or until the shrimp is fully cooked.

PER SERVING | Calories: 116 | Fat: 3 g | Protein: 18 g | Sodium: 127 mg | Fiber: 1 g | Carbohydrates: 5 g

Slow-Cooking with Shrimp

When slow-cooking with shrimp, resist the temptation to put the shrimp in at the beginning of the recipe. While it takes longer to overcook foods in the slow cooker, delicate shrimp can go from tender to rubbery very quickly. For most recipes, 20 minutes on high is sufficient cooking time for shrimp.

Ginger-Lime Salmon

The slow cooker does all the work in this recipe, creating a healthy yet impressive dish that requires virtually no hands-on time.

INGREDIENTS | SERVES 12

1 (3-pound) salmon fillet, bones removed
¼ cup minced fresh ginger
¼ cup lime juice
1 lime, thinly sliced
1 large onion, thinly sliced

Cracked!

Before each use, check your slow cooker for cracks. Even small cracks in the glaze can allow bacteria to grow in the ceramic insert. If there are cracks, replace the insert or the whole slow cooker.

1. Place the salmon skin-side down in an oval 6- or 7-quart slow cooker. Pour the ginger and lime juice over the fish. Arrange the lime slices and then the onion slices in single layers over the fish.

2. Cook on low for 3–4 hours or until the fish is fully cooked and flaky. Remove the skin before serving.

PER SERVING | Calories: 166 | Fat: 7 g | Protein: 22 g | Sodium: 50 mg | Fiber: 0 g | Carbohydrates: 2 g

Salmon with Lemon, Capers, and Rosemary

Salmon is amazingly moist and tender when cooked in the slow cooker.

INGREDIENTS | SERVES 2

8 ounces salmon
⅓ cup water
2 tablespoons lemon juice
3 thin slices fresh lemon
1 tablespoon nonpareil capers
½ teaspoon minced fresh rosemary

1. Place the salmon on the bottom of a 2-quart slow cooker. Pour the water and lemon juice over the fish.

2. Arrange the lemon slices in a single layer on top of the fish. Sprinkle with capers and rosemary.

3. Cook on low for 2 hours. Discard lemon slices prior to serving.

PER SERVING | Calories: 165 | Fat: 7 g | Protein: 22 g | Sodium: 54 mg | Fiber: 0 g | Carbohydrates: 2 g

Romaine-Wrapped Halibut Steaks

Enjoy this very healthy, lean seafood dish that is so tender it'll flake with just a light touch of a fork.

INGREDIENTS | SERVES 4

1 cup chicken broth
10–14 large romaine leaves
4 (4-ounce) halibut fillets
1 teaspoon bouquet garni or dried tarragon
Pepper, to taste
½ cup thinly sliced fresh spinach

Bouquet Garni

Bouquet garni is a classic herb mixture frequently used for flavoring in meat and vegetable dishes. The herbs are typically contained within a cheesecloth pouch, which is removed before the dish is served. The herbs traditionally used include: dried parsley, thyme, bay leaf, and sage.

1. Pour broth into a 4-quart slow cooker. Cover and cook on high for 20 minutes.

2. Immerse leaves of romaine (removing center stem) in boiling water for about 30 seconds, until wilted. Drain leaves.

3. Sprinkle halibut with herbs, pepper, and spinach. Wrap each fillet in 2–4 romaine leaves, placing lettuce seam-side down, and place in slow cooker.

4. Cover and cook on high for 1 hour or until the fish is tender and can be flaked with a fork.

PER SERVING | Calories: 132 | Fat: 3 g | Protein: 24 g | Sodium: 69 mg | Fiber: 0 g | Carbohydrates: 1 g

Foiled Fish Fillets

This recipe makes a simple, low-calorie, high-protein dish, that is ready in just 2 hours.

INGREDIENTS | SERVES 2

2 firm white fish fillets (e.g., tilapia)
1 small bulb fennel, thinly sliced
1 tomato, thinly sliced
1 red onion, sliced into rings
1 teaspoon dried dill
Juice of 1 lime
Pepper, to taste

1. Place fish fillets on aluminum foil and top with fennel, tomato, and onion.

2. Sprinkle on dill and lime juice. Fold the foil over and connect the edges, making a packet.

3. Place the packets in a 6-quart slow cooker. Cover and cook on high for 2 hours. Season to taste with pepper.

PER SERVING | Calories: 159 | Fat: 1 g | Protein: 26 g | Sodium: 83 mg | Fiber: 3 g | Carbohydrates: 11 g

Caveman's Catfish

First time trying catfish? This recipe is easily spruced up with any combination of flavorful veggies (i.e., tomatoes, onions, peppers, spinach, etc.).

INGREDIENTS | SERVES 4

4 catfish fillets
½ teaspoon dried dill
½ teaspoon dried basil
½ teaspoon dried thyme
2 lemons (1 juiced, 1 sliced into rings)

1. Place fish fillets on aluminum foil, sprinkle with spices, and squeeze the juice of 1 lemon over fish.

2. Place the lemon slices on the fish, and fold the foil over and connect the edges, making a packet.

3. Place the packets in a 6-quart slow cooker. Cover and cook on high for 2 hours.

PER SERVING | Calories: 160 | Fat: 5 g | Protein: 26 g | Sodium: 69 mg | Fiber: 1 g | Carbohydrates: 3 g

Orange Tilapia

This dish provides a sweet taste of the sea. Serve it with a medley of colorful summer vegetables.

INGREDIENTS | SERVES 4

4 tilapia fillets

2 tablespoons lime juice

1 tablespoon raw honey

1 (10-ounce) can mandarin oranges, drained

Pepper, to taste

1. Place fish fillets on aluminum foil, drizzle with lime juice and honey, and top with oranges.

2. Fold the foil over the fish and connect the edges, making a packet. Place the packets in a 6-quart slow cooker.

3. Cover and cook on high for 2 hours. Add pepper to taste.

PER SERVING | Calories: 194 | Fat: 5 g | Protein: 27 g | Sodium: 72 mg | Fiber: 1 g | Carbohydrates: 11 g

Mahi Mahi and Green Vegetable Medley

This is a super-healthy (and simply prepared) meal, packed with fiber, protein, iron, omega-3s, B-vitamins, and phytonutrients.

INGREDIENTS | SERVES 2

8 stalks asparagus

2 cups broccoli florets

2 cups fresh spinach

1 tablespoon walnut oil

¼ teaspoon black pepper

½ teaspoon red pepper flakes

¼ cup lemon juice, divided

1 pound mahi mahi

1. Place the vegetables in a 6-quart slow cooker.

2. In a separate bowl, combine the oil, pepper, red pepper flakes, and 1 tablespoon of lemon juice. Brush mixture on both sides of the mahi mahi, and place fish on top of vegetables in the slow cooker.

3. Add remaining lemon juice. Cover and cook on low for 2–3 hours. The fish should flake easily with a fork.

PER SERVING | Calories: 296 | Fat: 9 g | Protein: 45 g | Sodium: 258 mg | Fiber: 3 g | Carbohydrates: 10 g

Shrimp Creole

This Big Easy-inspired recipe may also be made by substituting meat or another seafood for the shrimp.

INGREDIENTS | SERVES 2

1 (8-ounce) can tomato sauce

1 (28-ounce) can whole tomatoes, broken up

1½ cups diced celery

1¼ cups chopped onion

1 cup chopped bell pepper

1 clove garlic, minced

¼ teaspoon pepper

6 drops hot sauce

1 pound medium-size shrimp, deveined and shelled

1. Combine all the ingredients in a 4-quart slow cooker, except shrimp. Cook on high for 3–4 hours or on low for 6–8 hours.

2. Add shrimp during last hour of cooking if cooking on low, or during final 20 minutes if cooking on high. Serve over hot veggies.

PER SERVING | Calories: 337 | Fat: 4 g | Protein: 49 g | Sodium: 998 mg | Fiber: 6 g | Carbohydrates: 24 g

Herbed Tilapia Stew

Any type of white fish fillets (such as haddock or cod) will also work in this recipe. Fish cooks very, very quickly even on the low setting in a slow cooker, so this is one recipe you will need to set a timer for.

INGREDIENTS | SERVES 6

2 pounds frozen boneless tilapia fillets

4 tablespoons organic butter or ghee, melted

1 (14.5-ounce) can diced tomatoes, undrained

4 cloves garlic, minced

½ cup sliced green onions

2 teaspoons Asian fish sauce

2 tablespoons chopped fresh thyme or 1 teaspoon dried

1. Place all the ingredients in a 4-quart slow cooker.

2. Cover and cook on high for 1½–2 hours or on low for 2½–3 hours. Watch the cooking time. If your fish fillets are very thin you may need to reduce the cooking time.

3. When fish is cooked through, fillets will easily separate and flake with a fork. Break up the fish in the tomatoes and cooking liquids.

PER SERVING | Calories: 87 | Fat: 9 g | Protein: 0 g | Sodium: 2 mg | Fiber: 0 g | Carbohydrates: 1 g

Scallop and Shrimp Jambalaya

This version of a "red" jambalaya originated in the French Quarter of New Orleans when saffron wasn't readily available. This Creole-type jambalaya contains tomatoes, whereas a rural Cajun jambalaya (also known as "brown jambalaya") does not.

INGREDIENTS | SERVES 8

2 tablespoons organic butter or ghee

1 large onion, chopped

2 medium celery stalks, chopped

1 medium green bell pepper, chopped

3 garlic cloves, minced

1 (28-ounce) can diced tomatoes, undrained

1 tablespoon dried parsley

½ teaspoon dried thyme

½ teaspoon salt

¼ teaspoon pepper

¼ teaspoon hot sauce

2 teaspoons Creole seasoning

¾ pound uncooked, frozen scallops, thawed

¾ pound uncooked, peeled, deveined medium shrimp, thawed if frozen

¼ cup fresh parsley, chopped

1. In a large frying pan, melt the butter over medium heat. Sauté the onions, celery, and bell pepper until softened, about 3–5 minutes. Add garlic and cook for 1 minute more.

2. Grease a 4-quart slow cooker and add sautéed vegetables and all the remaining ingredients, except the shrimp and fresh parsley.

3. Cover and cook on low for 6 hours or on high for 3 hours.

4. Add shrimp and continue to cook on low for 45 minutes to 1 hour, or until shrimp is bright pink. Serve jambalaya over a root-vegetable medley and garnish with fresh parsley.

PER SERVING | Calories: 103 | Fat: 4 g | Protein: 10 g | Sodium: 204 mg | Fiber: 2 g | Carbohydrates: 7 g

Mix It Up

Use your favorite type of seafood instead of shrimp or scallops. Try a combination of scallops, cod, or diced tilapia, halibut, mahi mahi, etc.

Fish "Bake"

The stewed tomatoes help prevent the fish from overcooking and make the perfect sauce for serving the fish over steamed cabbage or alongside a vegetable dish of your choice.

INGREDIENTS | SERVES 4

2 tablespoons organic butter or ghee
4 flounder or cod fillets
1 clove garlic, minced
1 small onion, thinly sliced
1 green bell pepper, seeded and diced
1 (14.5-ounce) can stewed tomatoes
½ teaspoon dried basil
½ teaspoon dried oregano
1 teaspoon dried parsley
Freshly ground black pepper, to taste

1. Add the butter to a preheated 2- or 4-quart slow cooker. Use the melted butter to coat the bottom and the sides of the insert.

2. Rinse the fish fillets and pat dry with paper towels. Add to the slow cooker in a single layer over the butter.

3. Evenly distribute the garlic, onion, and green bell pepper over the fish. Pour the stewed tomatoes over the fish. Evenly sprinkle the basil, oregano, parsley, and pepper over the tomatoes.

4. Cover and cook on low for 6 hours or until the fish is opaque and flakes apart.

PER SERVING | Calories: 223 | Fat: 8 g | Protein: 31 g | Sodium: 134 mg | Fiber: 1 g | Carbohydrates: 3 g

Cioppino

Cioppino is a versatile summer dish. You can replace the cod with haddock and add lobster, crab, crayfish, and clams. Enjoy this beautiful and healthy bounty from the sea!

INGREDIENTS | SERVES 6

2 tablespoons organic butter or ghee

1 large sweet onion, diced

2 stalks celery, finely diced

2 cloves garlic, minced

3 cups bottled clam juice or fish stock

2 cups water

1 (28-ounce) can diced or whole peeled tomatoes

1 cup dry red wine or chicken broth

2 teaspoons dried parsley

1 teaspoon dried basil

1 teaspoon dried thyme

Red pepper flakes, to taste

1 teaspoon raw honey

1 bay leaf

1 pound cod, cut into 1" pieces

½ pound medium or large raw shrimp, peeled and deveined

½ pound scallops

1. Add the butter, onion, celery, and garlic to a 4-quart slow cooker. Stir to mix the vegetables together with the butter. Cover and cook on high for 30 minutes or until the onions are transparent.

2. Add the clam juice or fish stock, water, tomatoes, wine or broth, parsley, basil, thyme, red pepper flakes, honey, and bay leaf. Stir to combine. Cover, reduce the slow cooker setting to low, and cook for 5 hours.

3. If you used whole peeled tomatoes, use a spoon to break them apart. Gently stir in the cod, shrimp, and scallops. Increase the slow cooker setting to high. Cover and cook for 30 minutes or until the seafood is cooked through. Ladle into soup bowls and serve immediately.

PER SERVING | Calories: 232 | Fat: 6 g | Protein: 29 g | Sodium: 168 mg | Fiber: 1 g | Carbohydrates: 6 g

Almond-Stuffed Flounder

Making this dish in the slow cooker lets you layer the fish and stuffing rather than stuffing and rolling the fillets. You can substitute sole for the flounder. Serve with a tossed salad and a seasoned vegetable medley of choice.

INGREDIENTS | SERVES 4

2 teaspoons coconut oil

4 (4-ounce) fresh or frozen flounder fillets

½ cup slivered almonds

1 tablespoon freeze-dried chives (optional)

Sweet paprika, to taste

¼ cup dry white wine or chicken broth (optional)

1 tablespoon coconut oil

½ cup grated carrot

1 tablespoon almond flour

¼ teaspoon dried tarragon

White pepper, to taste

1 cup (full-fat) coconut milk

1. Lightly grease the insert of a 2- or 4-quart slow cooker with coconut oil.

2. Rinse the fish and pat dry with paper towels. Lay 2 fillets flat in the slow cooker. Sprinkle the almonds and chives (if using) over the fillets. Place the remaining fillets on top. Sprinkle paprika over the top fillets. Pour the wine or broth around the fish.

3. Add the oil and carrots to a microwave-safe bowl. Cover and microwave on high for 1 minute; stir and microwave on high for 1 more minute. Stir in the flour, tarragon, and pepper. Whisk in half the coconut milk. Cover and microwave on high for 1 minute. Stir in the remaining coconut milk. Pour the sauce over the fish.

4. Cover and cook on low for 2 hours or until the fish is cooked through and the sauce is thickened.

5. Turn off the slow cooker and let rest for 15 minutes. To serve, use a knife to cut into four wedges. Spoon each wedge onto a plate (so that there is fish and filling in each serving). Sprinkle with additional paprika before serving if desired.

PER SERVING | Calories: 309 | Fat: 20 g | Protein: 25 g | Sodium: 108 mg | Fiber: 2 g | Carbohydrates: 6 g

Poached Swordfish with Lemon-Parsley Sauce

Swordfish steaks are usually cut thicker than most fish fillets, plus it's a firmer fish so it takes longer to poach. You can speed up the poaching process a little if you remove the steaks from the refrigerator and put them in room-temperature water during the 30 minutes that the onions and water are cooking.

INGREDIENTS | SERVES 4

1 tablespoon coconut butter

4 thin slices sweet onion

2 cups water

4 (6-ounce) swordfish steaks

1 lemon

2 tablespoons extra-virgin olive oil

2 teaspoons fresh lemon juice

¼ teaspoon Dijon mustard

Freshly ground white or black pepper, to taste (optional)

1 tablespoon fresh flat-leaf parsley, minced

Swordfish Salad

Triple the amount of lemon-parsley sauce and toss two-thirds of it together with 8 cups of salad greens. Arrange 2 cups of greens on each serving plate. Place a hot or chilled swordfish steak over each plate of the dressed greens. Spoon the additional sauce over the fish.

1. Use the coconut butter to grease the bottom and halfway up the sides of a 4-quart slow cooker.

2. Arrange the onion slices in the bottom of the slow cooker, pressing them into the butter so that they stay in place. Pour in the water. Cover and cook on high for 30 minutes.

3. Place a swordfish steak over each onion slice.

4. Thinly slice the lemon; discard the seeds, and place the slices over the fish. Cover and cook on high for 45 minutes or until the fish is opaque. Transfer the (well-drained) fish to individual serving plates or to a serving platter.

5. In a small bowl add the oil, lemon juice, mustard, and white or black pepper, if using, and whisk to combine.

6. Immediately before serving the swordfish, fold the parsley into the sauce. Evenly divide the sauce between the swordfish steaks.

PER SERVING | Calories: 274 | Fat: 14 g | Protein: 34 g | Sodium: 160 mg | Fiber: 1 g | Carbohydrates: 3 g

Manhattan Scallop Chowder

Serve this chowder with a tossed salad. Unlike the popular New England version, this clam chowder is red!

INGREDIENTS | SERVES 6

2 tablespoons coconut butter, melted

2 stalks celery, finely diced

1 medium green bell pepper, seeded and diced

1 large carrot, peeled and finely diced

1 medium onion, diced

2 medium butternut squash or turnips, scrubbed, peeled, and diced

1 (15-ounce) can diced tomatoes

1 (15-ounce) can tomato purée

2 cups bottled clam juice

1 cup dry white wine or chicken broth

¾ cup water

1 teaspoon dried thyme

1 teaspoon dried parsley

1 bay leaf

¼ teaspoon freshly ground black pepper

1½ pounds bay scallops

Fresh parsley, minced (optional)

Fresh basil (optional)

1. Add the butter, celery, bell pepper, and carrot to a 4- or 6-quart slow cooker; stir to coat the vegetables in the butter. Cover and cook on high for 15 minutes. Stir in the onion. Cover and cook on high for 30 minutes or until the vegetables are soft.

2. Stir in the squash or turnips, tomatoes, tomato purée, clam juice, wine or broth, water, thyme, parsley, bay leaf, and pepper. Cover, reduce the temperature to low, and cook for 7 hours or until the squash is cooked through.

3. Cut the scallops into 1" pieces. Add to the slow cooker.

4. Increase the temperature to high, cover, and cook for 15 minutes or until the scallops are firm.

5. Remove and discard the bay leaf. Taste and adjust seasonings if necessary. Ladle into soup bowls. If desired, sprinkle minced fresh parsley over each serving and garnish with fresh basil.

PER SERVING | Calories: 188 | Fat: 1 g | Protein: 21 g | Sodium: 583 mg | Fiber: 3 g | Carbohydrates: 17 g

Hatteras Clam Chowder

This cozy, Paleo-creamy chowder is thickened by turnip in place of potatoes.
Serve it with a fresh green salad or hearty main dish of your choice.

INGREDIENTS | SERVES 4

1 small onion, diced and sautéed in 1 tablespoon olive oil

2 medium turnips, peeled and diced

1 (8-ounce) bottle clam juice

2–3 cups water

½ teaspoon freshly ground black pepper

2 (6.5-ounce) cans minced clams, undrained

1. Add cooked onions to a greased 2½-quart slow cooker.

2. Add turnips, clam juice, and enough water to cover. Add pepper.

3. Cover and cook on high for 3 hours until turnips are very tender.

4. One hour prior to serving, add in the clams along with broth from the cans and cook until heated through.

PER SERVING | Calories: 159 | Fat: 2 g | Protein: 24 g | Sodium: 149 mg | Fiber: 1 g | Carbohydrates: 10 g

Mahi Mahi Wraps with Avocado and Fresh Cabbage

These California-style "tacos" can be prepared with any meaty, mild fish or shrimp.

INGREDIENTS | SERVES 4

1 pound mahi mahi

1 teaspoon salt

½ teaspoon freshly ground black pepper

1 teaspoon avocado oil

1 avocado

4–6 Bibb lettuce cups

2 cups shredded cabbage

2 limes, quartered

Salsa Verde

Fish tacos taste great with a citrusy salsa to brighten them up. Try these fish "tacos" accompanied by Salsa Verde (see Chapter 3). You'll love this combination!

1. Season fish with salt and pepper. Heat oil in a large pan over medium heat. Once the oil is hot, sauté fish for about 3–4 minutes on each side. Slice or flake fish into 1-ounce pieces.

2. Slice avocado in half. Remove seed and, using a spoon, remove the flesh from the skin. Slice the avocado halves into ½"-thick slices.

3. Place one-fourth of the mahi mahi on each lettuce leaf; top with avocado and cabbage. Serve with lime wedges.

PER SERVING | Calories: 209 | Fat: 9 g | Protein: 23 g | Sodium: 707 mg | Fiber: 6 g | Carbohydrates: 11 g

CHAPTER 9

Sides

Sautéed Asparagus
222

Roasted Asparagus
222

Citrus-Steamed
Carrots
223

Sautéed Brussels
Sprouts
223

Baked Sweet Potato
Sticks
224

Celeriac Slaw
224

Napa Cabbage with
Asian Sauce
225

Chipotle-Lime Mashed
Sweet Potatoes
225

Okra Stuffed with
Green Peppercorns
226

Eggplant Soufflé
227

Brussels Sprouts Hash
with Caramelized
Shallots
228

Mashed Cauliflower
229

Marinated Baby
Artichoke Hearts
229

Baked Stuffed
Artichokes
230

Pineapple Onion Salad
231

Roasted Peppers
231

Paleo Stuffed Peppers
232

Candied Butternut
Squash
233

Bison-Stuffed Zucchini
234

Stuffed Tomatoes
235

Vegetable Kebabs on
Rosemary Skewers
236

Spiced "Baked"
Eggplant
237

Slow-Cooked Broccoli
237

"Roasted" Roots
238

Zucchini Casserole
238

Sautéed Fennel with
Orange
239

Slow-Cooked Sweet
Potatoes
239

Dill Carrots
240

Stewed Tomatoes
240

Caramelized Onions
241

Sautéed Asparagus

*Asparagus makes a healthy and filling side complement to any main course.
Try this dish with any meat, poultry, or fish recipe.*

INGREDIENTS | SERVES 4

1 bunch asparagus
2 tablespoons walnut oil
2 cloves garlic, chopped

1. Cut bottoms off asparagus, then cut remainder of stalks into 2" pieces.

2. Add walnut oil to a frying pan set on medium heat.

3. Add garlic and cook for about 30 seconds, then add asparagus.

4. Stir-fry until asparagus is tender when pierced with fork, approximately 5–8 minutes.

PER SERVING | Calories: 86 | Fat: 7 g | Protein: 4 g | Sodium: 4 mg | Fiber: 4 g | Carbohydrates: 4 g

Roasted Asparagus

*Use thicker asparagus to withstand the heat of the grill. Be sure to
remove the woody ends of the stalks first.*

INGREDIENTS | SERVES 6

2 bunches asparagus
1 tablespoon walnut oil
1 tablespoon lemon juice
Freshly ground black pepper, to taste

Preheat grill to medium. Toss the asparagus in the oil, then drain on a rack and season with lemon juice and pepper. Grill the asparagus for 1–2 minutes on each side (cook to desired doneness). Serve immediately.

PER SERVING | Calories: 30 | Fat: 2 g | Protein: 1 g | Sodium: 1 mg | Fiber: 1 g | Carbohydrates: 2 g

Asparagus

Asparagus is low in calories and sodium and offers numerous vitamins and minerals, most notably folate and potassium. The tender stalks also offer a blast of inflammation-fighting antioxidants.

Citrus-Steamed Carrots

*This recipe includes figs, which are said to be the fruit of gods and goddesses.
Enjoy the pleasure yourself!*

INGREDIENTS | SERVES 6

1 pound carrots
1 cup orange juice
2 tablespoons lemon juice
2 tablespoons lime juice
3 fresh figs
1 tablespoon extra-virgin olive oil
1 tablespoon capers

1. Peel and julienne the carrots. In a pot, combine the citrus juices and heat over medium-high heat. Add the carrots, cover, and cook until al dente, about 5 minutes. Remove from heat, strain, and let cool.

2. Cut the figs into wedges. Mound the carrots on a serving plate and arrange the figs around the carrots. Sprinkle the olive oil and capers on top and serve.

PER SERVING | Calories: 93 | Fat: 2.5 g | Protein: 1.5 g | Sodium: 94 mg | Fiber: 3 g | Carbohydrates: 18 g

Sautéed Brussels Sprouts

*Brussels sprouts will no longer be boring when they are spiced up with bacon and garlic.
These are a great appetizer or side dish for any main meal.*

INGREDIENTS | SERVES 4

4 cups fresh Brussels sprouts
3 ounces uncured, nitrate-free bacon, diced
½ cup minced shallots
½ cup sliced mushrooms
4 cloves garlic, minced

1. Steam Brussels sprouts until tender, about 10 minutes.

2. Cook bacon in a medium-size frying pan over medium heat. Remove bacon from pan and set aside.

3. In the same pan, sauté shallots, mushrooms, and garlic until caramelized, approximately 5 minutes.

4. Add Brussels sprouts and bacon to the shallot mixture and cook over medium heat for 5 minutes. Remove from heat and serve.

PER SERVING | Calories: 155 | Fat: 10 g | Protein: 6 g | Sodium: 200 mg | Fiber: 3 g | Carbohydrates: 13 g

Baked Sweet Potato Sticks

These fries are good for you and make a delicious and energizing side dish that substitutes for traditional French fries. Great for kids!

INGREDIENTS | SERVES 2

1 large sweet potato, peeled and cut like French fries
1 tablespoon almond oil
1 teaspoon salt
½ teaspoon freshly ground black pepper
1 teaspoon dried thyme
1 teaspoon dried sage

1. Cook the potato slices in boiling water for 4–5 minutes. Drain potatoes and dry on paper towels.

2. Sprinkle with oil, salt, pepper, and herbs. Bake on an aluminum pan at 350°F until crisp, about 10 minutes.

PER SERVING | Calories: 104 | Fat: 2 g | Protein: 2 g | Sodium: 1,215 mg | Fiber: 2 g | Carbohydrates: 21 g

Sweet Potato Benefits

Full of fiber, potassium, and beta carotene, sweet potatoes are an often-neglected healthy and delicious vegetable—most people forget about them until Thanksgiving! Their bright orange flesh adds color to any meal, they can be cooked like regular potatoes, and they taste best when baked.

Celeriac Slaw

Celeriac is a vegetable in the celery family. You can put this slaw next to most meat, fish, or poultry for a tasty counterpoint.

INGREDIENTS | SERVES 6

1 bulb celeriac, peeled and coarsely grated
1 tablespoon Homemade Mayonnaise (see Chapter 3)
1 tablespoon white wine vinegar
Pinch dried thyme
½ teaspoon salt
½ teaspoon freshly ground black pepper
1 teaspoon ground mustard

Place the celeriac in a bowl. In a separate bowl, mix Homemade Mayonnaise, vinegar, thyme, salt, pepper, and mustard. Pour over the celeriac and serve as a garnish or as part of an appetizer tray.

PER SERVING | Calories: 30 | Fat: 2 g | Protein: 0 g | Sodium: 236 mg | Fiber: 1 g | Carbohydrates: 2 g

Napa Cabbage with Asian Sauce

You can use napa cabbage (cooked or raw) instead of pasta as a bed for sauces and meats or as a salad green. Try it steamed with various sauces. It's an easy way to add fiber and antioxidants to your meals. This sauce can be adapted to your taste, from fruity to hot.

INGREDIENTS | SERVES 2

4 tablespoons sesame oil

6 scallions, sliced

1 (1") piece fresh ginger, peeled and minced

1 clove garlic, minced

½ cup coconut aminos

½ head napa cabbage, cut crosswise in thin slices and separated into ribbons

Heat the oil in a medium skillet over medium-high heat. Sauté the scallions, fresh ginger, and garlic. Add the coconut aminos. Rinse the cabbage and drain on paper towels; toss with sauce.

PER SERVING | Calories: 341 | Fat: 27 g | Protein: 7 g | Sodium: 3,640 mg | Fiber: 7 g | Carbohydrates: 21 g

Asian-Style Garnishes

To add flair to the presentation of this dish, try topping it with 1 tablespoon toasted sesame seeds and the juice of half a lime. Serve with lime wedges and chopsticks.

Chipotle-Lime Mashed Sweet Potatoes

Sweet potatoes are a great post-workout food. These chipotle-lime mashed potatoes will be a favorite at any family table.

INGREDIENTS | SERVES 10

3 pounds sweet potatoes

1½ tablespoons coconut oil

1¼ teaspoons chipotle powder

Juice from ½ large lime

1. Peel the sweet potatoes and cut into cubes.

2. Steam the cubes until soft, approximately 5–8 minutes. Transfer to a large bowl.

3. In a small saucepan, heat coconut oil and whisk in the chipotle powder and lime juice.

4. Pour the mixture into the bowl with the sweet potato cubes and mash with fork or potato masher.

PER SERVING | Calories: 135 | Fat: 2 g | Protein: 2.5 g | Sodium: 75 mg | Fiber: 4 g | Carbohydrates: 27 g

Alternatives to Sweet Potatoes

If you don't like sweet potatoes, you can easily substitute rutabagas, turnips, or beets. Additionally, cauliflower makes a great "mashed potato" substitute.

Okra Stuffed with Green Peppercorns

This is a delightful Indian dish. You can make it in advance and warm it up before serving. It's a great side dish for curry, and okra is a nice vegetable alternative if you get sick of the usual broccoli, asparagus, and zucchini.

INGREDIENTS | SERVES 2

6 okra, stemmed

½ cup vegetable broth

3 teaspoons green peppercorns, packed in brine and drained

1 teaspoon organic butter or ghee

1 teaspoon cumin

½ teaspoon salt

½ teaspoon freshly ground black pepper

1. In a large saucepan, poach the okra in the vegetable broth until slightly softened, about 4 minutes. Remove from the broth and place on a work surface, reserving broth in the saucepan.

2. Rinse peppercorns and poke them down into the center of the okra. Return to broth; add butter, cumin, salt, and pepper.

PER SERVING | Calories: 30 | Fat: 2 g | Protein: 1 g | Sodium: 680 mg | Fiber: 1 g | Carbohydrates: 4 g

Eggplant Soufflé

Smooth and creamy in texture, this is an Indian favorite. Often the eggplant is simply puréed and spiced—this is more of a fusion dish.

INGREDIENTS | SERVES 4

2 medium eggplants

1 teaspoon water

1 tablespoon avocado oil

2 cloves garlic, minced

1 small white onion, minced

4 eggs, separated

1 teaspoon salt

½ teaspoon freshly ground black pepper

1 teaspoon curry powder, or to taste

1. Wrap the eggplant in aluminum foil with water. Roast the eggplant at 400°F in a roasting pan for 1 hour, or until very soft when pricked with a fork. Cool, cut in half, scoop out flesh, and discard skin. Keep oven on.

2. In a medium-size frying pan, heat oil and sauté garlic and onion over medium heat until softened, about 8–10 minutes. Mix with eggplant and purée in a food processor or blender until very smooth. Mix in egg yolks and pulse, adding salt, pepper, and curry powder. Place in a greased 1-quart soufflé dish.

3. Beat the egg whites until stiff. Fold into the eggplant mixture. Bake until puffed and golden, about 45 minutes.

PER SERVING | Calories: 126 | Fat: 9 g | Protein: 9 g | Sodium: 665 mg | Fiber: 8 g | Carbohydrates: 13 g

Brussels Sprouts Hash with Caramelized Shallots

Even people who say they dislike Brussels sprouts will love this dish.

INGREDIENTS | SERVES 6

1 pound Brussels sprouts
2 shallots, thinly sliced
¼ cup avocado oil
1 teaspoon salt
½ teaspoon freshly ground black pepper
3 tablespoons balsamic vinegar

1. Preheat oven to 400°F.

2. Trim stems off Brussels sprouts and slice in half lengthwise. Place Brussels sprouts and shallots in a shallow baking dish. Coat Brussels sprouts with oil; season with salt and pepper.

3. Bake for 20 minutes. Remove dish from the oven, and drizzle vinegar evenly over Brussels sprouts. Return dish to the oven and bake for 3–4 more minutes.

PER SERVING | Calories: 121 | Fat: 9 g | Protein: 3 g | Sodium: 414 mg | Fiber: 3 g | Carbohydrates: 9 g

Mashed Cauliflower

A healthier alternative to mashed potatoes, mashed cauliflower is lower in calories, fat, and carbohydrates.

INGREDIENTS | SERVES 6

1 head cauliflower, chopped
2 tablespoons organic butter or ghee
1 tablespoon chopped fresh chives
1 teaspoon salt
½ teaspoon freshly ground black pepper

1. Place cauliflower in a large pot of boiling water, and cook for 10 minutes. Drain well, reserving ¼ cup cooking liquid.

2. Place cauliflower in blender or food processor with butter and ¼ cup cooking liquid and purée until smooth. Pour puréed cauliflower into a serving dish and stir in chives, salt, and pepper.

PER SERVING | Calories: 95 | Fat: 7 g | Protein: 3 g | Sodium: 422 mg | Fiber: 2 g | Carbohydrates: 7 g

Marinated Baby Artichoke Hearts

Here's where frozen artichoke hearts work perfectly! They save you the time and energy of cutting out the choke and removing the leaves of fresh artichokes, and they taste delicious when marinated.

INGREDIENTS | SERVES 4

2 (10-ounce) boxes frozen artichoke hearts
½ cup white wine vinegar
¼ cup olive oil
1 teaspoon Dijon mustard
½ teaspoon ground coriander
Salt and freshly ground black pepper

1. Thaw and cook the artichokes according to package directions. Drain and set aside.

2. Whisk the rest of the ingredients together in a bowl large enough to hold the artichokes. Add the warm artichokes and cover with dressing. Cover and marinate for 2–4 hours. Serve as antipasto.

PER SERVING | Calories: 142 | Fat: 15 g | Protein: 1 g | Sodium: 18 mg | Fiber: 0 g | Carbohydrates: 4 g

Baked Stuffed Artichokes

These are worth a bit of effort. You can make them in advance, then finish cooking just before serving.

INGREDIENTS | SERVES 4

2 large artichokes

2 tablespoons avocado oil

2 cloves garlic, chopped

½ sweet onion, chopped

1 cup almond meal

1 tablespoon minced lemon peel

8 medium shrimp, peeled and deveined

4 tablespoons fresh parsley

½ teaspoon freshly ground black pepper

4 quarts plus ½ cup water

Juice and rind of ½ lemon

½ teaspoon ground coriander

1. Remove any tough or brown outside leaves from the artichokes. Using a sharp knife, cut off artichoke tops, about ½" down. Slam the artichokes against a countertop to loosen leaves. Cut in half, from top to stem, and set aside.

2. Heat the oil in a large frying pan over medium heat. Add the garlic and onion and sauté for 5 minutes, stirring. Add the almond meal, lemon peel, shrimp, parsley, and pepper. Cook until shrimp turns pink. Pulse in the food processor or blender.

3. Boil the artichokes in 4 quarts water with lemon juice, lemon rind, and coriander for 18 minutes. Remove the artichokes but reserve the cooking water. Place the artichokes in a baking dish with ½ cup water on the bottom. Pile with shrimp filling. Drizzle with a bit of the cooking water and bake for 25 minutes. Serve.

PER SERVING | Calories: 403 | Fat: 16 g | Protein: 15 g | Sodium: 127 mg | Fiber: 8 g | Carbohydrates: 54 g

Pineapple Onion Salad

This sweet and tangy recipe does not keep well, so make sure to throw it together right before eating. If you prefer a little more zing, add another tablespoon of lime juice and a sprinkle of cayenne pepper.

INGREDIENTS | SERVES 4

1 cup cubed fresh pineapple
½ cup chopped red onion
3 cups mixed baby greens
1 tablespoon lime juice

1. Place pineapple cubes in a large salad bowl. Mix onion and baby greens into the pineapple.

2. Sprinkle lightly with lime juice. Toss to coat and serve immediately.

PER SERVING | Calories: 28 | Fat: 0 g | Protein: 0 g | Sodium: 1 mg | Fiber: 1 g | Carbohydrates: 5.5 g

Roasted Peppers

Many people don't know that peppers become very sweet when roasted.

INGREDIENTS | SERVES 6

2 tablespoons avocado oil
2 green peppers
2 yellow peppers
2 red peppers
6 cloves garlic, minced
Freshly ground black pepper, to taste

1. Pour the oil in a stainless-steel bowl. Dip the peppers in the oil, then roast or grill them over an open flame (reserve the bowl with the oil in it). Shock the peppers in ice water and remove the skins.

2. Julienne the peppers and add them to the bowl with the oil, along with the garlic and black pepper.

3. Let sit at room temperature in serving bowl until ready to serve.

PER SERVING | Calories: 76 | Fat: 4.5 g | Protein: 1.5 g | Sodium: 1 mg | Fiber: 2.5 g | Carbohydrates: 9 g

Paleo Stuffed Peppers

Peppers are chock-full of great vitamins and minerals that everyone needs. These peppers are so fun to eat, you won't even guess how healthy they are.

INGREDIENTS | SERVES 4

4 red bell peppers
2 tablespoons avocado oil
3 cloves garlic, chopped
1 large onion, chopped
1 pound ground chicken
2 green bell peppers, chopped
1 cup diced celery
1 cup sliced mushrooms
2 tablespoons chili powder
1 tablespoon cumin
1 (28-ounce) can organic, no-salt-added diced tomatoes
1 (6-ounce) can organic, no-salt-added tomato paste

1. Cut off the tops of red peppers and remove seeds and ribs. Set aside.

2. Heat the oil in a large frying pan over medium-high heat and sauté garlic and onion for 2 minutes.

3. Add ground chicken and cook until browned, about 5 minutes.

4. Add green peppers, celery, mushrooms, chili powder, and cumin and continue cooking for 5 minutes.

5. Stuff mixture into red peppers and place in a 4-quart slow cooker.

6. Stir in diced tomatoes and tomato paste and cook on high for 5 hours.

PER SERVING | Calories: 385 | Fat: 25 g | Protein: 23 g | Sodium: 159 mg | Fiber: 6 g | Carbohydrates: 17 g

Candied Butternut Squash

Butternut squash has a delicious natural sweetness and is an excellent replacement for sweet potatoes. Also, you can now buy cut-and-peeled butternut squash in many grocery stores (in the produce section), making this recipe incredibly easy to assemble.

INGREDIENTS | SERVES 4

4–5 cups peeled, seeded, and cubed butternut squash

⅓ cup raw honey

1 tablespoon orange zest

½ teaspoon cinnamon

½ teaspoon ground cloves

Add all the ingredients to a greased 4-quart slow cooker. Cook on high for 3–4 hours or on low for 6–8 hours, until squash is fork-tender.

PER SERVING | Calories: 168 | Fat: 0 g | Protein: 2 g | Sodium: 9 mg | Fiber: 4 g | Carbohydrates: 44 g

Butternut Squash versus Sweet Potatoes

Wondering which might be better for you? Actually both are extremely healthy choices. Per serving, sweet potatoes have more fiber than the squash, but one cup of butternut squash contains fewer calories and fewer total carbohydrates. Both are high in vitamins A and C. In many recipes, they can be used interchangeably.

Bison-Stuffed Zucchini

Bison meat is both low in fat and high in protein. It has a great taste that resembles beef but with a little more flavor. This is sure to be a big hit at any party or holiday gathering.

INGREDIENTS | SERVES 6

3 large zucchini, halved

2 tablespoons coconut oil

1 cup diced onion

1 cup chopped cauliflower

1½ pounds bison meat, cubed

¼ teaspoon cayenne pepper

1 teaspoon oregano

1 (14.5-ounce) can no-salt-added diced tomatoes

1 (6-ounce) can, no-salt-added tomato paste

1 large egg

Bison: A Great Protein Choice

Bison meat is quite popular amongst Paleolithic-diet enthusiasts. It is especially great for women because of its high iron content. Bison has more nutrients, pound for pound, than chicken, pork, or beef. It contains high levels of vitamins E, B_6, B_{12}, and such minerals as zinc, potassium, selenium, and copper.

1. Preheat oven to 400°F.

2. Scrape out seeds of zucchini and save in a mixing bowl.

3. Heat coconut oil in a large frying pan over medium-high heat and sauté onion, cauliflower, and zucchini seeds until caramelized, about 12 minutes.

4. Add bison, cayenne pepper, and oregano to frying pan and brown meat, approximately 8–10 minutes. Drain.

5. Add tomatoes and tomato paste and stir to combine.

6. Add egg, mix, and stuff each zucchini half, forming a large mound on top.

7. Place in large baking dish with a little water on the bottom and bake 40 minutes.

PER SERVING | Calories: 214 | Fat: 7 g | Protein: 30 g | Sodium: 249 mg | Fiber: 3.5 g | Carbohydrates: 15 g

Stuffed Tomatoes

This is a great side dish or light vegetarian lunch that is packed with flavor.

INGREDIENTS | SERVES 3

3 large beefsteak tomatoes
6 small white mushrooms, sliced
4 cloves garlic, minced
6 sun-dried tomatoes, chopped
1 teaspoon ground black pepper
½ teaspoon paprika
1 teaspoon thyme
8 leaves fresh basil, torn

1. Preheat oven to 350°F.

2. Cut tomatoes in half and hollow them out, reserving tomato pulp. Place tomatoes in a small baking dish.

3. Mix tomato pulp with mushrooms, garlic, sun-dried tomatoes, pepper, paprika, thyme, and basil.

4. Fill tomatoes with tomato pulp mixture and bake for 25 minutes.

PER SERVING | Calories: 116 | Fat: 2.5 | Protein: 7.5 g |
Sodium: 162 mg | Fiber: 5.5 g | Carbohydrates: 23 g

Vegetable Kebabs on Rosemary Skewers

Serve these kebabs as an appetizer at parties so your guests can easily handle the food without using cutlery. Using rosemary for the skewers adds an extra dimension of flavor to the grilled vegetables.

12 large rosemary sprigs with strong woody stems

1 large red bell pepper

1 large yellow bell pepper

1 large green bell pepper

1 medium red onion, peeled and cut into wedges

1 medium zucchini, sliced into 1" rounds

1 tablespoon avocado oil

Freshly ground black pepper, to taste

An Alternative to Rosemary Skewers

If you can't find sturdy rosemary sprigs, you can use wooden skewers. Make sure you soak them in water for an hour before spearing the vegetables. Soaking the skewers prevents them from burning on the grill.

1. Strip the leaves from the bottom two-thirds of the rosemary sprigs (reserve the leaves for another use).

2. Trim and seed the bell peppers and cut them into 2" squares.

3. Thread the bell peppers, onions, and zucchini onto the rosemary sprigs and brush all sides of the vegetables with oil. Season with black pepper.

4. Place the skewers on the grill or under the broiler, paying close attention as they cook, as they can easily burn. Cook for 8–10 minutes, turning occasionally, until the vegetables are fork-tender.

PER SERVING | Calories: 38 | Fat: 2.5 g | Protein: 1 g | Sodium: 3.5 mg | Fiber: 2 g | Carbohydrates: 4 g

Spiced "Baked" Eggplant

Serve this as a main dish over a garden salad, or as a side dish.

INGREDIENTS | SERVES 4

1 pound cubed eggplant
⅓ cup sliced onion
½ teaspoon red pepper flakes
½ teaspoon crushed rosemary
¼ cup lemon juice

Place all the ingredients in a 2-quart slow cooker. Cook on low for 3 hours or until the eggplant is tender.

PER SERVING | Calories: 37 | Fat: 0 g | Protein: 1 g | Sodium: 6 mg | Fiber: 4 g | Carbohydrates: 9 g

Cold Snap

Take care not to put a cold ceramic slow-cooker insert directly into the slow cooker. The sudden shift in temperature can cause it to crack. If you want to prepare your ingredients the night before use, refrigerate them in reusable containers, not in the insert.

Slow-Cooked Broccoli

This is a great way to cook a large amount of broccoli while preserving all its nutrients.

INGREDIENTS | SERVES 5

1 pound broccoli
½ cup water or chicken broth
2 tablespoons organic butter or ghee
½ teaspoon lemon juice
¼ teaspoon black pepper

1. Cut the main stalk off of broccoli with a sharp kitchen knife, and then rinse the broccoli under cool running water. Place the broccoli in a 2-quart slow cooker.

2. Add water or broth, butter, lemon juice, and pepper to the slow cooker with the broccoli. Cover and cook on low for 3 hours or until the broccoli is tender.

3. Serve immediately or allow to stay warm in the slow cooker for another hour.

PER SERVING | Calories: 89 | Fat: 6 g | Protein: 3 g | Sodium: 135 mg | Fiber: 2 g | Carbohydrates: 7 g

"Roasted" Roots

This is a perfect substitute for a starchy side dish such as potatoes.

INGREDIENTS | SERVES 6

1 pound baby carrots

12 ounces turnips, peeled and cubed

1 medium onion, chopped

2 cloves garlic, minced

2 tablespoons water

3 tablespoons organic butter or ghee

¼ teaspoon lemon juice

⅛ teaspoon pepper

1. Combine all the ingredients in a 3- or 4-quart slow cooker and stir to mix.

2. Cover and cook on low for 7–9 hours or until vegetables are tender when pierced with a fork.

PER SERVING | Calories: 110 | Fat: 7 g | Protein: 1 g | Sodium: 97 mg | Fiber: 4 g | Carbohydrates: 12 g

Zucchini Casserole

This highly nutritious and delicious vegetable compilation is great for a side dish or a light lunch.

INGREDIENTS | SERVES 4

4 medium zucchini, sliced and unpeeled

1 red onion, sliced

1 green pepper, cut in thin strips

1 (16-ounce) can diced tomatoes, undrained

1 teaspoon lemon juice

½ teaspoon pepper

½ teaspoon dried basil

1 tablespoon avocado oil

1. Combine all the ingredients, except the oil, in a 2-quart slow cooker. Cook on low for 3 hours.

2. Drizzle casserole with oil. Cook on low for 1½ hours more.

PER SERVING | Calories: 101 | Fat: 4 g | Protein: 4 g | Sodium: 193 mg | Fiber: 4 g | Carbohydrates: 16 g

Sautéed Fennel with Orange

Fennel is crunchy and a bit sweet and is most often associated with Italian cuisine.

INGREDIENTS | SERVES 4

3 small bulbs fennel, halved
1 (13.5-ounce) can chopped tomatoes
Juice and zest of 1 small orange
2 tablespoons raw honey
Pepper, to taste

1. Place the halved fennel in a 4- or 6-quart slow cooker.

2. In a large mixing bowl, combine the remaining ingredients. Pour mixture over the fennel in the slow cooker.

3. Cover and cook on high for 4–5 hours.

PER SERVING | Calories: 59 | Fat: 0 g | Protein: 1 g | Sodium: 131 mg | Fiber: 2 g | Carbohydrates: 15 g

Slow-Cooked Sweet Potatoes

This is the simplest way to prepare this carbohydrate-rich side dish, perfect for the Paleo-athlete.

INGREDIENTS | SERVES 2

2 large sweet potatoes

1. Wash off the sweet potatoes, but don't dry them. You'll want the moisture in the slow cooker.

2. Stab each sweet potato with a fork 5–6 times. Place the sweet potatoes in the slow cooker.

3. Cover the slow cooker and cook on low for 5–6 hours.

PER SERVING | Calories: 112 | Fat: 0 g | Protein: 2 g | Sodium: 72 mg | Fiber: 4 g | Carbohydrates: 26 g

Dill Carrots

The carrots in this side dish keep a firm texture even when fully cooked.

INGREDIENTS | SERVES 6

1 pound carrots, cut into coins

1 tablespoon minced fresh dill

⅓ teaspoon almond oil

3 tablespoons water

Place all the ingredients in a 2-quart slow cooker. Stir. Cook on low 1½–2 hours or until the carrots are fork-tender. Stir before serving.

PER SERVING | Calories: 31 | Fat: 0 g | Protein: 1 g | Sodium: 53 mg | Fiber: 2 g | Carbohydrates: 7 g

Dill Details

Dill is a delicate plant that has many culinary uses. The seeds are used as a spice, and the fresh and dried dill plant is used as an herb. Dill is an essential ingredient in dill pickles and gravlax, a type of cured salmon.

Stewed Tomatoes

For an Italian variation on these tomatoes, add basil and Italian parsley.

INGREDIENTS | SERVES 6

1 (28-ounce) can whole tomatoes in purée, cut up and undrained

1 tablespoon minced onion

1 stalk celery, diced

½ teaspoon oregano

½ teaspoon thyme

Place all the ingredients in a 2-quart slow cooker. Stir. Cook on low for up to 8 hours.

PER SERVING | Calories: 24 | Fat: 0 g | Protein: 1 g | Sodium: 192 mg | Fiber: 2 g | Carbohydrates: 6 g

Caramelized Onions

These are wonderful on salads and as a garnish for roasts and stews.

INGREDIENTS | YIELDS 1 CUP

3 large Vidalia or other sweet onions, sliced ⅛" thick

1 tablespoon avocado oil

Timesaving Tip

This recipe can be made ahead of time and kept on hand in a small glass jar for 3–5 days to use as a condiment and add flavor to many lunch and dinner dishes.

Place the onions in a large frying pan with oil. Over very low heat, sauté for 20 minutes or until onions are browned but not burned.

PER SERVING (½ CUP) | Calories: 110 | Fat: 4 g | Protein: 2 g | Sodium: 20 mg | Fiber: 2 g | Carbohydrates: 19 g

CHAPTER 10

Children's Favorites

Mini Caveman's Squash
(Baby Food)
244

Mini Caveman's Sweet Potatoes
(Baby Food)
244

Mini Caveman's Carrots
(Baby Food)
245

Chicken Tenders
245

Turnip Tots
246

Slow-Cooked Sloppy Joeys
246

Sweet Potato "Fries"
247

"Roasted" Fall Vegetables
247

Soft "Shell" Beef Tacos
248

Turkey Lettuce Wraps
249

Baked Apples
250

Blueberry Cookie Balls
251

Paleo Chocolate Bars
252

Kids' Favorite Trail Mix
253

Old-Fashioned Sweet Potato Hash
Browns
254

Carrot Pudding
254

Awesome Applesauce
255

Mini Caveman's Squash (Baby Food)

Babies seem to love this nutrient-rich and creamy sweet squash. It's full of Vitamins A and C, along with the anti-inflammatory pigment, beta-carotene.

INGREDIENTS | SERVES 6

2 butternut squash, peeled and cubed
¼ cup water

1. Place the squash in a 4- or 6-quart slow cooker, add water, cover, and cook on high for 3 hours.

2. Use a blender or food processor to purée into baby food.

PER SERVING | Calories: 126 | Fat: 0 g | Protein: 4 g | Sodium: 15 mg | Fiber: 6 g | Carbohydrates: 32 g

Mini Caveman's Sweet Potatoes (Baby Food)

Turnips could also be used here in place of the sweet potatoes.

INGREDIENTS | SERVES 6

2 medium-size sweet potatoes, peeled
¾ cup water

1. Place the sweet potatoes in a 4- or 6-quart slow cooker, add water, cover, and cook on high for 3 hours.

2. Use a blender or food processor to purée into baby food.

PER SERVING | Calories: 37 | Fat: 0 g | Protein: 1 g | Sodium: 25 mg | Fiber: 1 g | Carbohydrates: 9 g

Mini Caveman's Carrots (Baby Food)

These puréed carrots can be incorporated into another recipe—to thicken a soup, for example.

INGREDIENTS | SERVES 6

12 ounces carrots, peeled and chopped
¼ cup water

1. Place the carrots in a 4- or 6-quart slow cooker, add water, cover, and cook on high for 3 hours.

2. Use a blender or food processor to purée into baby food.

PER SERVING | Calories: 23 | Fat: 0 g | Protein: 1 g |
Sodium: 39 mg | Fiber: 2 g | Carbohydrates: 5 g

Chicken Tenders

Here's a Paleo-approved version of a traditional kid-friendly favorite. These flavorful chicken tenders partner perfectly with a side of Turnip Tots (see recipe in this chapter).

INGREDIENTS | SERVES 4

2 tablespoons avocado oil
1 clove garlic, minced
6 sprigs fresh thyme, stripped and chopped
1 tablespoon lemon zest
¼ cup lemon juice
1 pound chicken breast tenders
Pepper, to taste

1. In a large mixing bowl, combine the oil, garlic, chopped thyme, lemon zest, and lemon juice.

2. Season the chicken tenders with pepper.

3. Place chicken in the slow cooker, and pour avocado oil mixture over chicken, stirring until coated.

4. Cover and cook on low for 4–6 hours.

PER SERVING | Calories: 65 | Fat: 7 g | Protein: 0 g |
Sodium: 4 mg | Fiber: 0 g | Carbohydrates: 2 g

Turnip Tots

This is a healthier, Paleo-approved substitute for frozen Tater Tots, and the perfect accompaniment to Chicken Tenders (see previous recipe). Serve with Homemade Ketchup (see Chapter 3).

INGREDIENTS | SERVES 4

4 medium turnips, peeled and cubed
2 tablespoons avocado oil
2 tablespoons raw honey
1 tablespoon brown mustard
¼ teaspoon pepper

1. Place the turnips in a 2- or 4-quart slow cooker, drizzle with oil, and toss.

2. In a small bowl, mix together the honey, brown mustard, and pepper. Drizzle over turnips, and toss.

3. Cover and cook on low for 5 hours. Serve alongside Chicken Tenders.

PER SERVING | Calories: 127 | Fat: 7 g | Protein: 1 g | Sodium: 82 mg | Fiber: 2 g | Carbohydrates: 17 g

Slow-Cooked Sloppy Joeys

Serve over mashed cauliflower, turnips, or winter squash.

INGREDIENTS | SERVES 4

1 pound lean ground beef or turkey
1 (6-ounce) can tomato paste
2 tablespoons raw honey
1 tablespoon onion flakes
1 tablespoon paprika
1 teaspoon cumin
1 teaspoon lemon juice
½ teaspoon garlic powder
¼ teaspoon dry mustard
¼ teaspoon celery seed
¼ teaspoon black pepper
1 cup warm water
1 teaspoon almond meal

1. Place meat, tomato paste, honey, and seasonings into a 4-quart slow cooker. Add water and almond meal and stir.

2. Cover and cook on low for 6–7 hours or on high for 3–5 hours. Serve warm.

PER SERVING | Calories: 234 | Fat: 6 g | Protein: 26 g | Sodium: 414 mg | Fiber: 3 g | Carbohydrates: 18 g

Sweet Potato "Fries"

Serve alongside a burger and drizzle with Homemade Ketchup (see Chapter 3), honey, or honey mustard. If you like, sprinkle the fries with fine sea salt before serving.

INGREDIENTS | SERVES 2

2 medium-size sweet potatoes, sliced into thin wedges
¼ cup water
2 tablespoons coconut oil, melted

1. Place sweet potato wedges in a 4-quart slow cooker and add water.

2. Drizzle oil over sweet potatoes. Cover and cook on high for 2–3 hours.

3. Remove cover and continue cooking for 20–30 minutes, until desired browning occurs.

PER SERVING | Calories: 232 | Fat: 14 g | Protein: 2 g | Sodium: 72 mg | Fiber: 4 g | Carbohydrates: 26 g

"Roasted" Fall Vegetables

You won't have to beg the kids to eat their veggies with this yummy recipe.
You won't even have to ask them twice!

INGREDIENTS | SERVES 10

1½ pounds sweet potatoes
1 pound parsnips
1 pound carrots
2 large red onions, coarsely chopped
¾ cup chopped cranberries
1 tablespoon raw honey
3 tablespoons avocado oil
2 tablespoons lemon juice
½ teaspoon freshly ground black pepper
⅓ cup chopped fresh flat-leaf parsley

1. Peel the sweet potatoes, parsnips, and carrots and cut into 1½" pieces.

2. Combine the parsnips, carrots, onions, and cranberries in a lightly greased 6-quart slow cooker; layer sweet potatoes over the top.

3. In a small bowl, mix together the honey, oil, lemon juice, and pepper; pour over vegetable mixture. (Do not stir.)

4. Cover and cook on high for 4–5 hours or until vegetables are tender. Toss with parsley just before serving.

PER SERVING | Calories: 193 | Fat: 4 g | Protein: 2 g | Sodium: 75 mg | Fiber: 7 g | Carbohydrates: 38 g

Soft "Shell" Beef Tacos

The romaine leaves could also be placed under the broiler until crispy, for use as a "hard" taco shell.

INGREDIENTS | SERVES 12

2 (16-ounce) jars mild or medium tomato-based salsa

2 tablespoons lime juice

5 teaspoons chili powder

1½ pounds beef chuck pot roast, fat trimmed

12 large leaves romaine lettuce

3 cups shredded lettuce

1 avocado, diced

1. Spoon 1 cup salsa into a small bowl; set aside.

2. In a 4-quart slow cooker, combine remaining salsa with lime juice and chili powder.

3. Stir in beef, cover, and turn heat to low. Cook for 10–12 hours. Shred the meat, using 2 forks, and spoon into a serving bowl.

4. Lay out the romaine leaves for use as taco "shells," and place a small portion of slow-cooked beef on each.

5. Place shredded lettuce, diced avocado, and reserved salsa in small separate bowls for serving. Add toppings to tacos, wrap lettuce leaves tightly, and enjoy.

PER SERVING | Calories: 56 | Fat: 3 g | Protein: 2 g | Sodium: 464 mg | Fiber: 3 g | Carbohydrates: 8 g

Turkey Lettuce Wraps

Turkey is a low-fat protein source that kids are sure to love. Although these wraps are a bit complex to make, you can make a larger batch of the filling and serve it over salad at a later meal.

INGREDIENTS | SERVES 4

3 tablespoons walnut oil
3 shallots, chopped
1 piece lemongrass, thinly sliced
1 serrano chili pepper, thinly sliced
½ teaspoon fresh ground black pepper
1½ pounds ground turkey
⅓ cup fresh lime juice
2 tablespoons sesame oil
4 tablespoons coconut oil
½ cup thinly sliced basil leaves
8 large butter lettuce leaves

1. In a large frying pan, heat walnut oil over medium heat.

2. Add shallots, lemongrass, serrano pepper, and black pepper. Cook until the shallots soften, about 4 minutes.

3. Add ground turkey and stir frequently until cooked through, approximately 8–10 minutes.

4. Add lime juice, sesame oil, and coconut oil and cook for 1 minute.

5. Turn the heat off and mix in basil leaves.

6. Wrap mixture in lettuce leaves and serve.

PER SERVING | Calories: 381 | Fat: 29 g | Protein: 40 g | Sodium: 1 mg | Fiber: 1 g | Carbohydrates: 1 g

Baked Apples

You will feel as if you're eating apple pie when you eat these, and your house will smell like Thanksgiving dinner.

INGREDIENTS | SERVES 6

6 Pink Lady apples
1 cup unsweetened coconut flakes
Cinnamon, to taste

1. Preheat oven to 350°F.

2. Remove cores to ½" above the bottom of the apples.

3. Place apples in a medium baking dish.

4. Fill apple hollows with coconut flakes and sprinkle with cinnamon.

5. Bake for 10–15 minutes. Apples are done when they are completely soft and brown on top.

PER SERVING | Calories: 159 | Fat: 9.5 g | Protein: 1 g | Sodium: 6.5 mg | Fiber: 4.5 g | Carbohydrates: 21 g

Blueberry Cookie Balls

These antioxidant-packed cookie balls are a great alternative to commercial cookies. They taste great, are all natural, and will give your kids energy from all macronutrient categories.

INGREDIENTS | SERVES 12

2 egg whites
5 cups blueberries
4 teaspoons cinnamon
1½ teaspoons ginger
¼ cup raw honey
1 teaspoon vanilla extract

Glycemic Load and Kids

It is particularly important to limit children's sugar intake, because they are more sensitive to mood changes than adults and lack the ability to control their emotions. Recipes that combine fat, protein, and carbohydrates minimize blood sugar spikes and pitfalls.

1. Preheat oven to 350°F.

2. Whisk egg whites in a bowl until frothy. Add all other ingredients and mix well.

3. Scoop out tablespoons of dough and form into balls. Place balls on a baking sheet. Bake for 12–15 minutes.

4. Remove cookies from baking pan and cool on a rack. When cookies are completely cool, place in a single layer on a clean baking sheet and refrigerate for 1 hour before serving.

PER SERVING | Calories: 60 | Fat: 0.5 g | Protein: 1.5 g | Sodium: 12 mg | Fiber: 1.5 g | Carbohydrates: 14 g

Paleo Chocolate Bars

Your kids will be thrilled when they see these chocolate bars in their lunch boxes. These bars are quick to whip up and quick to eat. The amount of honey can be varied depending on your desired sweetness level.

INGREDIENTS | SERVES 8

1 tablespoon raw honey
4 tablespoons coconut oil
¼ cup ground almonds
¼ cup ground hazelnuts
¼ cup sunflower seeds
¼ cup cacao powder
¾ cup shredded unsweetened coconut flakes

Natural Sugars

Although natural honey is an acceptable Paleo-lithic diet food, you should still eat it in moderation. It does cause an increase in blood-sugar levels and therefore a spike in insulin.

1. Melt honey and coconut oil in saucepan over medium heat.

2. In a mixing bowl, combine almonds, hazelnuts, sunflower seeds, cacao powder, and coconut. Mix thoroughly.

3. Add honey mixture to bowl and mix well.

4. Pour dough into an 8" × 8" baking pan and store in refrigerator or freezer until firm, about 10 minutes in the freezer or 1 hour in the refrigerator.

5. Cut into squares and enjoy.

PER SERVING | Calories: 154 | Fat: 15 g | Protein: 2 g | Sodium: 2 mg | Fiber: 2 g | Carbohydrates: 5 g

Kids' Favorite Trail Mix

For kids who love potato chips, this recipe will be a nice alternative.
It has a sweet and salty taste that will satisfy all their cravings.

INGREDIENTS | SERVES 8

½ cup raw sunflower seeds
½ cup almonds
½ cup macadamia nuts
½ cup pistachios, shelled
4 tablespoons raw honey
1 teaspoon sea salt
½ teaspoon ground black pepper
¼ teaspoon cumin
1 teaspoon curry powder
Pinch ground cloves
1 teaspoon cinnamon

1. Preheat oven to 300°F.

2. Place sunflower seeds and nuts on a large baking sheet and bake for 10–12 minutes, taking care they do not burn. Remove from oven and let cool approximately 5 minutes.

3. In a small bowl, mix honey, salt, pepper, cumin, curry powder, cloves, and cinnamon.

4. In a large saucepan over medium heat, place the nuts and half of the honey mixture. When the mixture begins to melt, mix in the remaining honey mixture.

5. Shake the pan until all the nuts are coated, about 5 minutes.

6. Cool on wax paper. Use a spoon to separate nuts that stick together.

PER SERVING | Calories: 207 | Fat: 16 g | Protein: 5 g | Sodium: 292 mg | Fiber: 2.5 g | Carbohydrates: 15 g

Old-Fashioned Sweet Potato Hash Browns

These sweet potato hash browns are likely to become a family favorite. They are easy to make and packed with flavor your entire family will love.

INGREDIENTS | SERVES 6

3 tablespoons coconut oil

3 medium sweet potatoes, peeled and grated

1 tablespoon cinnamon

1. Heat the coconut oil in large frying pan over medium-high heat.

2. Cook grated sweet potatoes in hot oil for 7 minutes, stirring often.

3. Once brown, sprinkle with cinnamon and serve.

PER SERVING | Calories: 116 | Fat: 7 g | Protein: 1.5 g | Sodium: 36 mg | Fiber: 2 g | Carbohydrates: 13 g

Carrot Pudding

Serve this pudding chilled in the summer and enjoy warm in the winter.

INGREDIENTS | SERVES 4

4 large carrots, cooked and mashed

1 small onion, grated

¼ teaspoon nutmeg

1 tablespoon raw honey

1 cup canned unsweetened coconut milk

3 eggs, beaten

½ teaspoon lemon juice

1. Mix together all ingredients.

2. Pour into a 2- or 4-quart slow cooker and cook on high for 3–4 hours.

PER SERVING | Calories: 218 | Fat: 16 g | Protein: 7 g | Sodium: 110 mg | Fiber: 2 g | Carbohydrates: 15 g

Awesome Applesauce

Serve warm or chilled, or as a complement to a main pork, chicken, or beef dish.
Or freeze for an icy, sweet summer treat!

INGREDIENTS | SERVES 6

3 pounds Jonathan apples, peeled, cored, and coarsely chopped

½ cup water

½ cup pure maple syrup

Cinnamon, to taste

1. Combine all ingredients, except cinnamon, in a 6-quart slow cooker and cover.

2. Cook on high until apples are very soft and form applesauce when stirred, about 2–2½ hours. Sprinkle with cinnamon just before serving.

PER SERVING | Calories: 150 | Fat: 0 g | Protein: 1 g | Sodium: 2 mg | Fiber: 3 g | Carbohydrates: 30 g

CHAPTER 11

Grilling Time

Grilled Lemon-and-Dill Swordfish
Steaks
258

Salmon Skewers
258

Tilapia with Tomato and Basil
259

Spicy Grilled Flank Steak
259

Lime-Thyme Grilled Swordfish
260

Shrimp Skewers
261

Asian Grilled Salmon
262

Jalapeño Steak
263

BBQ Chicken
264

Grilled Trout
265

Grilled Pineapple
266

Grilled Watermelon
266

Grilled Salmon
267

Grilled Lemon-and-Dill Swordfish Steaks

This recipe calls for preparation on the grill but could easily be cooked in the oven using the broiler.

INGREDIENTS | SERVES 4

4 (4-ounce) swordfish steaks
1 tablespoon almond oil
1 lemon
4 sprigs dill

1. Lightly coat swordfish steaks with oil.

2. Slice lemon into rings and place on top of swordfish steaks.

3. Place 1 fresh dill sprig on each swordfish steak.

4. Grill over medium-high heat, about 5 minutes per side, depending on thickness of steaks.

PER SERVING | Calories: 134 | Fat: 6.5 g | Protein: 17 g | Sodium: 77 mg | Fiber: 0 g | Carbohydrates: 0 g

Salmon Skewers

Salmon has a wonderful omega profile—it is one of the highest sources of omega-3 fatty acid.

INGREDIENTS | SERVES 4

8 ounces salmon fillets
1 red onion, cut into wedges
2 red bell peppers, seeded and cut into 2" pieces
12 mushrooms
12 cherry tomatoes
12 (2") cubes fresh pineapple

1. Cut salmon into cubes.

2. Thread all ingredients on metal skewers, alternating vegetables, pineapple, and meat.

3. Grill over medium-high heat until salmon is light pink, about 10 minutes, depending on thickness of salmon cubes.

PER SERVING | Calories: 214 | Fat: 4 g | Protein: 15 g | Sodium: 35 mg | Fiber: 5 g | Carbohydrates: 32 g

Wild-Caught versus Farm-Raised Salmon

Salmon is one of the best sources of omega-3 fatty acids, but be sure to purchase wild-caught salmon. Farm-raised salmon are not exposed to the colder water, and therefore their fat reserves are not as robust as in wild salmon.

Tilapia with Tomato and Basil

Tilapia is a very low-fat fish choice with a light flavor. It cooks quickly and absorbs flavors from spices quite nicely.

INGREDIENTS | SERVES 6

6 tilapia fillets
2 large beefsteak tomatoes, sliced
12 whole basil leaves

1. Place each tilapia fillet on a square of aluminum foil.

2. Cover each fillet with 2–3 slices of tomato and 2 basil leaves.

3. Fold and seal foil over each fillet and grill over medium heat for 6–8 minutes, or until fish flakes easily.

PER SERVING | Calories: 122 | Fat: 2.5 g | Protein: 23 g | Sodium: 53 mg | Fiber: 0.5 g | Carbohydrates: 2.5 g

Spicy Grilled Flank Steak

Flank steak is one of the leanest steak cuts. It is usually the best and safest choice of steak to order when going out to dinner as well.

INGREDIENTS | SERVES 4

2 tablespoons raw honey
1 teaspoon cinnamon
1 teaspoon chili powder
½ teaspoon salt-free lemon-pepper seasoning
1½ pounds lean flank steak
½ cup sliced green onions

1. Combine honey, cinnamon, chili powder, and lemon-pepper seasoning in a small bowl.

2. Grill flank steak over medium-high heat for 6 minutes on each side. Baste often with honey mixture. Remove steak from grill.

3. Thinly slice the steak against the grain.

4. Serve sprinkled with green onions as garnish.

PER SERVING | Calories: 368 | Fat: 12 g | Protein: 52 g | Sodium: 113 mg | Fiber: 0.5 g | Carbohydrates: 9.5 g

Flank Steak and Good Fat

Flank steak is a terrific choice when you want a lower-fat version of red meat. This steak usually contains less than 13 grams of fat per serving, while some other more fatty cuts have about 20 grams of fat per serving.

Lime-Thyme Grilled Swordfish

Thyme is a useful spice that adds flavor without overpowering a dish, and it blends well with other spices.

INGREDIENTS | SERVES 4

4 (4-ounce) swordfish steaks
1 cup water
3 tablespoons fresh lime juice
1 bay leaf
1 teaspoon crushed dried thyme

1. Preheat grill to 350°F.

2. Place each swordfish steak on a large sheet of heavy-duty aluminum foil.

3. Pour the water and lime juice over fish. Add bay leaf.

4. Sprinkle the thyme over the fish and wrap the foil closed.

5. Cook for 10 minutes or until the fish flakes easily when tested with a fork and is opaque all the way through.

PER SERVING | Calories: 107 | Fat: 3.5 g | Protein: 17 g | Sodium: 77 mg | Fiber: 0 g | Carbohydrates: 1 g

Shrimp Skewers

These skewers are easy to make and can be served as a main dish or an appetizer.
They are fantastic at parties or holiday celebrations.

INGREDIENTS | SERVES 4

1½ pounds large shrimp, peeled and deveined

Juice of ½ lime

1 teaspoon ground black pepper

12 white mushrooms

1 medium summer squash, sliced in 1" pieces

1 large red bell pepper, sliced in 2" pieces

1 large green bell pepper, sliced in 2" pieces

4 cloves garlic, finely minced

2 tablespoons coconut oil, melted

Shrimp and Omega-3

Shrimp is a good source of omega-3 fatty acids. This terrific shellfish is naturally low in fat and high in protein. If you have high cholesterol, you might want to watch your intake. They do have higher levels than other protein sources.

1. Soak 8 wooden skewers in water for at least 30 minutes.

2. In a large bowl, drizzle shrimp with lime juice and season with pepper. Set aside for 5 minutes.

3. Add vegetables, garlic, and oil to the shrimp and toss to coat.

4. Alternate vegetables and shrimp on skewers.

5. Grill over medium heat for 5 minutes or until shrimp turns pink, then turn skewers to cook other side an additional 5 minutes.

PER SERVING | Calories: 209 | Fat: 9.5 g | Protein: 26 g | Sodium: 190 mg | Fiber: 0.5 g | Carbohydrates: 4.5 g

Asian Grilled Salmon

Salmon is a traditional barbecue item and a staple in the Paleolithic diet.

INGREDIENTS | SERVES 4

2 pounds salmon fillets, skin on

¼ cup sesame oil

¼ cup coconut aminos

¼ cup lemon juice

4 green onions, thinly sliced

3 tablespoons minced fresh parsley

2 teaspoons minced fresh rosemary

¼ teaspoon sea salt

⅛ teaspoon pepper

1. Place salmon in a shallow dish.

2. Combine remaining ingredients in a medium-size bowl and mix well. Set aside ¼ cup for basting and pour the rest over the salmon.

3. Cover and refrigerate salmon for 30 minutes.

4. Grill salmon over medium heat, skin side down, for 15–20 minutes. Baste with marinade often.

PER SERVING | Calories: 446 | Fat: 28 g | Protein: 45 g | Sodium: 281 mg | Fiber: 0 g | Carbohydrates: 2 g

Olive Oil and Grilling

Although there are many oils to choose from, many recipes in this book use olive oil. Olive oil has a high heat tolerance and low smoke value. This makes it ideal for cooking, particularly on the grill.

Jalapeño Steak

When you want a little kick of flavor instead of the more traditional steak meals, give this recipe a shot. Jalapeños and lime juice give this meal a multicultural feel.

INGREDIENTS | SERVES 6

4 jalapeño peppers, stemmed, seeded, and roughly chopped

4 cloves garlic

¼ cup fresh cilantro leaves

1½ teaspoons fresh cracked black pepper

1 tablespoon sea salt

¼ cup lime juice

1½ pounds top sirloin steak

1. Combine jalapeños, garlic, cilantro, pepper, sea salt, and lime juice in a blender. Blend until smooth.

2. Place steak in a shallow pan and pour marinade over it. Cover and marinate for 8 hours in the refrigerator.

3. Drain and discard marinade. Grill steak over high heat for 5 minutes per side, or to desired doneness.

PER SERVING | Calories: 229 | Fat: 8 g | Protein: 35 g | Sodium: 1,238 mg | Fiber: 0 g | Carbohydrates: 2 g

Sea Salt

Strict Paleolithic-diet followers would not use salt in any form, but looser followers add organic sea salt to recipes where salt is desired. Sea salt is often used for steaks and other grilled meats.

BBQ Chicken

This mouthwatering chicken will become a staple in your home regardless of the season.

INGREDIENTS | SERVES 4

3 tablespoons avocado oil

¼ cup tomato paste

1½ cups apple cider vinegar

½ cup raw honey

Juice of 1 lemon

¼ teaspoon ground black pepper

5 sprigs fresh sage

2 pounds bone-in chicken breasts

Cage-Free and Barn-Roaming

Cage-free and barn-roaming chickens are the best chickens to purchase. Chickens that are given feedlot grains derived from corn have a less healthy fat profile. Commercial farms tend to use antibiotics and growth hormones. All of these products eventually leach into our bodies where they can magnify over time.

1. In a small bowl combine oil, tomato paste, vinegar, honey, lemon juice, pepper, and sage.

2. Place chicken breasts on hot grill and baste with sauce.

3. Cook for 45–60 minutes, turning every 10–15 minutes. Baste with sauce after each turning.

PER SERVING | Calories: 463 | Fat: 15 g | Protein: 39 g | Sodium: 344 mg | Fiber: 2 g | Carbohydrates: 41 g

Grilled Trout

Cooking the fish inside the foil packets keeps it tender and moist.

INGREDIENTS | SERVES 2

2 whole trout, heads removed, cleaned and butterflied
1 teaspoon ground black pepper
2 cloves garlic, minced
½ teaspoon chopped fresh rosemary
1 teaspoon chopped fresh parsley
6 sprigs fresh rosemary
1 lemon, halved; one half thinly sliced

Oily Fishes

There are many fishes that are good sources of beneficial fatty acids. These fish include trout, sardines, swordfish, whitebait, fresh tuna, anchovies, eel, kipper, mackerel, carp, bloater, smelt, and bluefish. The more varieties of fish that you try, the better fatty acid profile you will compile.

1. Place each trout on a square piece of aluminum foil.

2. Season both sides of trout with pepper, garlic, rosemary, and parsley.

3. Fold fish closed and top with rosemary sprigs and a few slices of lemon.

4. Squeeze the lemon half over each fish.

5. Wrap each fish securely inside the sheet of aluminum foil.

6. Grill packets over medium-high heat for 7 minutes on each side or until fish is flaky.

PER SERVING | Calories: 176 | Fat: 8 g | Protein: 25 g | Sodium: 62 mg | Fiber: 0 g | Carbohydrates: 0 g

Grilled Pineapple

Pineapple has such a profound flavor, and grilling just intensifies it. The addition of some raw honey will make this a really special treat at any barbecue or party.

INGREDIENTS | SERVES 6

1 tablespoon avocado oil

1 fresh pineapple, cored, peeled, and cut into 1" rings

¼ cup raw honey

2 tablespoons chopped macadamia nuts

1. Coat grill rack with oil before starting the grill.

2. Grill pineapple over medium heat for 5 minutes.

3. Turn pineapple over and grill 5 more minutes.

4. Brush with honey and sprinkle with macadamia nuts.

PER SERVING | Calories: 102 | Fat: 2 g | Protein: 1 g | Sodium: 1.5 mg | Fiber: 1 g | Carbohydrates: 22 g

Grilled Watermelon

If you haven't tried grilled fruit, you are missing out. Not only does the heat enhance the flavor, but the little bit of sea salt really brings out the natural sweetness of the fruit.

INGREDIENTS | SERVES 6

1 tablespoon avocado oil

1 small (4-pound) watermelon, sliced

2 teaspoons sea salt

1. Coat grill rack with oil before starting the grill. Season both sides of watermelon slices with salt.

2. Grill watermelon over medium heat for 5 minutes.

3. Turn watermelon over and grill 5 more minutes.

PER SERVING | Calories: 110 | Fat: 3 g | Protein: 2 g | Sodium: 789 mg | Fiber: 1 g | Carbohydrates: 23 g

Grilled Salmon

Grilling salmon is a nice way to get maximum flavor while cooking. The marinade in this recipe doubles as a basting sauce to really seal in the flavor.

INGREDIENTS | SERVES 4

2 pounds skin-on salmon fillets
½ cup avocado oil
½ cup lemon juice
4 green onions, thinly sliced
3 tablespoons minced fresh parsley
1½ teaspoons minced fresh rosemary
⅛ teaspoon pepper

1. Place salmon in a shallow dish.

2. In a medium-size bowl, combine remaining ingredients and mix well. Set aside ¼ cup for basting; pour the rest over the salmon.

3. Cover and refrigerate for 30 minutes. Drain, discarding marinade.

4. Grill salmon over medium heat, skin side down, for 15–20 minutes or until fish flakes easily with a fork. Baste occasionally with reserved marinade.

PER SERVING | Calories: 492 | Fat: 39 g | Protein: 34 g | Sodium: 75 mg | Fiber: 0.5 g | Carbohydrates: 0.5 g

Paleo "Yes" Foods

In order to ensure your success on the Paleolithic diet, you need to stock your pantry with fresh, organic produce and grass-fed and barn-roaming meats. This list contains both the basics and the obscure. Feel free to experiment with items you would not normally choose. That will spice things up and keep you interested in the diet.

Protein

alligator
bass
bear
beef
bison
bluefish
caribou
chicken
chuck steak
clams
cod
crab
crayfish
egg whites
eggs
flank steak
game hen breasts
goat
grouper
haddock
halibut
hamburger
herring
liver (beef, lamb, goat, or chicken)
lobster
London broil
mackerel
marrow (beef, lamb, or goat)
mussels
orange roughy
ostrich
oysters

pheasant
pork chops
pork loin
pork
quail
rabbit
rattlesnake
red snapper
salmon, wild-caught
scallops
scrod
shrimp
tilapia
tongue (beef, lamb, or goat)
trout
tuna, canned, unsalted
tuna, fresh
turkey breast
veal
venison

Leafy Vegetables

arugula
beet greens
bitterleaf
bok choy
broccoli rabe
Brussels sprouts
cabbage
celery
chard
chicory
Chinese cabbage
collard greens
dandelion
endive
fiddlehead
kale
lettuce
radicchio
spinach
Swiss chard
turnip
watercress
yarrow

Fruiting Vegetables

avocado
bell pepper
cucumber
eggplant
squash
sweet pepper
tomatillo
tomato
zucchini

Flowers and Flower Buds

artichoke
broccoli
cauliflower

Bulb and Stem Vegetables

asparagus
celery
Florence fennel
garlic
kohlrabi
leek
onion
sea vegetables and herbs of all types

Fruits

apple
apricot
banana
blackberries
blueberries
cantaloupe
cherries
coconut
cranberries
figs
grapefruit
grapes
guava
honeydew melon
kiwi
lemon
lime
mandarin orange
mango
nectarine
orange
passion fruit
peaches
pears
persimmon
pineapple
plums
pomegranate
raspberries
rhubarb
star fruit
strawberries
tangerine
watermelon

Fats, Nuts, Seeds, Oils, and Fatty Proteins

almond butter
almonds
avocado
brazil nuts
cashew
cashew butter
chestnuts
coconut oil
avocado oil
almond oil
macadamia nut oil
olive oil
hazelnuts (filberts)
macadamia nut butter
macadamia nuts
pecans
pine nuts
pistachios
pumpkin seeds
sesame seeds
sunflower butter, unsweetened
sunflower seeds
walnut oil
walnuts

Paleo "No" Foods

Legume Vegetables

American groundnut
azuki beans
black-eyed peas
chickpeas (garbanzo beans)
common beans
fava beans
green beans
guar
Indian peas
kidney beans
lentils
lima beans
mung beans
navy beans
okra
peanuts
peanut butter
peas
pigeon peas
pinto beans
red beans
ricebeans
snow peas
soybeans and soy products
string beans
sugar snap peas
white beans

Dairy Foods

cheese
dairy spreads
frozen yogurt
ice cream
ice milk
low-fat milk
nonfat dairy creamer
powdered milk
skim milk
whole milk
yogurt

Cereal Grains

barley
corn
millet
oats
rice
rye
sorghum
wheat
wild rice

Cereal Grain–Like Seeds

amaranth
buckwheat
quinoa

Starchy Vegetables

cassava root
manioc
white potatoes and all potato products
tapioca pudding

Salt-Containing Foods, Fatty Meats, and Sugar

almost all commercial salad dressings and condiments
bacon (uncured, nitrate-free bacon is okay)
candy
deli meats
frankfurters
processed ketchup
pork rinds
processed meats
salted nuts
processed sausages
soft drinks and fruit juice
refined sugar

Paleo Substitutions

▼ PALEO SUBSTITUTIONS

cow's milk	coconut, almond, macadamia, or hazelnut milk (unsweetened)
bacon	uncured nitrite-free bacon and meats
deli meat	fresh cut chicken or turkey breast, thinly sliced
salad dressing	oil and lemon or lime juice (add herbs and mustard for flavoring)
starch	spaghetti squash, butternut squash, acorn squash
sugar	raw honey, coconut palm sugar, pure maple syrup
soda	water, iced tea
salt	lemon juice, spices, fresh herbs
butter	nut oils, coconut butter, ghee
peanut butter	all other nut and seed butters
cookies	fresh fruit
chocolate	cacao (72% or higher dark chocolate is acceptable)
commercially prepared meat	grass-fed, free-roaming meat
farm-raised fish	sustainable wild-caught fish
baked desserts	baked fruit

Six Weeks of Weeknight Paleo Meals

Monday	Tuesday	Wednesday	Thursday	Friday
Week 1				
Chicken and Mushroom Stew (Chapter 5)	London Broil with Onions and Sweet Potato Sticks (Chapter 6)	Turkey Club Salad with Bacon, Lettuce, and Tomato (Chapter 4)	Paleo Pulled Pork (Chapter 6); Mashed Cauliflower (Chapter 9)	Crunchy Fruit Salad (Chapter 4); Spicy Bison Stew (Chapter 5)
Week 2				
Foolproof Chicken (Chapter 7); Citrus-Steamed Carrots (Chapter 9)	Fresh Tuna with Sweet Lemon Leek Salsa (Chapter 8); Red Pepper and Fennel Salad (Chapter 4)	Pork Tenderloin with Nectarines (Chapter 6); Celeriac Slaw (Chapter 9)	Chicken Cacciatore (Chapter 7)	Scallop and Shrimp Jambalaya (Chapter 8); Okra Stuffed with Green Peppercorns (Chapter 9)
Week 3				
Zesty Pecan Chicken and Grape Salad (Chapter 4); Simple Tomato Soup (Chapter 5)	Orange Tilapia (Chapter 8); Roasted Asparagus (Chapter 9)	Coconut Mango Spiced Chicken (Chapter 7); Chipotle-Lime Mashed Sweet Potatoes (Chapter 9)	Ginger Beef and Napa Cabbage (Chapter 6); Stuffed Tomatoes (Chapter 9)	Mediterranean Seafood Soup (Chapter 5); Greek Salad (Chapter 4)
Week 4				
Baked Coconut Shrimp (Chapter 8); Fire-Kissed Cantaloupe Salad (Chapter 4)	Beef Tenderloin with Chimichurri (Chapter 6); Mashed Cauliflower (Chapter 9)	Lime-Thyme Grilled Swordfish (Chapter 11); Vegetable Kebabs on Rosemary Skewers (Chapter 9)	Avocado Chicken Salad (Chapter 4)	Filet Mignon and Roasted Red Pepper Wraps (Chapter 6)
Week 5				
Ground Turkey Joes (Chapter 7)	Chicken Chili Verde (Chapter 5)	Paleo Meatballs and Sauce (Chapter 6)	Hot Buffalo Chicken Bites (Chapter 7); Baked Sweet Potato Sticks (Chapter 9)	Sausage and Spicy Eggs (Chapter 6); Floret Salad (Chapter 4)
Week 6				
Mahi Mahi and Green Vegetable Medley (Chapter 8)	Beef and Broccoli Stir-Fry (Chapter 6)	Thai Chicken Stew with Vegetables in Coconut Cream (Chapter 7)	Salmon in Parchment with Baby Brussels Sprouts (Chapter 8)	Lone Star State Chili (Chapter 5)

Standard U.S./Metric Measurement Conversions

VOLUME CONVERSIONS

U.S. Volume Measure	Metric Equivalent
⅛ teaspoon	0.5 milliliter
¼ teaspoon	1 milliliter
½ teaspoon	2 milliliters
1 teaspoon	5 milliliters
½ tablespoon	7 milliliters
1 tablespoon (3 teaspoons)	15 milliliters
2 tablespoons (1 fluid ounce)	30 milliliters
¼ cup (4 tablespoons)	60 milliliters
⅓ cup	90 milliliters
½ cup (4 fluid ounces)	125 milliliters
⅔ cup	160 milliliters
¾ cup (6 fluid ounces)	180 milliliters
1 cup (16 tablespoons)	250 milliliters
1 pint (2 cups)	500 milliliters
1 quart (4 cups)	1 liter (about)

WEIGHT CONVERSIONS

U.S. Weight Measure	Metric Equivalent
½ ounce	15 grams
1 ounce	30 grams
2 ounces	60 grams
3 ounces	85 grams
¼ pound (4 ounces)	115 grams
½ pound (8 ounces)	225 grams
¾ pound (12 ounces)	340 grams
1 pound (16 ounces)	454 grams

OVEN TEMPERATURE CONVERSIONS

Degrees Fahrenheit	Degrees Celsius
200 degrees F	95 degrees C
250 degrees F	120 degrees C
275 degrees F	135 degrees C
300 degrees F	150 degrees C
325 degrees F	160 degrees C
350 degrees F	180 degrees C
375 degrees F	190 degrees C
400 degrees F	205 degrees C
425 degrees F	220 degrees C
450 degrees F	230 degrees C

BAKING PAN SIZES

U.S.	Metric
8 × 1½ inch round baking pan	20 × 4 cm cake tin
9 × 1½ inch round baking pan	23 × 3.5 cm cake tin
11 × 7 × 1½ inch baking pan	28 × 18 × 4 cm baking tin
13 × 9 × 2 inch baking pan	30 × 20 × 5 cm baking tin
2 quart rectangular baking dish	30 × 20 × 3 cm baking tin
15 × 10 × 2 inch baking pan	30 × 25 × 2 cm baking tin (Swiss roll tin)
9 inch pie plate	22 × 4 or 23 × 4 cm pie plate
7 or 8 inch springform pan	18 or 20 cm springform or loose bottom cake tin
9 × 5 × 3 inch loaf pan	23 × 13 × 7 cm or 2 lb narrow loaf or pâté tin
1½ quart casserole	1.5 liter casserole
2 quart casserole	2 liter casserole

Index

Note: Page numbers in **bold** indicate recipe category lists.

Acorn Squash Autumn Bisque, 126
Aioli, 61
Almonds. *See* Nuts and seeds
Appetizers and snacks, **33**–56
    about: good snack choices, 23
    Appetizer Meatballs, 51
    Asparagus and Avocado Lettuce
        Wraps, 56
    Baked Chicken Wings, 38
    Baked Stuffed Clams, 35
    Buffalo Chicken Wings, 39
    Clams Casino, 43
    Deviled Eggs, 34
    Deviled Eggs with Capers, 44
    Eggplant Relish, 50
    Exotic Fruit Guacamole, 38
    Hot and Spicy Nuts, 48
    Hot Cinnamon-Chili Walnuts, 54
    Lollipop Lamb Chops, 40
    Paleo Chips, 45
    Roasted Kale, 34
    Roasted Parsnip Chips, 46
    Roasted Pistachios, 55
    Roasted Spicy Pumpkin Seeds, 48
    Sardines in Red Pepper Cups, 46
    Scallop Ceviche, 36
    Scallops Wrapped in Bacon, 36
    Shrimp Cocktail, 47
    Slow-Cooked Almonds with a Kick,
        50
    Slow-Cooked Paleo Party Mix, 52
    Spiced Hazelnuts, 51
    Spinach Dip, 53
    Stuffed Grape Leaves, 49
    Stuffed Mushroom Caps, 37
    Stuffed Mushrooms (Bacon and
        Herbs), 42
    Stuffed Mushrooms (Crabmeat or
        Shrimp), 41

Stuffed Mushrooms (Spicy Beef), 42
Apples
    Apple Chutney, 71
    Apple Coleslaw, 87
    Apples-and-Onions Pork Chops,
        155
    Awesome Applesauce, 255
    Baked Apples, 250
    Broccoli, Pine Nut, and Apple Salad,
        102
    Cran-Apple Sauce, 77
    Pork and Apple Stew, 124
    Pork Tenderloin with Sweet and
        Savory Apples, 168
Approved and non-approved Paleo
    foods. *See* "No" foods; "Yes" foods
Artichokes
    Artichoke Sauce, 70
    Baked Stuffed Artichokes, 230
    Marinated Baby Artichoke Hearts,
        229
Arugula and Fennel Salad with
    Pomegranate, 99
Asian Dressing, 82
Asian Grilled Salmon, 262
Asian-style garnishes, 225
Asparagus
    about: nutritional benefits, 222
    Asparagus and Avocado Lettuce
        Wraps, 56
    Chicken and Vegetable Frittata, 183
    Roasted Asparagus, 222
    Sautéed Asparagus, 222
Avocados
    Asparagus and Avocado Lettuce
        Wraps, 56
    Avocado and Shrimp Salad, 88
    Avocado Chicken Salad, 86
    Crisp Avocado Salad, 86

Exotic Fruit Guacamole, 38
    Mahi Mahi Wraps with Avocado and
        Fresh Cabbage, 220
    Party Guacamole, 58
Awesome Applesauce, 255

Baby food
    Mini Caveman's Carrots, 245
    Mini Caveman's Squash, 244
    Mini Caveman's Sweet Potatoes,
        244
Bacon
    Scallops Wrapped in Bacon, 36
    Stuffed Mushrooms (Bacon and
        Herbs), 42
    Turkey Club Salad with Bacon,
        Lettuce, and Tomato, 95
Baked Apples, 250
Baked Chicken Legs, 188
Baked Chicken Wings, 38
Baked Coconut Shrimp, 203
Baked Stuffed Clams, 35
Baked Sweet Potato Sticks, 224
Balsamic barbecue sauce, fruity, 68
Balsamic Vinaigrette and Marinade, 81
Balsamic vinegar, 62
Bananas
    Crunchy Fruit Salad, 105
    Rainbow Fruit Salad, 92
Basil
    about: other spices/herbs and, 30
    Habanero-Basil Sauce, 66
    Tilapia with Tomato and Basil, 259
Bay leaves, 187
BBQ Chicken, 264
Beans and legumes
    to avoid, 274
    nutritional benefits, 16, 17

Beef, **145**
  about: filet mignon, 97; flank steak and good fat, 259; grass-fed, 19; London broil, 157; preparing, 27–28
  Appetizer Meatballs, 51
  Beef and Broccoli Stir-Fry, 163
  Beef and Cabbage, 169
  Beef and Coconut Curry, 169
  Beef and Ginger Curry, 170
  Beef and Vegetable Stew, 114
  Beef Brisket with Onions and Mushrooms, 160
  Beef Tenderloin with Chimichurri, 158
  Beef with Bell Peppers, 155
  Boeuf Bourguignon, 164
  Bolognese Sauce, 74
  Brown Stock, 109
  Caveman's Chili, 116
  Cincinnati Chili, 128
  Corned Beef and Cabbage, 158
  Filet Mignon and Red Onion Salad, 97
  Filet Mignon and Roasted Red Pepper Wraps, 156
  Ginger Beef and Napa Cabbage, 161
  Jalapeño Steak, 263
  London Broil with Onions and Sweet Potato Sticks, 157
  Lone Star State Chili, 129
  Paleo Meatballs and Sauce, 146
  Pot Roast with a Touch of Sweet, 165
  Pot Roast with Vegetables and Gravy, 159
  Slow-Cooked Sloppy Joeys, 246
  Soft "Shell" Beef Tacos, 248
  Spicy Grilled Flank Steak, 259
  Steak-and-Mushroom Kebabs, 162
  Stuffed Grape Leaves, 49
  Stuffed Mushrooms (Spicy Beef), 42
  Stuffed Pepper Soup, 142
  Texas Firehouse Chili, 130
Berries
  about: tasting before sweetening, 69
  Blueberry Cookie Balls, 251
  Cranberry Sauce, 77
  Minty Blueberry Melon Salad, 91

  Rainbow Fruit Salad, 92
  Raspberry Coulis, 69
  Rosemary Rack of Lamb in Berries Sauce, 147
  Summer Berry Sauce, 70
Bison
  about: grass-fed, 19; nutritional benefits, 234
  Bison-Stuffed Zucchini, 234
  Spicy Bison Stew, 138
Blood Orange Salad with Shrimp and Baby Spinach, 93
Blood sugar
  glycemic levels, 19–20, 21, 251
  insulin levels and, 16, 19, 21, 22–23
  mood swings and, 22–23
  sugar consumption and, 21–22, 252
Blueberries. See Berries
Body mass index (BMI), 14
Boeuf Bourguignon, 164
Bolognese Sauce, 74
Bouillabaisse, 115
Bouquet garni, 210
Braised Chicken with Citrus, 185
Braised Chicken with Kale, 186
Broccoli
  about: superfood nutrition of, 104
  Beef and Broccoli Stir-Fry, 163
  Broccoli, Pine Nut, and Apple Salad, 102
  Chicken and Vegetable Frittata, 183
  Floret Salad, 104
  Mahi Mahi and Green Vegetable Medley, 212
  Paleo "Cream" of Broccoli Soup, 119
  Slow-Cooked Broccoli, 237
Brown Stock, 109
Brussels sprouts
  Brussels Sprouts Hash with Caramelized Shallots, 228
  Salmon in Parchment with Baby Brussels Sprouts, 197
  Sautéed Brussels Sprouts, 223
Buffalo Chicken Wings, 39
Butternut squash. See Squash

Cabbage, 87
  Beef and Cabbage, 169
  Caveman's Cabbage Soup, 125

  Corned Beef and Cabbage, 158
  Five-Spice Crabmeat Salad, 94
  Ginger Beef and Napa Cabbage, 161
  Grilled Tuna Salad with Asian Vegetables and Spicy Dressing, 96
  Mahi Mahi Wraps with Avocado and Fresh Cabbage, 220
  Napa Cabbage with Asian Sauce, 225
  Thai Chicken Stew with Vegetables in Coconut Cream, 190
Cancer, Paleo diet and, 13
Candied Butternut Squash, 233
Cantaloupe. See Melons
Capers
  about, 177; brine-packed, 44
  Deviled Eggs with Capers, 44
  Fennel and Caper Sauce, 69
  Salmon with Lemon, Capers, and Rosemary, 209
Caramelized Onions, 241
Carbohydrates
  glycemic levels and, 19–20, 21, 251
  good, 16–17, 19
  omega-3 sources, 19
  sugar consumption and, 21–22, 252, 274
Carrots
  Basic Vegetable Stock, 108
  Carrot-Lemon Soup, 137
  Carrot Pudding, 254
  Citrus-Steamed Carrots, 223
  Dill Carrots, 240
  Mini Caveman's Carrots (Baby Food), 245
  "Roasted" Fall Vegetables, 247
  "Roasted" Roots, 238
  Stewed Chicken with Vegetables, 187
Cauliflower
  Chicken and Vegetable Frittata, 183
  Cream of Cauliflower Soup, 134
  Curried Cauliflower Soup, 115
  Floret Salad, 104
  Mashed Cauliflower, 229
Caveman's Cabbage Soup, 125
Caveman's Catfish, 211
Caveman's Chili, 116

Celeriac Slaw, 224
Celery
    Basic Vegetable Stock, 108
    Stewed Chicken with Vegetables, 187
Chicken, **171**
    about: cage-free and barn-roaming, 101, 264; cooking with skin on, 274; preparing, 27–28
    Avocado Chicken Salad, 86
    Baked Chicken Legs, 188
    Baked Chicken Wings, 38
    Basic Chicken Soup, 113
    BBQ Chicken, 264
    Braised Chicken with Citrus, 185
    Braised Chicken with Kale, 186
    Buffalo Chicken Wings, 39
    Chicken and Mushroom Stew, 120
    Chicken and Vegetable Frittata, 183
    Chicken Bolognese, 141
    Chicken Cacciatore, 189
    Chicken Chili Verde, 131
    Chicken Chowder, 138
    Chicken Enchiladas, 179
    Chicken Piccata, 177
    Chicken Salad, 90
    Chicken Tenders, 245
    Chicken with Eggplant, 182
    Chicken with Sautéed Tomatoes and Pine Nuts, 180
    Coconut Mango Spiced Chicken, 192
    Curried Chicken Salad, 101
    Foolproof Chicken, 175
    Ginger-Orange Chicken Breast, 193
    Grilled San Francisco–Style Chicken, 184
    Hot Buffalo Chicken Bites, 176
    Jerk Chicken, 191
    Lemon Chicken, 185
    No-Crust Chicken Potpie, 181
    Paleo Stuffed Peppers, 232
    Pecan-Crusted Chicken, 180
    Poached Chicken, 175
    Poached Chicken with Pears and Herbs, 184
    Rosemary-Thyme Stew, 140
    Shredded Chicken Wraps, 178
    Spicy Chicken Sliders, 181
    Stewed Chicken with Vegetables, 187
    Stuffed Grape Leaves, 49

    Thai Chicken Stew with Vegetables in Coconut Cream, 190
    Tomato and Chicken Sausage Sauce, 72
    Tuscan Chicken, 192
    Zesty Pecan Chicken and Grape Salad, 84
Children
    glycemic load, 251
    good snack choices, 23
    list of food items for, 23–24
    mood swings and blood sugar levels, 22–23
    nut butters and, 25
    Paleo lifestyle and, 20–21
Children's favorites, **243**–55
    Awesome Applesauce, 255
    Baked Apples, 250
    Blueberry Cookie Balls, 251
    Carrot Pudding, 254
    Chicken Tenders, 245
    Kids' Favorite Trail Mix, 253
    Mini Caveman's Carrots (Baby Food), 245
    Mini Caveman's Squash (Baby Food), 244
    Mini Caveman's Sweet Potatoes (Baby Food), 244
    Old-Fashioned Sweet Potato Hash Browns, 254
    Paleo Chocolate Bars, 252
    "Roasted" Fall Vegetables, 247
    Slow-Cooked Sloppy Joeys, 246
    Soft "Shell" Beef Tacos, 248
    Sweet Potato "Fries," 247
    Turkey Lettuce Wraps, 249
    Turnip Tots, 246
Chili. See Stocks, soups, and stews
Chipotle-Lime Mashed Sweet Potatoes, 225
Chipotle Mayonnaise, 64
Chipotle Tomato Sauce, 73
Chips, 45, 46
Chive, 136
Chocolate bars, Paleo, 252
Chutneys. See Sauces and spreads
Cincinnati Chili, 128
Cioppino, 216
Citrus
    about: using lemons, 137

    Blood Orange Salad with Shrimp and Baby Spinach, 93
    Braised Chicken with Citrus, 185
    Carrot-Lemon Soup, 137
    Citrus-Baked Snapper, 198
    Citrus-Steamed Carrots, 223
    Ginger-Lime Salmon, 209
    Ginger-Orange Chicken Breast, 193
    Grilled Lemon-and-Dill Swordfish Steaks, 258
    Lemon Chicken, 185
    Lemon-Dill Dressing, 83
    Lemon-Dill Sauce, 68
    Lemon-Parsley Sauce, 218
    Lime-Poached Flounder, 202
    Lime-Thyme Grilled Swordfish, 260
    Orange Salad, 89
    Orange Tilapia, 212
    Salmon with Lemon, Capers, and Rosemary, 209
    Shaved Fennel Salad with Orange Sections and Toasted Hazelnuts, 100
    Sweet Lemon Leek Salsa, 201
Clams. See Fish and seafood
Coconut
    about: cream, milk, and juice, 190
    Baked Coconut Shrimp, 203
    Beef and Coconut Curry, 169
    Coconut Mango Spiced Chicken, 192
    Coconut Shrimp, 205
    Thai Chicken Stew with Vegetables in Coconut Cream, 190
Cookie balls, blueberry, 251
Cooking day, 27
Cooking/flavoring meals, 27–30
Corned Beef and Cabbage, 158
Cranberries. See Berries
Cream of Cauliflower Soup, 134
"Cream" of soups. See Paleo "Cream" of references
Cucumbers
    Gazpacho, 135
    Mackerel with Tomato and Cucumber Salad, 85
Curry
    about: other spices/herbs and, 30
    Beef and Coconut Curry, 169

Beef and Ginger Curry, 170
Curried Cauliflower Soup, 115
Curried Chicken Salad, 101
Curry Salad Dressing, 82

Dairy, 17, 274
Desserts/sweets
    about: glycemic load, kids and, 251;
        natural sugars, 252
    Awesome Applesauce, 255
    Baked Apples, 250
    Blueberry Cookie Balls, 251
    Carrot Pudding, 254
    Paleo Chocolate Bars, 252
Deviled Eggs, 34
Deviled Eggs with Capers, 44
Dill
    Dill Carrots, 240
    Grilled Lemon-and-Dill Swordfish
        Steaks, 258
    Lemon-Dill Dressing, 83
    Lemon-Dill Sauce, 68
Dips. See Appetizers and snacks
Diseases, in prehistoric times, 12
Dressings. See Salads and dressings
Duck breast, mango, 174

Eggplant
    Chicken with Eggplant, 182
    Eggplant Relish, 50
    Eggplant Soufflé, 227
    Grilled Tuna Salad with Asian
        Vegetables and Spicy Dressing,
        96
    Spiced "Baked" Eggplant, 237
Eggs
    about: eating raw, 63
    Aioli, 61
    Chicken and Vegetable Frittata,
        183
    Chipotle Mayonnaise, 64
    Deviled Eggs, 34
    Deviled Eggs with Capers, 44
    Homemade Mayonnaise, 63
    Sausage and Spicy Eggs, 166
    Wasabi Mayonnaise, 63
Enchiladas, chicken, 179
Exotic Fruit Guacamole, 38

Family, Paleo lifestyle and, 20–21,
    23–25. See also Children's favorites
Fats
    about: for Paleo diet, 271
    benefits of, 16
    fighting inflammation, 196
    flank steak and, 259
    good vs. bad, 15–16
    obtaining in diet, 29
    oils and, 28–29, 83, 262
    omega-3, 18–19, 83, 87, 196, 198,
        199, 201, 258, 261
    omega-6, 16, 83, 87
    pork and, 152
    sources of omega-3, 19
    truth about fat-free, 15
Fennel
    about, 99
    Arugula and Fennel Salad with
        Pomegranate, 99
    Fennel and Caper Sauce, 69
    Red Pepper and Fennel Salad, 103
    Sautéed Fennel with Orange, 239
    Stewed Chicken with Vegetables,
        187
Filet mignon. See Beef
Fire-Kissed Cantaloupe Salad, 100
Fish and seafood, **195**–220
    about: buying, 35; eating raw food,
        36; frozen, 202; littleneck clams,
        121; mercury in, 199; nutritional
        benefits, 47, 196, 198, 199, 201,
        261; oily fishes, 265; omega-
        3s in, 196, 198, 199, 201, 261;
        preparing, 27–28; salmon, 196,
        258; sardines, 199; shrimp, 47,
        261; slow-cooking with shrimp,
        208; smell test for, 35; snapper,
        198; stock in a hurry, 112; tuna, 96,
        201; wild-caught vs. farm-raised
        salmon, 258
    Almond-Crusted Salmon, 204
    Almond-Stuffed Flounder, 217
    Asian Grilled Salmon, 262
    Avocado and Shrimp Salad, 88
    Baked Coconut Shrimp, 203
    Baked Stuffed Artichokes, 230
    Baked Stuffed Clams, 35
    Blood Orange Salad with Shrimp
        and Baby Spinach, 93

Bouillabaisse, 115
Caveman's Catfish, 211
Cioppino, 216
Citrus-Baked Snapper, 198
Clams Casino, 43
Coconut Shrimp, 205
Fish "Bake," 215
Fish Stock, 111
Five-Spice Crabmeat Salad, 94
Foiled Fish Fillets, 211
Fresh Tuna Salad à la Niçoise, 98
Fresh Tuna with Sweet Lemon Leek
    Salsa, 201
Fried Sardines, 199
Ginger-Lime Salmon, 209
Grilled Halibut Herb Salad, 207
Grilled Lemon-and-Dill Swordfish
    Steaks, 258
Grilled Salmon, 267
Grilled Trout, 265
Grilled Tuna Salad with Asian
    Vegetables and Spicy Dressing,
    96
Haddock Fish Cakes, 200
Hatteras Clam Chowder, 220
Herbed Tilapia Stew, 213
Lime-Poached Flounder, 202
Lime-Thyme Grilled Swordfish, 260
Mackerel with Tomato and
    Cucumber Salad, 85
Mahi Mahi and Green Vegetable
    Medley, 212
Mahi Mahi Wraps with Avocado and
    Fresh Cabbage, 220
Manhattan Scallop Chowder, 219
Mediterranean Seafood Soup, 121
Orange Tilapia, 212
Pecan-Crusted Chicken, 204
Poached Swordfish with Lemon-
    Parsley Sauce, 218
Romaine-Wrapped Halibut Steaks,
    210
Salmon Cakes, 196
Salmon in Parchment with Baby
    Brussels Sprouts, 197
Salmon Skewers, 258
Salmon-Spinach Salad, 92
Salmon with Leeks, 206
Salmon with Lemon, Capers, and
    Rosemary, 209

Sardines in Red Pepper Cups, 46
Scallop and Shrimp Jambalaya, 214
Scallop Ceviche, 36
Scallops Wrapped in Bacon, 36
Seafood Stock, 112
Shrimp Cocktail, 47
Shrimp Creole, 213
Shrimp Fra Diavolo, 208
Shrimp Skewers, 261
Steamed King Crab Legs, 196
Stuffed Mushrooms (Crabmeat or
    Shrimp), 41
Swordfish Salad, 218
Tilapia with Tomato and Basil, 259
Five-Spice Crabmeat Salad, 94
Flavoring foods, 29–30
Flax oil, 29
Floret Salad, 104
Foiled Fish Fillets, 211
Foolproof Chicken, 175
French Dressing, 80
Fried Sardines, 199
Fruits. *See also specific fruits*
    about: great for young children, 23–
        24; lowering glycemic levels, 19–
        20; for Paleo diet, 271; preparing,
        26; seasonal, 105
    Crunchy Fruit Salad, 105
    Exotic Fruit Guacamole, 38
    Rainbow Fruit Salad, 92
Fruity Balsamic Barbecue Sauce, 68

Garlic, fresh vs. powder, 176
Garnishes, Asian-style, 225
Gazpacho, 135
Ginger
    Beef and Ginger Curry, 170
    Ginger Beef and Napa Cabbage,
        161
    Ginger-Lime Salmon, 209
    Ginger-Orange Chicken Breast, 193
    Pumpkin and Ginger Soup, 132
Glycemic levels. *See* Blood sugar
GMOs (genetically modified
    organisms), 17–18
Goat, grass-fed, 19
Grains, about/to avoid, 16, 274
Grape leaves, stuffed, 49

Grapes
    Crunchy Fruit Salad, 105
    Rainbow Fruit Salad, 92
    Zesty Pecan Chicken and Grape
        Salad, 84
Grass-Fed Lamb Meatballs, 149
Grass-fed meat, 19
Greek Salad, 89
Grilling time, **257**–67
    about: olive oil and, 262
    Asian Grilled Salmon, 262
    BBQ Chicken, 264
    Grilled Halibut Herb Salad, 207
    Grilled Lemon-and-Dill Swordfish
        Steaks, 258
    Grilled Pineapple, 266
    Grilled Salmon, 267
    Grilled San Francisco–Style
        Chicken, 184
    Grilled Trout, 265
    Grilled Tuna Salad with Asian
        Vegetables and Spicy Dressing,
        96
    Grilled Watermelon, 266
    Jalapeño Steak, 263
    Lime-Thyme Grilled Swordfish,
        260
    Salmon Skewers, 258
    Shrimp Skewers, 261
    Spicy Grilled Flank Steak, 259
    Tilapia with Tomato and Basil, 259
Ground Turkey Joes, 172
Ground Turkey Tomato Sauce, 76
Guacamole, 58

Habanero-Basil Sauce, 66
Haddock Fish Cakes, 200
Hash browns, sweet potato, 254
Hatteras Clam Chowder, 220
Health benefits, of Paleo diet, 13–14
Heart health, 13
Herbed Lamb Chops, 150
Herbed Tilapia Stew, 213
Herbs. *See* Spices and herbs
Honey-Mustard Pork Loin, 167
Hot and Spicy Nuts, 48
Hot Buffalo Chicken Bites, 176
Hot Cinnamon-Chili Walnuts, 54

Insulin. *See* Blood sugar
Italian Dressing, 80

Jalapeño Steak, 263
Jalapeño-Tomatillo Sauce, 67
Jambalaya, 214
Jerk Chicken, 191

Kale
    about: nutritional benefits, 186
    Braised Chicken with Kale, 186
    Roasted Kale, 34
Kebabs and skewers
    about: soaking skewers, 236
    Salmon Skewers, 258
    Steak-and-Mushroom Kebabs,
        162
    Vegetable Kebabs on Rosemary
        Skewers, 236
Ketchup, homemade, 64
Kids. *See* Children; Children's favorites

Lamb, **145**
    about: disliking, 148; grass-fed, 19;
        preparing, 27–28; removing fat
        from, 148
    Easy Leg of Lamb, 149
    Grass-Fed Lamb Meatballs, 149
    Herbed Lamb Chops, 150
    Lamb Stew, 143
    Lamb with Garlic, Lemon, and
        Rosemary, 151
    Lollipop Lamb Chops, 40
    Rosemary Rack of Lamb in Berries
        Sauce, 147
    Rustic Lamb Shanks, 148
Leeks
    about: nutritional benefits, 206
    Salmon with Leeks, 206
    Sweet Lemon Leek Salsa, 201
Lemon and lime. *See* Citrus
Lettuce wraps, turkey, 249
Lollipop Lamb Chops, 40
London Broil with Onions and Sweet
    Potato Sticks, 157
Lone Star State Chili, 129

Mackerel with Tomato and Cucumber Salad, 85

Mangoes
  Coconut Mango Spiced Chicken, 192
  Exotic Fruit Guacamole, 38
  Fruity Balsamic Barbecue Sauce, 68
  Mango Chutney, 71
  Mango Duck Breast, 174
  Rainbow Fruit Salad, 92

Manhattan Scallop Chowder, 219
Marinated Baby Artichoke Hearts, 229
Mashed Cauliflower, 229
Mayonnaise, 63, 64
Meal planning, 26, 276
Meals, menus, 276

Meatballs
  Appetizer Meatballs, 51
  Grass-Fed Lamb Meatballs, 149
  Paleo Meatballs and Sauce, 146
  Turkey Meatballs, 173

Meats. See also specific meats
  about: to avoid, 274
  grass-fed, 19
  ground, fat content in, 173
  preparing, 27–28

Medicine, health without, 14
Mediterranean Seafood Soup, 121
Mediterranean Tomato Salad, 91

Melons
  Fire-Kissed Cantaloupe Salad, 100
  Grilled Watermelon, 266
  Melon Salsa, 60
  Minty Blueberry Melon Salad, 91

Menus, six weeks of, 276
Metabolism, prehistoric, 14
Metric conversion tables, 277
Mini Caveman's Carrots (Baby Food), 245
Mini Caveman's Squash (Baby Food), 244
Mini Caveman's Sweet Potatoes (Baby Food), 244

Mint
  Mint Chimichurri Sauce, 67
  Minty Blueberry Melon Salad, 91
  Serrano-Mint Sauce, 66

Mood swings, blood sugar and, 22–23
Mortar and pestle, 160

Mushrooms
  about: buying, 41
  Beef Brisket with Onions and Mushrooms, 160
  Chicken and Mushroom Stew, 120
  Mushroom and Onion Soup, 119
  Mushroom Pork Medallions, 154
  Mushroom Stock, 114
  Paleo "Cream" of Mushroom Soup, 118
  Rosemary-Mushroom Sauce, 78
  Steak-and-Mushroom Kebabs, 162
  Stuffed Mushroom Caps, 37
  Stuffed Mushrooms (Bacon and Herbs), 42
  Stuffed Mushrooms (Crabmeat or Shrimp), 41
  Stuffed Mushrooms (Spicy Beef), 42
  Stuffed Tomatoes, 235

Mustard, about, 81

Napa Cabbage with Asian Sauce, 225
Nectarines
  Pork Tenderloin with Nectarines, 153
  Rainbow Fruit Salad, 92

No-Bean Chili, 117
No-Crust Chicken Potpie, 181
"No" foods, 273–74
Nuts and seeds
  about: to avoid, 274; butters for children, 25; flax oil, 29; omega-3 and omega-6 content, 87; omega-3s, omega-6s and, 19; for Paleo diet, 271; pumpkin seed benefits, 48; toasting nuts, 84; walnut oil, 103
  Almond-Crusted Salmon, 204
  Almond-Stuffed Flounder, 217
  Broccoli, Pine Nut, and Apple Salad, 102
  Chicken with Sautéed Tomatoes and Pine Nuts, 180
  Hot and Spicy Nuts, 48
  Hot Cinnamon-Chili Walnuts, 54
  Kids' Favorite Trail Mix, 253
  Pecan-Crusted Chicken, 180, 204
  Roasted Spicy Pumpkin Seeds, 48

Shaved Fennel Salad with Orange Sections and Toasted Hazelnuts, 100
Slow-Cooked Almonds with a Kick, 50
Slow-Cooked Paleo Party Mix, 52
Spiced Hazelnuts, 51
Walnut-Parsley Pesto, 65
Zesty Pecan Chicken and Grape Salad, 84

Oils, 28–29, 83, 103, 262
Oily fishes, 265
Okra Stuffed with Green Peppercorns, 226
Old-Fashioned Sweet Potato Hash Browns, 254
Omega fatty acids. See Fats
Onions
  about: cutting without crying, 113
  Apples-and-Onions Pork Chops, 155
  Basic Vegetable Stock, 108
  Beef Brisket with Onions and Mushrooms, 160
  Caramelized Onions, 241
  Filet Mignon and Red Onion Salad, 97
  London Broil with Onions and Sweet Potato Sticks, 157
  Mushroom and Onion Soup, 119
  Pineapple Onion Salad, 231
  "Roasted" Fall Vegetables, 247
  "Roasted" Roots, 238
  Scallion Chive Soup, 136
  Stewed Chicken with Vegetables, 187

Orange. See Citrus

Paleo Chocolate Bars, 252
Paleo "Cream" of Broccoli Soup, 119
Paleo "Cream" of Mushroom Soup, 118
Paleo diet/lifestyle
  about: overview of, 11, 12
  children and, 20–21
  cooking day, 27
  cooking/flavoring meals, 27–30
  family and, 20–21, 23–25

following, 31–32
health benefits, 13–14
"no" foods, 273–74
planning meals, 26, 276
prehistoric metabolism and, 14
prepping food, 26
six weeks of meals, 276
Standard American Diet (SAD) and, 15–18
starting, 25–27, 31–32
storing foods, 27
substitutions, 275
today's diet, 12
"yes" foods, 18–20, 269–71
Paleo Meatballs and Sauce, 146
Paleopathology, 12
Paleo Pulled Pork, 153
Paleo Stuffed Peppers, 232
Papaya
    Crunchy Fruit Salad, 105
    Exotic Fruit Guacamole, 38
Parsley
    Basic Vegetable Stock, 108
    Walnut-Parsley Pesto, 65
Parsnips
    "Roasted" Fall Vegetables, 247
    Roasted Parsnip Chips, 46
Party Guacamole, 58
Party mix, slow-cooked, 52
Pears, poached chicken with, 184
Pecans. See Nuts and seeds
Peppercorns, 68
Peppers
    about: handling hot peppers, 129
    Beef with Bell Peppers, 155
    Filet Mignon and Roasted Red Pepper Wraps, 156
    Paleo Stuffed Peppers, 232
    Red Pepper and Fennel Salad, 103
    Roasted Peppers, 231
    Sardines in Red Pepper Cups, 46
    sauces and salsas with. See Sauces and spreads
    Stuffed Pepper Soup, 142
    Vegetable Kebabs on Rosemary Skewers, 236
Pestos, 65
Pheasantly Pleasant, 172
Pineapple
    Crunchy Fruit Salad, 105

Grilled Pineapple, 266
    Pineapple Onion Salad, 231
Plum Sauce, 72
Poached Chicken, 175
Poached Chicken with Pears and Herbs, 184
Poached Swordfish with Lemon-Parsley Sauce, 218
Pomegranate, arugula and fennel salad with, 99
Pork, 145. See also Bacon
    about: as low-fat protein, 152; making roast and stock simultaneously, 110; preparing, 27–28; slow-cooking with boneless, 155; tenderloin tip, 168
    Apples-and-Onions Pork Chops, 155
    Easy Slow-Cooker Pork Tenderloin, 152
    Honey-Mustard Pork Loin, 167
    Mushroom Pork Medallions, 154
    Paleo Pulled Pork, 153
    Pork and Apple Stew, 124
    Pork Broth, 110
    Pork Tenderloin with Nectarines, 153
    Pork Tenderloin with Sweet and Savory Apples, 168
    Roasted Pork Tenderloin, 152
    Sausage and Spicy Eggs, 166
    Southwestern Soup, 139
    Stuffed Grape Leaves, 49
    Tomato-Braised Pork, 167
Potatoes, abou. See also Sweet potatoes
Potatoes, about, 16
Potpie, no-crust chicken, 181
Pot Roast with a Touch of Sweet, 165
Pot Roast with Vegetables and Gravy, 159
Poultry, 171–93. See also Chicken; Turkey
    about: cooking with skin on, 274
    Mango Duck Breast, 174
    Pheasantly Pleasant, 172
Prehistoric metabolism, 14
Prepping food, 26
Protein. See also specific meats
    about: for Paleo diet, 270, 271
    eating raw, 36, 63

preparing, 27–28
    sources, 18, 19, 270
Pumpkin
    about: making purée, 123; seed benefits, 48
    Pumpkin and Ginger Soup, 132
    Pumpkin Bisque, 123
    Pumpkin Soup, 122
    Pumpkin Turkey Chili, 127
    Roasted Spicy Pumpkin Seeds, 48

Rainbow Fruit Salad, 92
Raspberries. See Berries
Raw food, eating, 36, 63
Red peppers. See Peppers; Sauces and spreads
Relishes. See Sauces and spreads
Roasted Asparagus, 222
"Roasted" Fall Vegetables, 247
Roasted Kale, 34
Roasted Parsnip Chips, 46
Roasted Peppers, 231
Roasted Pistachios, 55
Roasted Pork Tenderloin, 152
"Roasted" Roots, 238
Roasted Spicy Pumpkin Seeds, 48
Rocking Salsa, 59
Romaine-Wrapped Halibut Steaks, 210
Rosemary-Mushroom Sauce, 78
Rosemary Rack of Lamb in Berries Sauce, 147
Rosemary-Thyme Stew, 140
Rustic Lamb Shanks, 148

SAD (Standard American Diet), 15–18
Salads and dressings, 79–105
    about: commercial dressings, 95; commercial salads, 274; oils and, 28–29, 83, 103; spinach instead of lettuce, 93
    Apple Coleslaw, 87
    Arugula and Fennel Salad with Pomegranate, 99
    Asian Dressing, 82
    Avocado and Shrimp Salad, 88
    Avocado Chicken Salad, 86
    Balsamic Vinaigrette and Marinade, 81

Blood Orange Salad with Shrimp and Baby Spinach, 93
Broccoli, Pine Nut, and Apple Salad, 102
Celeriac Slaw, 224
Chicken Salad, 90
Crisp Avocado Salad, 86
Crunchy Fruit Salad, 105
Curried Chicken Salad, 101
Curry Salad Dressing, 82
Filet Mignon and Red Onion Salad, 97
Fire-Kissed Cantaloupe Salad, 100
Five-Spice Crabmeat Salad, 94
Floret Salad, 104
French Dressing, 80
Fresh Tuna Salad à la Niçoise, 98
Greek Salad, 89
Grilled Halibut Herb Salad, 207
Grilled Tuna Salad with Asian Vegetables and Spicy Dressing, 96
Italian Dressing, 80
Lemon-Dill Dressing, 83
Mackerel with Tomato and Cucumber Salad, 85
Mediterranean Tomato Salad, 91
Minty Blueberry Melon Salad, 91
Orange Salad, 89
Pineapple Onion Salad, 231
Rainbow Fruit Salad, 92
Red Pepper and Fennel Salad, 103
Salmon-Spinach Salad, 92
Shaved Fennel Salad with Orange Sections and Toasted Hazelnuts, 100
Swordfish Salad, 218
Turkey Club Salad with Bacon, Lettuce, and Tomato, 95
Zesty Pecan Chicken and Grape Salad, 84
Salmon. See Fish and seafood
Salsas. See Sauces and spreads
Salt, sea, 263
Salt-containing foods, to avoid, 274
Sardines, 46, 199
Sauces and spreads, 57–78. See also Salads and dressings
Aioli, 61
Apple Chutney, 71

Artichoke Sauce, 70
Bolognese Sauce, 74
Chipotle Mayonnaise, 64
Chipotle Tomato Sauce, 73
Cran-Apple Sauce, 77
Cranberry Sauce, 77
Fennel and Caper Sauce, 69
Fresh Pepper Salsa, 59
Fresh Tomato Drizzle, 62
Fruity Balsamic Barbecue Sauce, 68
Ground Turkey Tomato Sauce, 76
Habanero-Basil Sauce, 66
Homemade Ketchup, 64
Homemade Mayonnaise, 63
Jalapeño-Tomatillo Sauce, 67
Lemon-Dill Sauce, 68
Lemon-Parsley Sauce, 218
Mango Chutney, 71
Melon Salsa, 60
Mint Chimichurri Sauce, 67
Party Guacamole, 58
Plum Sauce, 72
Raspberry Coulis, 69
Red Pepper Coulis, 65
Red Pepper Relish, 78
Rocking Salsa, 59
Rosemary-Mushroom Sauce, 78
Salsa Verde, 60
Serrano-Mint Sauce, 66
Slow-Cooked Salsa, 58
Spinach Marinara Sauce, 75
Summer Berry Sauce, 70
Sun-Dried Tomato Sauce, 74
Sweet Lemon Leek Salsa, 201
Tomato and Chicken Sausage Sauce, 72
Walnut-Parsley Pesto, 65
Wasabi Mayonnaise, 63
Sausage
about: to avoid, 274
Sausage and Spicy Eggs, 166
Tomato and Chicken Sausage Sauce, 72
Sautéed Asparagus, 222
Sautéed Brussels Sprouts, 223
Sautéed Fennel with Orange, 239
Scallion Chive Soup, 136
Scallions. See Onions
Scallops. See Fish and seafood
Seafood. See Fish and seafood

Sea salt, 263
Seasonings, 29–30
Serrano-Mint Sauce, 66
Shallots, caramelized, 228
Shaved Fennel Salad with Orange Sections and Toasted Hazelnuts, 100
Shredded Chicken Wraps, 178
Shrimp. See Fish and seafood
Sides, 221–41
Baked Stuffed Artichokes, 230
Baked Sweet Potato Sticks, 224
Bison-Stuffed Zucchini, 234
Brussels Sprouts Hash with Caramelized Shallots, 228
Candied Butternut Squash, 233
Caramelized Onions, 241
Celeriac Slaw, 224
Chipotle-Lime Mashed Sweet Potatoes, 225
Citrus-Steamed Carrots, 223
Dill Carrots, 240
Eggplant Soufflé, 227
Marinated Baby Artichoke Hearts, 229
Mashed Cauliflower, 229
Napa Cabbage with Asian Sauce, 225
Okra Stuffed with Green Peppercorns, 226
Paleo Stuffed Peppers, 232
Pineapple Onion Salad, 231
Roasted Asparagus, 222
Roasted Peppers, 231
"Roasted" Roots, 238
Sautéed Asparagus, 222
Sautéed Brussels Sprouts, 223
Sautéed Fennel with Orange, 239
Slow-Cooked Broccoli, 237
Slow-Cooked Sweet Potatoes, 239
Spiced "Baked" Eggplant, 237
Stewed Tomatoes, 240
Stuffed Tomatoes, 235
Vegetable Kebabs on Rosemary Skewers, 236
Zucchini Casserole, 238
Skewers. See Kebabs and skewers
Sloppy Joeys, Slow-Cooked, 246
Slow-Cooked Almonds with a Kick, 50
Slow-Cooked Broccoli, 237
Slow-Cooked Paleo Party Mix, 52

Slow-Cooked Salsa, 58
Slow-Cooked Sloppy Joeys, 246
Slow-Cooked Sweet Potatoes, 239
Slow cookers
    advantages of, 141
    cleaning, 70
    knowing and using, 73
    temperature change precaution,
        237
Soft "Shell" Beef Tacos, 248
Southwestern Soup, 139
Spiced "Baked" Eggplant, 237
Spiced Hazelnuts, 51
Spices and herbs, 29–30, 68, 117, 124,
    187, 210
Spicy Bison Stew, 138
Spicy Chicken Sliders, 181
Spinach
    about: instead of lettuce, 93
    Blood Orange Salad with Shrimp
        and Baby Spinach, 93
    Mahi Mahi and Green Vegetable
        Medley, 212
    Salmon-Spinach Salad, 92
    Spinach Dip, 53
    Spinach Marinara Sauce, 75
Squash. See also Zucchini
    about: butternut vs. sweet potatoes,
        233
    Acorn Squash Autumn Bisque, 126
    Butternut Squash Soup, 127
    Candied Butternut Squash, 233
    Chicken and Vegetable Frittata, 183
    Mini Caveman's Squash (Baby
        Food), 244
Standard American Diet (SAD), 15–18
Starting Paleo diet, 25–27, 31–32
Steamed King Crab Legs, 196
Stewed Chicken with Vegetables, 187
Stewed Tomatoes, 240
Stews. See Stocks, soups, and stews
Stocks, soups, and stews, 107–43
    about: cream soup variations, 118;
        homemade stocks, 108; sautéing
        meat when making chili, 116
    Acorn Squash Autumn Bisque, 126
    Basic Chicken Soup, 113
    Basic Vegetable Stock, 108
    Beef and Vegetable Stew, 114
    Bouillabaisse, 115

Brown Stock, 109
Butternut Squash Soup, 127
Carrot-Lemon Soup, 137
Caveman's Cabbage Soup, 125
Caveman's Chili, 116
Chicken and Mushroom Stew, 120
Chicken Bolognese, 141
Chicken Chili Verde, 131
Chicken Chowder, 138
Cincinnati Chili, 128
Cioppino, 216
Cream of Cauliflower Soup, 134
Curried Cauliflower Soup, 115
Fish Stock, 111
Gazpacho, 135
Hatteras Clam Chowder, 220
Herbed Tilapia Stew, 213
Lamb Stew, 143
Lone Star State Chili, 129
Manhattan Scallop Chowder, 219
Mediterranean Seafood Soup, 121
Mushroom and Onion Soup, 119
Mushroom Stock, 114
No-Bean Chili, 117
Paleo "Cream" of Broccoli Soup, 119
Paleo "Cream" of Mushroom Soup,
    118
Pork and Apple Stew, 124
Pork Broth, 110
Pumpkin and Ginger Soup, 132
Pumpkin Bisque, 123
Pumpkin Soup, 122
Pumpkin Turkey Chili, 127
Rosemary-Thyme Stew, 140
Scallion Chive Soup, 136
Seafood Stock, 112
Simple Ground Turkey and
    Vegetable Soup, 142
Simple Tomato Soup, 126
Southwestern Soup, 139
Spicy Bison Stew, 138
Stuffed Pepper Soup, 142
Texas Firehouse Chili, 130
Thai Chicken Stew with Vegetables
    in Coconut Cream, 190
Tomato Vegetable Soup, 132
Turkey Stock, 110
Zucchini Soup, 133
Storing foods, 27
Strawberries. See Berries

Stuffed Grape Leaves, 49
Stuffed Mushroom Caps, 37
Stuffed Mushrooms (Bacon and
    Herbs), 42
Stuffed Mushrooms (Crabmeat or
    Shrimp), 41
Stuffed Mushrooms (Spicy Beef), 42
Stuffed Pepper Soup, 142
Stuffed Tomatoes, 235
Sugars and sugar consumption, 21–22,
    252, 274
Summer Berry Sauce, 70
Sun-Dried Tomato Sauce, 74
Sweet potatoes
    about: alternatives to, 225; butternut
        squash vs., 233
    Baked Sweet Potato Sticks, 224
    Chipotle-Lime Mashed Sweet
        Potatoes, 225
    London Broil with Onions and
        Sweet Potato Sticks, 157
    Mini Caveman's Sweet Potatoes
        (Baby Food), 244
    Old-Fashioned Sweet Potato Hash
        Browns, 254
    "Roasted" Fall Vegetables, 247
    Slow-Cooked Sweet Potatoes, 239
    Sweet Potato "Fries," 247
Swordfish. See Fish and seafood

Tacos, soft "shell" beef, 248
Texas Firehouse Chili, 130
Thai Chicken Stew with Vegetables in
    Coconut Cream, 190
Thyme-Roasted Turkey Breast, 174
Toasting nuts, 84
Tomatillos
    Jalapeño-Tomatillo Sauce, 67
    Salsa Verde, 60
Tomatoes
    Chicken with Sautéed Tomatoes
        and Pine Nuts, 180
    Paleo Stuffed Peppers, 232
    salads with. See Salads and
        dressings
    sauces and salsas with. See
        Sauces and spreads
    soups and stews with. See Stocks,
        soups, and stews

Stewed Tomatoes, 240
Stuffed Tomatoes, 235
Tilapia with Tomato and Basil, 259
Tomato-Braised Pork, 167
Trail mix, kids,' 253
Tuna. *See* Fish and seafood
Turkey, **171**
about: cooking with skin on, 274; preparing, 27–28
Ground Turkey Joes, 172
Ground Turkey Tomato Sauce, 76
Pumpkin Turkey Chili, 127
Simple Ground Turkey and Vegetable Soup, 142
Slow-Cooked Sloppy Joeys, 246
Stuffed Mushroom Caps, 37
Thyme-Roasted Turkey Breast, 174
Turkey Club Salad with Bacon, Lettuce, and Tomato, 95
Turkey Lettuce Wraps, 249
Turkey Meatballs, 173
Turkey Stock, 110
Turnips
"Roasted" Roots, 238
Stewed Chicken with Vegetables, 187
Turnip Tots, 246
Tuscan Chicken, 192

Vegetables. *See also specific vegetables*
about: bulb and stem, 271; flowers and flower buds, 271; fruiting options, 271; good carbs and, 16–17; great for young children, 23–24; leafy options, 270; lowering glycemic levels, 19–20; for Paleo diet, 270–71; preparing, 28–29; starchy, to avoid, 274
Chicken and Vegetable Frittata, 183
Mahi Mahi and Green Vegetable Medley, 212
Pot Roast with Vegetables and Gravy, 159
"Roasted" Fall Vegetables, 247
soups and stews with. *See* Stocks, soups, and stews
Stewed Chicken with Vegetables, 187

Vegetable Kebabs on Rosemary Skewers, 236
Vinegar, 62, 94

Walnuts. *See* Nuts and seeds
Wasabi Mayonnaise, 63
Watermelon. *See* Melons
Wraps
Filet Mignon and Roasted Red Pepper Wraps, 156
Mahi Mahi Wraps with Avocado and Fresh Cabbage, 220
Shredded Chicken Wraps, 178
Turkey Lettuce Wraps, 249

"Yes" foods, 18–20, 269–71

Zucchini
Bison-Stuffed Zucchini, 234
Chicken and Vegetable Frittata, 183
Zucchini Casserole, 238
Zucchini Soup, 133